GOETHE'S *FAUST*

GOETHE'S *FAUST*

THE MAKING OF PART I

John Gearey

New Haven and London   Yale University Press

Published with assistance from the foundation established in memory
of Amasa Stone Mather of the Class of 1907, Yale College.

Designed by Nancy Ovedovitz
and set in IBM Baskerville type.
Printed in the United States of America by
Halliday Lithograph, West Hanover, Mass.

Library of Congress Cataloging in Publication Data

Gearey, John, 1926–
  Goethe's Faust.

  Bibliography: p.
  Includes index.
  1. Goethe, Johann Wolfgang von, 1749-1832.
Faust. I. Title.
PT1925.G4   832'.6   80-25826
ISBN 0-300-02571-8

10   9   8   7   6   5   4   3   2   1

One cannot get to know works of art and of nature as finished products; one must grasp them as they come into being in order to understand them to some extent.
—Goethe in a letter to Zelter, August 4, 1803

CONTENTS

PREFACE

As a work of national literature, Goethe's *Faust* rests secure, with the basis of its security in the very intellectual and cultural milieu it helped to create and which, in turn, sustains it. No such background or context is afforded *Faust* in the realm of world literature. While its intellectual stature and the truly dramatic impact of its first part may thereby be in no way diminished, in this setting the all-important question of its unique form, of its significance and greatness as a work of art, most often goes unasked or is peremptorily, and wrongly, answered. The question goes unasked when *Faust* is regarded as a philosophical poem, with little attention paid to the manner in which its vision is presented; it is quickly, and negatively, answered when the work is measured against the great tradition of order and beauty in art and found wanting—the poetic grandeur of the whole notwithstanding.

Yet it is precisely in the matter of form that *Faust* gains its broadest importance, as a challenge to the tradition, as a separate but equal world classic. Not that the challenge was the reflection of a will to break with the past, although that will played its part in the creation of the work in its earliest stage. Rather, it was the natural outgrowth of the struggle to express a new sense of reality and life as process, as evolution, in a poetic form inherited from a world where reality and life were experienced as given, as being. The some sixty years that Goethe took to complete his *Faust* are an indication of the struggle. They also proved a vindication. For the Goethe who began was not the Goethe who finished his *Faust*. Over the years a somewhat different poet and thinker seems each time to have returned to his task, and a somewhat different conception of the task to have presented itself each time he approached. We have in *Faust* not only the

expression of a new philosophy of life but also the demon-
stration *through* the work of the faith in that same philosophy
of evolution and change. In that lies its truly exceptional
nature.

I have described this artistic and intellectual development
in the belief that only in the knowledge of the actual composition of *Faust*—its making—do we fully understand its
meaning. I have concentrated on Part I, which best illustrates
the evolutionary process of the work, but I make constant
reference to both the content and the form of Part II, so that
the present study may be considered complete in itself.

Since the study is in English, I have chosen English titles
for reference wherever feasible. These titles in turn contain
further reference to extensive literature in both German and
English, as well as in other languages. This forced some
limits on a bibliography which otherwise would have been
formidable. The most recently compiled *Faust-Bibliographie*
(ed. Hans Henning [Weimar, 1966–76]) runs to five volumes.
And since the purpose of this study is to provide an apologia
for *Faust* as a masterpiece of world literature, a knowledge
of the original on the part of the reader could not automati-
cally be assumed, and so I have quoted from the play in
English translation and given the German in footnotes. I
have used the translation of Anna Swanwick, which I found
most serviceable, that is, requiring least adjustment to conform to the intent of the original. A prose translation might
have served in this regard, but, again, since the concern of
the present study is *Faust* as a work of art and not merely as
a philosophical poem, some suggestion of its poetic quality
better suited our needs. I have not made reference to page
and line numbers in Swanwick, however, but to act and scene,
which will be the same in any complete translation. In quoting the original in footnotes I use the numbering that is
standard in modern editions of *Faust*.

I wish to express my thanks to the Research Foundation
of the City University of New York for a grant for the
academic year 1970–71, when this study was begun. I also

wish to thank Ellen Graham, Sheila Huddleston, and Maura
Shaw Tantillo of Yale University Press for their help and
advice in preparing the manuscript.

The City College of New York
August 1980

THE MEANING IN THE MAKING OF THE POEM

One begins by thinking about Goethe and ends by thinking like him. There is a kind of giving-in in the process. Not that his genius overwhelms, as might be said to be the case with Shakespeare. But its spontaneous, free, or as Schiller called it, "naive" (as opposed to reflective), quality prompts recognition and acceptance rather than thought. If there is thought in Goethe, it is rarely distinguishable from experience. This may not be surprising in the lyric poet and may be of only relative importance in the dramatist and novelist, who created from whole experience, often personal. But it is to be noted in the scientist, who when he ranged beyond the descriptive to the theoretical, as in his "Theory of Color," found his natural mode of thinking at odds with established concepts and could only stubbornly persist. And it is to be noted in his *Faust,* which, written sporadically over a lifetime, could hardly have been the product of whole experience and yet, conceived as a philosophical poem, would have demanded a guiding thought or principle to make it comprehensible, at least in the traditional sense of the word.

Goethe rejected the traditional and persisted in his own view. To Eckermann, in a conversation of May 6, 1827, he is reported to have said:

> "The Germans are strange people! They make life harder than it is by their deep thoughts and ideas which they seek everywhere and impose everywhere. Have the courage . . . to give in to impressions, to let yourselves be moved, uplifted, even taught, and fired and encouraged to something great; and not always think

that it is all in vain if it is not somehow abstract thought and idea!

"They come and ask which idea I tried to embody in my *Faust*. As if I myself knew and could express it! From heaven through the world to hell—that would be something in a pinch. But it is not an idea, but the course of the action. And further, that the devil loses the bet and that a man gone astray who still strives for the better is to be saved—that, to be sure, is a good, effective thought that explains much, but it is not an idea that lies at the base of the whole and each scene in particular. It would have been a fine thing indeed if I had tried to string out the rich, colorful and varied life which I presented in *Faust* on the thin thread of a single . . . idea!

"In general, it was not my way as a poet to strive for the embodiment of something abstract. I received impressions in my inner mind, and impressions of a sensual, vivacious, pleasant, colorful, manifold kind, as my imagination presented them to me; and I had as a poet nothing more to do than to form and develop these visions and impressions artistically within me and through lively presentation bring them out in such a way that others when they heard or read what I had presented would receive the same impressions.

"If I did want as a poet to present some kind of an idea, then I did it in small poems, where a distinct unity could prevail and be comprehended, as for example, the evolution of animals, that of the plant, the poem 'Testament,' and many others. The only product of greater scope where I was conscious of having worked toward the representation of a pervasive idea was perhaps my *Elective Affinities*. With that, the novel became more intelligible to the mind; but I do not want to say that it had thereby become better. Rather, I am of the opinion that the more incommensurable and, for the mind, less intelligible a poetic product, the better."[1]

1. "Je inkommensurabeler und für den Verstand unfaßlicher eine

Whatever the extent to which Eckermann may have filtered the details of this statement through his own understanding, the position is clear. It may also be valid. But initially it presents difficulties. I would appear to preempt in *Faust* the very approach to Goethe which has proved so effective in regard to his other writings and which he himself, in his famous allusion to the confessional element in his art, apparently had sanctioned. "All my writings so far," he said in 1808, in his autobiography *Poetry and Truth,* "are fragments of a great confession." "Thus began," he wrote further in Book Seven, "that tendency I adhered to throughout my life, namely, to transform whatever pleased or pained, or otherwise occupied me, into an image, a poem, and come to terms with myself about it, both in order to rectify my ideas of external things as well as to console myself inwardly."[2] And he seems to have been willing, up to the point

----

poetische Produktion, desto besser." My translation of the passage. Except where I quote from *Faust* itself (where I use the English translation by Anna Swanwick) and in some few other instances, which are noted, all translations are my own. In quoting from conversations, letters, and diaries, I use dates rather than volume and page numbers for reference, in the text and in footnotes. In quoting from plays of Goethe other than *Faust,* for which line numbers are given, I cite act and scene. The present passage is from J. P. Eckermann, *Gespräche mit Goethe,* part 3, first published in 1847. A selection of the *Conversations* is available in English as *J. P. Eckermann: Conversations with Goethe,* ed. Hans Kohn, trans. Gisela O'Brien (New York, 1964), and a more complete version in *Conversations with Eckermann and Soret,* trans. John Oxenford, 2 vols. (London, 1884). For reference to English translations of works by Goethe, or others referred to in the present study, see B. Q. Morgan, *A Critical Bibliography of German Literature in English Translation.*

2. ". . . dasjenige was mich erfreute oder quälte, oder sonst beschäftigte, in ein Bild, ein Gedicht zu verwandeln und darüber mit mir selbst abzuschließen, um sowohl meine Begriffe von den äußern Dingen zu berichtigen, als mich im Innern deshalb zu beruhigen. . . . Alles was daher von mir bekannt geworden, sind nur Bruckstücke einer grossen Konfession. . . ." The title of the autobiography is difficult to translate. Goethe wrote of his writings as well as his life up to the point, in 1775, where he left for Weimar. The literal meaning of the title is thus jus-

where the above conversation turned to *Faust,* to allow just
such a connection to be made between his life and his works.
Eckermann had asked him about *Torquato Tasso.* Goethe,
immediately dismissing the notion that an *idea* underlay this
drama, nevertheless supplied one meaning for the work by
pointing out the relation between himself and his subject,
whose traits, he said, he had combined with his own in order
to create the image of his protagonist. This one meaning is
the kind of meaning that is generally sought and found in
Goethe and provides for the unique study of the man. In this
particular case he went even farther by mentioning the
resemblance between the political, social, and amorous relations at his German court in Weimar and those at the Italian
court of his counterpart in Ferrara. He concluded of
this work: "It is bone of my bone and flesh of my
flesh."[3]

To admit of an autobiographical element in his writings
and to find that element identifiable in most of them is not
to preclude the possibility that in one particular work Goethe
had simply proceeded differently. But that this work should
be *Faust* is the difficulty. One would wish that Goethe had
remained tacit or evasive, or had played hide-and-seek, as he
admitted he sometimes did,[4] with the intent of almost any

---

tified, although it is clear that the broader implication of life in relation
to art, truth in relation to fiction, was also intended. *The Autobiography of Johann Wolfgang von Goethe,* trans. John Oxenford (London,
1872), has been reissued, with an introduction by Gregor Sebba (New
York, 1969). A broader picture emerges from *Goethe's World: As Seen
in His Letters and Memoirs,* ed. Berthold Biermann (New York, 1949).

3. In the same conversation, May 6, 1827: ". . . sie ist Bein von
meinem Bein und Fleisch von meinem Fleisch." For February 16,
1826 (Part Two), we find: ". . . das war doch Bein von meinem Bein
und Fleisch von meinem Fleisch, und es war schon etwas damit zu
machen," said of *Götz von Berlichingen.*

4. "The public does not always know what poems are about, and
very seldom what poets are about. I do not deny, since I became aware
of this very early, that I have always enjoyed playing hide-and-seek"

of his other writings. As subjective in content as they may be, they contain a first, objective, or intelligible meaning independent of the added meaning they gain by being read in the special light of his own experience. This is true of *Tasso,* as of *Werther*—to mention only the other most obvious examples. As finished products they stand on their own. They are distinguishable in the basic matter of form, the one as drama, if a closet drama, the other as novel, if a novel composed of letters. It is also true of the lyric poetry into which Goethe poured his private feelings, yet which remains unesoteric in manner. If the question of form in a work of art is answered, the intent is definable, and the meaning usually not far away.

But it is the very question of form in *Faust* that has not been answered. The best interpretations of the work are those that have struggled most with the problem.[5] Not that solutions have been found. The only solution is to see *Faust* as a unique literary form. But the attempts to identify the various impulses or visions that went into its composition have created an awareness of what is experienced in confronting this phenomenon, whether we know what the phenom-

------

(in a letter to Karl F. Reinhard, June 22, 1808); see covering letter of August 13, 1780. This apropos of the dedicatory poem to *Faust,* "Zueignung."

5. In English, notably Barker Fairley, *Goethe's Faust: Six Essays,* especially the first two chapters, "Goethe's Dramatic Characters" and "The Form of Faust." Even in a relatively short, serviceable study, Liselotte Dieckmann in *Goethe's Faust: A Critical Reading* approaches the work from the standpoint of "Modes of Presentation," "Elements of Form," etc. On the general question of form, see "Goethe's Conception of Form," in E. M. Wilkinson and L. A. Willoughby, *Goethe, Poet and Thinker;* R. Peacock, *Goethe's Major Plays.* The Wilkinson essay is included in *Goethe: A Collection of Critical Essays,* ed. Victor Lange, as are essays relevant to the subject by Fairley, Peacock, and Willoughby. Harold Jantz's *The Form of Goethe's Faust* is polemical, and in its own findings hardly convincing.

I cite here, as throughout wherever feasible, English titles for further reference on matters at hand. These titles, in turn, make reference to more extensive literature.

enon is or not. The experience is not entirely that of dramatic, nor lyric, nor epic, nor didactic poetry, but of all these
forms together.[6] It soon becomes apparent that here Goethe
extended artistic license to the point where it became almost
a law of composition. There may even appear to be an element of willfulness in a way he changed perspective or approach, allowing characters to speak sometimes in their own
voices, sometimes in what can only be heard as his; or per-
mitting fantasy free rein in the midst of realistic dramatic
tension, and employing that fantasy not only to symbolic or
poetic purpose but also for literary satire and local allusion.
Faust at times is as introverted, as conscious of itself as art,
as it is at other times extroverted, wholly objective or epic
in vision. But whether this variability is a fault can only be
determined after—or better, while—one determines the actual
intent of the work. It may be that ultimately *Faust* will be
shown to have served Goethe excellently in his purpose, once
that purpose is defined, and to be in that sense classic. And
it is true of this unique drama, epic, or poem that, as it
recedes in memory or becomes part of the unconscious
mind, in recall it emerges as a clear rather than a confused
experience, as though despite initial difficulties the profounder impression had been one of unity. (This is not true
of lesser works.) But that is not our present concern, which
rather is how, if Goethe demanded that one react spontaneity to his *Faust,* the spontaneity can be maintained while
Faust itself changes?

The conversation with Eckermann, in its tone rather than
its content, raises another question. The tone is one of mild
annoyance. Allowing again for some discrepancy between
what was heard and what was said, still the suspicion arises
that Goethe felt somehow uneasy about this particular work.
One begins to wonder whether his concern for the misin-
terpretations that *Faust* might suffer at the hands of the public did not mask a related concern with the unusual treatment
the poem had received at his own hand. Goethe never did

6. In using these terms I have in mind the essay by T. S. Eliot, *The
Three Voices of Poetry* (New York, 1954).

adopt a pious attitude toward his art, and yet his remarks concerning *Faust* were more than merely ironic or detached. We find him referring to the work as "this barbaric composition," as a "world of symbols, ideas, and mist," as a "poetic monster" (to Schiller, June 27, 1797, June 22, 1797, and September 16, 1800, respectively). He compared the finished product to human life, which has a beginning and an end but is not a whole. This last remark appears in an epilogue in which Goethe, in three short poems, takes leave of his endeavor. There is a notice of departure, which is the second poem, as well as an actual farewell. It is as if he could not end.[7] Nor could he easily begin. The "Prelude in the Theater" that opens the play is not, as we would expect of a prologue, an introduction to the action so much as an apology for the disparity of elements the work comprises. The prologue is in the form of a discussion between the director, the poet, and the common theatergoer. Each makes his demands and all remain partially unsatisfied. The play can begin only because the director takes a practical stand. "Enough words have been exchanged," he says, "Let us finally see action."[8]

If all this suggests uncertainty of intention, there is much

7. The poems are included in *Goethes Faust,* 2 vols., ed. Georg Witkowski, 1:511–15. They were probably written around 1800 but were not published with the completed work. Goethe's praise of the fourteenth-century Persian poet Hafiz is interesting in this regard, "Daß du nicht enden kannst, das macht dich groß, /Und daß du nie beginnst, das ist dein Los." From *West-östlicher Diwan,* the poem "Unbegrenzt." "That thou canst end, doth make thee great, / And that thou ne'er beginnest, is thy fate . . . ," in the translation by Bowring, included in *The Permanent Goethe,* edited, selected, and with an introduction by Thomas Mann (New York, 1948), p. 650. One also thinks of the remark by Paul Valéry that a poem is never completed, merely abandoned: ". . . un ouvrage n'est jamais *achevé* . . . mais abandonné" (in the standard edition of Valéry's works, *Oeuvres* [Paris, 1957], 1:1497).

8. "Der Worte sind genug gewechselt, /Laßt mich auch endlich Taten sehn! (Witkowski, l.214, so referred to throughout.) The line numbering is fairly standard in the editions of *Faust* in the original, and in more recent translations, e.g., Passage, Arndt.

that suggests the opposite. Goethe placed his faith in the
natural as opposed to the intentional in art. If he had doubts,
as he clearly had with the "natural" phenomenon that was
Faust, still the faith persisted, and he applied it to others as
to himself. Of Raphael, for example, one of whose master-
works he had heard criticized, he wrote under December
1787 in his *Italian Journey:* "Raphael distinguished himself
through the rightness of his thinking, and the godly gifted
man, whom one accepts for that very reason, should have in
the prime of his life thought falsely, proceeded falsely? No,
he is right at all times, like Nature, and most profoundly
right at the point where we least understand him." We are
tempted to believe the same of Goethe and of his *Faust.*
But we are tempted for other reasons. It is not our acceptance of his genius alone that accounts for the indulgence.
Perhaps it is that his other achievements, in the sciences as
well as in poetry, have reflected some glory upon his difficult masterpiece; *Faust* has its reputation from Goethe as
much as Goethe has his reputation from *Faust.* But it is also
true that the level of artistic accomplishment within the
work commands of itself a respect, if not beyond, at least
equal to any question of its inherent greatness.[9] There is
the highest degree of resolution in particular parts, for
example in the imagery and the characterization, which
makes us suspect the same quality in the whole, though at
first we may not perceive it. There is the theme itself. If
other great works derive their stature from the form in which
their contents are cast, the Faust theme, like the story of the
son who marries his mother, or the man who tilts at wind-
mills, or, more modernly, the individual who turns into a bug,
attracts attention in the simple telling. One does not sell
one's soul to the devil without arousing curiosity, a curiosity

9. "If you pretend to be poets, then command [the forces of]
poetry"—"Gebt ihr euch einmal für Poeten, /So kommandiert die
Poesie" (ll. 220-21)—are lines from the "Prelude in the Theater" that
Goethe had occasion to repeat. He noted the interesting effect of this
dictum on his own process of creating in a letter to Wilhelm von Humboldt, December 1, 1831.

which will surmount great obstacles in order to be satisfied.[10]

When in addition Goethe takes the traditional pact with its
clear conditions and limit of twenty-four years and turns it
into a precarious agreement open to interpretation, the
curiosity increases. The pact that his Faust makes is not a
simple pact but a wager that the Devil will not be able to
supply him with a moment of experience so fine that he
would wish it ever to continue. To the attraction in the idea
of sacrificing the soul to attain what is otherwise unattainable
is added the attraction to the question of what precisely is
or is not attainable and why, since here there are no restrictions imposed from without but only by the nature and
psychology of man himself. For answers to that question the
mind will extend itself, as Goethe himself in creating his
poem extended his own powers of perception and imagination in order to resolve the problem he had posed. Regarded
from this point of view, the "formal" freedom in *Faust*
seems less an expression of natural genius than a reflection
of the struggle to comprehend, that is, "take in," the implications of the initial changes he had made in the theme. And
to the extent that he refused to resolve artistically what he
could not resolve morally or philosophically, his poem remained honest. It was he who said that all art as art is a lie:
"Every form, even the most deeply felt, has something
untrue. . . . "[11] Without attempting to say whether this

10. The number of Fausts attests to the fact. See E. M. Butler, *The
Fortunes of Faust.* The author deals only with what she terms "literary
Fausts." The comprehensive *Faust-Bibliographie,* to which I referred
in the preface, provides evidence of the fascination with the theme in
its almost thirteen thousand entries in two half-volumes under "Das
Faustthema bis 1790," the year in which Goethe first came to print on
the subject.

11. "Jede Form, auch die gefühleste, hat etwas Unwahres. . . ." But
form, he noted, is once and for all the means by which human beings
truly comprehend nature: ". . . allein, sie ist ein—für allemal das Glas,
wordurch wir die heiligen Strahlen der verbreiteten Natur an das Herz
der Menschen zum Feuerblick sammeln" ("Aus Goethes Brieftasche,

reasoning truly justifies or merely rationalizes the unusual course that Goethe pursued, still we *incline* at least to the first assumption.[12] We incline toward it not only because of respect for genius, not only because it presents the greater challenge to interpretation, but also because it entails the belief that in a work of art, truth—and not merely artistic truth—may be revealed.

But if we speak at all of intention, even supposed intention, on the part of an author, we must also take him at his word when he speaks. This brings us back to the remarks to Ecker-mann, quoted at the outset, in which Goethe clearly rejected the assumption that a particular idea underlay his work. What we did not ask then and must ask now is what he meant by "idea." He seems to have distrusted the word while at the same time knowing the thing in everything but name. He himself told the story that best illustrates this distinction.

He recounted how he had attended a scientific meeting in Jena in 1794, at which he met Schiller, and on leaving the meeting Schiller remarked that the manner in which science deals with nature could hardly be attractive to the layman. Goethe agreed and added that even to the initiated the method might seem strange, and that there must be another way of

---

1775," in the Weimar edition, 1:37, 314); also, implicitly in the re-mark: "Content brings form with it; form is never without content"— "Gehalt bringt die Form mit; Form ist nie ohne Gehalt" (in the schema-tic notes to *Faust* written in 1800: in Witkowski, 2:526; in English, in *Faust: A Tragedy*, trans. Walter Arndt, ed. Cyrus Hamlin, p. 396 [re-ferred to as Ardnt/Hamlin throughout] and in *Goethe's Faust*, 2 vols., ed. Calvin Thomas, 2:vi, referred to as Thomas).

12. The question of the unity in *Faust* has long been debated. Rein-hard Buchwald in his *Führer durch Goethes Faust* speaks of the "unitarians" and "fragmentarians" as the opposing schools of thought, and finds a representative of the latter in Kuno Fischer, *Goethes Faust: Ueber die Entstehung und Composition des Gedichts*, and of the former in Heinrich Rickert, *Goethes Faust. Die dramatische Einheit der Dich-tung*. Stuart Atkins, in *Goethe's Faust: A Literary Analysis*, argues the essential unity of the completed work.

treating the subject, not separate and piecemeal, but in its dynamic and vital form, presenting the parts as they proceed from the whole. Schiller doubted whether that kind of method, as Goethe seemed to contend, grew naturally out of experience. To make his point Goethe took pen and paper—they had arrived at Schiller's house, where the conversation, as Goethe nicely put it, had "enticed me inside"— and, expounding his theory of the evolution of plants, made an image of a symbolic plant emerge before their eyes. Schiller listened and observed with great interest, but remarked finally: "That is not an experience, it is an idea." Goethe ended the discussion with the retort that he was pleased to discover that he had "ideas without knowing it, and could even actually see them."[13]

This anecdote serves well as an illustration of the difference in temperament and world view of the two poets, a difference which Schiller went on to explore in his essay *On Naive and Sentimental Poetry.* There he broadened the contrast to include all modern art with its tendency consciously to symbolize and allegorize, as distinct from the "unthinking" creativity of the art of the ancient world, in which order, as he saw it, Goethe uniquely still belonged.[14] But the more important distinction, for our purposes, is not that between Goethe and the tendencies in modern art, nor Goethe in his similarity to the ancients, but Goethe in relation to his own processes of thought. If what Schiller experienced as idea he experienced as experience, then the concept of experience in his mind must have been comprehensive or flexible enough to include virtually all mental activity, whether prompted from within or without, and the concept of idea, in turn, so limited as to exclude all but what appeared to him to have no true connection with the

13. In material intended for an extension of his autobiography, Artemis edition, vol. 11, "Tag-und Jahreshefte oder Annalen."

14. *Ueber naive und sentimentalische Dichtung* (1795). A new English translation has an excellent introduction to Schiller's aesthetic theories; see Julius Elias, trans. and ed., *"On Naive and Sentimental Poetry" and "On the Sublime."*

real world. He seems, in other words, truly to have had what
we, with Schiller, might well call ideas, without knowing
it, and to have *seen* them, since they always presented themselves to his mind attached with image and vision.[15]

There is a clue here to the understanding of *Faust,* but also
a danger. The clue perhaps is less a clue than simply a re-
minder to the critical mind that poetry may be creative as
well as descriptive, whether we mean by descriptive the
describing of objects and action or the reflecting of ideas.
Our initial question repeats itself in a new form. We can read
Faust with Goethe or with that opposite sense of things
which we may now for convenience identify with Schiller.
It was Schiller who, on reading the fragment of the poem
that Goethe had published in 1790, first pointed out that the
theme or plot—or, as he called it, "fable"—since it tended of
itself toward the formless and blatant could not stand on
its content alone but would have to be lead by content to ideas.

15. *Augenmensch* is a word often used to describe Goethe. There is
no single study in English on the all-important question of his *Weltanschauung.* Ilse Graham's *Goethe: Portrait of the Artist* touches on this
matter, as do all general studies of Goethe, Karl Viëtor, in *Goethe,
the Thinker,* presents the subject clearly but does not provide a critical
analysis of the way in which Goethe instinctively saw *(schauen)* the
world; the companion volume, *Goethe, the Poet,* aids greatly in this
matter. Rudolf Steiner's *Goethes Weltanschauung* (Weimar, 1897)
is directly to the point, but represents an extreme position. Arnold
Bergstraesser, *Goethe's Image of Man and Society,* is more serviceable,
as is, in a separate regard, Sir Charles Sherrington, *Goethe on Nature
and Science.* The penetrating study by Georg Simmel, which first
appeared in 1918 and has been reprinted in German numerous times, is
not available in English.

Comparative analysis is often enlightening: for example, Ernst
Cassirer, *Rousseau, Kant, Goethe;* Carl Hammer, *Goethe and Rousseau:
Resonances of the Mind;* or George Santayana, *Three Philosophical
Poets: Lucretius, Dante, and Goethe;* and the many similar titles listed
in Hans Pyritz, *Goethe-Bibliographie.* But see Wilkinson and Willough-
by, *Goethe, Poet and Thinker,* where poet and thinker are always
treated as one; also, F. M. Stawell and G. Lowes Dickinson, *Goethe's
Faust,* especially the first chapter, "Nature and Man."

"In short," he wrote to Goethe on June 23, 1797, in reply
to the request for his opinion on the work thus far, "the
demands on the Faust theme are at the same time philosophical and poetic, and turn whichever way you wish, the nature
of the subject will dictate a philosophical treatment, and the
imagination will have to submit itself to the service of a
rational idea." Schiller was quick to notice the general difficulty in particulars. For example, he noted in a subsequent
letter of June 26, that the Devil through his character, which
is realistic, contradicts his existence, which is ideological
("idealistisch"). It is a telling point which goes to the heart of
the matter of experience as opposed to idea. But the heart of
the matter is the dilemma. If Goethe failed to make Schiller
experience the existence of a primal plant, which the latter
believed to exist only in the mind, he succeeded in making
him experience a devil—"realistic"—in whose actual existence
he had equally little belief. Schiller, of course, made the
distinction between experience in poetry and experience in
the physical world. Yet as common, almost natural, a distinction as that may be, it is precisely the distinction that Goethe
avoided, or attempted to avoid.

His instinct was to comprehend experience *as* it is experienced, both in the sense of the moment of experience
and the manner. He only found himself as a poet, and distinguished himself as a scientist, when he broke through the
convention of "mind versus matter" of his day and posited
a unifying principle. For him the two were one, the former
partaking of the latter as much as the latter of the former.
That is why he can appear to us as much a neo-Platonist as an
empiricist;[16] why he could be the poet and the scientist at

16. His approach was not unusual at the time, if his results were. In
discussing the "Fundamental Problems of Aesthetics" in *The Philosophy
of the Enlightenment,* Ernst Cassirer says of the English philosopher
Shaftesbury: "The idea and the ideal of an intuitive understanding (*in-
tellectua archetypus*) Shaftesbury derived from his principal philosophical model, from Plotinus's doctrine of 'intelligible beauty.' But he
applies this idea in a fresh sense and imbues it with a tendency which
it does not possess either in Plato or Plotinus. For with its aid he wants

once; and why, as we can now better understand, he could
both reject Schiller in principle and still be disturbed by his
views. For we recall that in the conversation with Eckermann, Goethe singled out, as a rare example of his presenting
an idea in his writings, a poem on the very topic on which
he and Schiller supposedly found themselves uncompromisingly at odds, the primal plant. It would seem that something
from his first encounter with Schiller had remained with
Goethe and that on this one topic at least he would be wary
of his natural tendency to identify experience with idea.
This may have had its effect in the conception of the poem,
or on his memory of it as he spoke later with Eckermann.
But a more important point emerges when the apparent
discrepancy is resolved. What disturbed Goethe, and prompted
his remark about ideas he could actually see, was not simply
that Schiller conceived reality differently, but that, having
been witness to Goethe creating, "before his eyes" and with
accompanying commentary, and thus in the best position
to experience all that the latter experienced, *as* he experienced
it, still Schiller chose to abstract rather than to react. This
is precisely what Goethe feared, and so often found confirmed
in presenting *Faust* to his public. To read *Faust* with Schiller
is almost to read it against Goethe.

    We read then with the author. There is an inherent danger

------

to invalidate the objection which Plato raised against art and on the
basis of which Plato disfranchised art in the philosophical sense. Art is
not imitation in the sense that it is content with the surface of things
and with their mere appearance, and that it attempts to copy these
aspects as faithfully as possible. Artistic 'imitation' belongs to another
sphere and, so to speak, to another dimension; it imitates not merely
the product, but the act of producing, not that which has become, but
the process of becoming. The ability to immerse itself in this process
and to contemplate it from this standpoint is, according to Shaftesbury,
the real nature and mystery of genius." "Intelligible beauty" seems a
fit equivalent for the idea of beauty as freedom that has come into
being: "Schönheit ist Freiheit in der Erscheinung," which came to stand
as the motto for German classicism. In this context (p. 317), Cassirer
also cites Schiller's "Philosophische Briefe."

in this approach, however. We can, on the admonition of
Goethe, react to the individual parts of the poem spontaneously. We may even, as he remarked, become inspired
by them. Much of the imaginative criticism of *Faust* has
focused on the symbolic value of its motifs, not excluding
excursions into the cabalistic and alchemistic, which were
known to the author and incorporated in the work.[17] But in
the attempt to relate the parts to the whole, we can hardly
avoid making "ideal," that is, less than spontaneous, connections. Yet the attempt must be made. It is nothing more
nor less than what Goethe himself demanded in regard to
the approach to nature and thus, in his mind, the approach to
art, that it describe "the parts vitally developing from the
whole." The whole, however, is not given in *Faust,* on his
own admission. It is, therefore, no longer a matter of main-
taining a spontaneous reaction to a work which itself
changes; no longer, conversely, a decision to read the work
in one or another way; but a question of what in fact we do
when we read. We do not, at the very least, immediately
relate the parts to the whole, for the whole is not initially
there. We do, on the other hand, gradually form a comprehensive sense of what is being presented, with the assumption
that it was from the same general sense that the author himself created, consciously or unconsciously. When we are told
that this is not the case, and evidence from many sides—
from statements of the author through indications from the
text to the very nature of the theme of the work—tends
only to bear out the fact, it becomes clear that we must read
in an unusual way. But with *Faust,* the unusual way seems
the more natural and necessary as we ask basic questions of
the work and find we must answer them in an unusual way;

17. Ronald Gray makes the point well in *Goethe, the Alchemist,* and
Alice Raphael, a translator of *Faust,* extends the subject in *Goethe and
the Philosopher's Stone.* Rudolf Steiner draws constantly upon Goethe
in expounding his own views, e.g., *The Theory of Knowledge Implicit
in Goethe's World View.* The anthroposophists remain generally isolated in *Faust* criticism, although the subject lends itself to the search
for the "wisdom of men," as denoted in their name.

the more we listen to Goethe and accept what he says, the
more we remain open to the possible conclusion that nothing
meaningful can be said in an attempt to interpret the work.
For that, too, must be inferred from the conversation with
Eckermann.

The questions we have asked, without attempting to resolve them, do lead to a possible conclusion, which is not this
last, though it also implies a unique course. My main point,
and it could only be suggested after the difficulties were raised,
is to read *Faust as* it was written—again in the dual sense of
the manner and the moment of its creation. This, if nothing
else short of personal reaction or utter silence, could be said
at least to satisfy Goethe in his own demands. We may not
be able to speak of the parts evolving from the whole in the
same way that Goethe would have wished from the approach
to natural phenomena. Here, the whole is not the thing of
a moment, as was his vision or experience of the primal
plant. *Faust* was written over a period of sixty years. Its
content was constantly enlarged and reconceived to include
the experience that had accrued, and the meanings that had
occurred, to its author as well as to its protagonist, who also
had his being in process rather than as given. The *moment*
of creation for *Faust* was a moment only in the sense that an
individual life may be said to be a moment, in that it has a
beginning and an end. But that is what Goethe said of this
work. He believed, moreover, that the task of an author is to
offer not what is expected of him, but what reflects his
necessary, inner development. "The highest respect an author
can have for his public is that he never offer what is expected
but what he himself at the respective stages of his own . . .
development considers good and useful" (*Maxims and
Reflections*). We expect a description in *Faust* and find
rather a creation: a reflection of accumulated concept,
struggle, enlargement, reconception, and redefinition, like
life, if less like art as we are used to it. It could hardly have
been otherwise. The Faust theme as Goethe conceived it
demanded an open perspective, if only because the terms of
the wager depended upon eventuality, a *moment* of ex-

perience, and not upon preconception. If Goethe had written
a traditional *Faust,* he would have written it differently, in
the sense of both the form it might have taken and the time.
That he wrote it over a lifetime, at various stages of his
development, may have been a choice or a necessity, and may
not even be a virtue, but it is a fact about the poem and will
have something to do with its meaning.

If we regard it as having been choice, the sporadic and
prolonged course of its composition suggests a struggle to
give form to material initially only dimly perceived, then
gradually resolved in its parts. But it was not like Goethe as
an artist to struggle, at least not in that fashion. His own
remark to Eckermann about his mode of creating, the very
nature of his poetry, as Schiller recognized,[18] suggest virtually the opposite, an immediate, rather than deliberate,
receiving and forming of impression, a receiving and forming
almost in one. His first attempt at the *Faust* theme, the un-
published *Urfaust,* resulted, in fact, not in a fragment in the
usual sense but in a self-contained dramatic action, a *Faust* in
itself, if not the only *Faust* that Goethe was to create. It
was as though he knew clearly at each stage what he intended
but knew it each time differently. For Part I, when it appeared, proved to be not a continuation of the action as first
conceived but a reconception of its significance within a
broader context. The "Prologue in Heaven" places the actions
of the earthly Faust in new perspective, and the pact with
the Devil, which is only now introduced and defined, lends
deeper strains to the motivation, but the actions remain
much the same. Part II, in its turn, although it continues the
action, does so at a new level, the level of mind. Even the
"Prelude in the Theater," as we have mentioned, is not a
prelude to the action in the play so much as to the work as
work, as poetic production in its relation to the rest of
experience outside it, which is the most comprehensive

18. Schiller speaks of Goethe as a "poet in whom nature functions
more faithfully and purely than any other, and who, among modern
poets, is perhaps least removed from the sensuous truth of things" (in
the English translation and edition by Julius Elias, p. 138).

perspective we are offered. For a poetic product has no real existence, other than physically between two covers, when it is not being seen or read, and of that also Goethe seems to have been aware. Of course, the natural or spontaneous way need not be the only way of creativity; and we may say also that it is hardly a wonder, knowing the activity and other concerns of Goethe, that the composition of *Faust* was drawn out over so many years. But if we say that, we will be hard put to explain why it was *Faust* and not one of his other works that underwent such transformation; why, for that matter, he did not abandon the project after the initial start, as he had other projects of similar form and import from the early period, such as the dramatic poems *Prometheus* and *Mahomet.*

It appears rather to have been necessity. The struggle with the poem was the struggle in the poem. Not that Faust was Goethe, certainly not throughout. But his vision and understanding of life at the various stages of his development—and Faust lives to be a hundred—partook enough of the vision of his author at his various stages to be seen at times as coinciding, at others as diverging. This has to do not with any personal experience of Goethe's that might or might not have entered into the poem, but only with his attitude toward the hero he had created, or better, was creating—which changed. It was from this that the struggle arose, but also the development, and ultimately the truth, of the work. For the new comprehensive perspectives in which Faust is continually re-seen could not be called truly new and comprehensive if they did not include all that had come before, in the way that it had come. There has even been speculation, borne out by parts of the text, that Goethe up to a certain point intended to condemn rather than to save Faust (see below, chapter 5).

Yet these parts, if that is in fact what they imply, were not removed in rewriting. The process as well as the results remain in *Faust.* And when Goethe came finally to resolve the central problem in the poem, to have the hero express the essence of what he had learned and to envision the perfect

moment, he had to take into account all the experience that
had been described and reflected, not because it was his own
experience, but because only on that basis could he artistically justify its conclusion. He might have taken out parts to
justify a new conclusion, but that would have been poetic
truth and not the whole truth. Or he might have created final
words and a vision that were appropriate to his protagonist
and yet less than what he himself in a last analysis believed to
be true. But that would have necessitated the condemnation
or failure of Faust on the basis of an ultimate recognition
which his author knew to be not viable. The salvation of the
hero not only vindicates his own actions; it also assures us
that in the closing scenes Faust is speaking at one with
Goethe. And if he is so speaking, and draws his conclusions
about life from his experience as we know it from the poem,
then however much his experiences may have differed from
those of the author in detail, and in their understanding of
them at various times, finally and in essence they had come
to mean the same.

This might be said of many an author in his relationship
to a character or a work, but it must also be noted here. It
was not a practice with Goethe to conclude *with* his heroes,
but *for* them. That was the case with Werther and Tasso,
those two earlier figures with whom the author so closely
identified and yet from whom, through writing, he ultimately
stood detached. The great subjectivity of his approach, paradoxically, resulted in an objective view. Goethe was able to
externalize his feelings in the action of his characters and
thus begin to see them in the light of a greater reality of
which he, if not they, had become aware. Or the sense of
detachment might be there from the beginning and the actions
be seen throughout in that light, as in the novel of his middle
period, *Wilhelm Meister,* where the objectivity is so supreme
as to verge on mockery,[19] though the concerns of this hero

19. The so-called romantic irony. In his essay on *Wilhelm Meister's
Apprenticeship,* Friedrich Schlegel says: "One must not be misled into
thinking that because the author himself appears to take the characters
and events so lightly and humorously, almost never mentioning his

also were at one time the concerns of the author. But Faust is not an early or middle or late figure but an accumulative figure, who comes to take up so much of his creator's world, both real and of the mind, that it is difficult to imagine Goethe becoming aware of any greater reality that would encompass such broad experience and serve as focus for judgment on it. There are perspectives of truth beyond the realization of Faust in the "Prologue in Heaven" and in the Chorus Mysticus at the end, but these are speculative truths, views from eternity, and not conclusions from experience. It is as if Goethe, when he attempted to detach himself from Faust, had also to detach himself from the real world. His usual practice of therapy through art was not working in this case, or rather it came only ultimately to work. He could not easily get Faust out of his system, as he had Werther and Tasso, any more than he could "get out" the poem in the sense of completion and publication. It was only at the end of his own life, under pressure from necessity, that he could bring himself to conclude for Faust and with him. This necessity proved, however, to be a virtue. For Goethe to have expressed "wisdom's final conclusion," as the words of Faust in a closing scene have it, at any earlier time would have lessened its meaning. It is this I meant when I spoke of the importance of the moment as well as the manner of creation in the work.

I alluded above to a kind of complete or conclusive truth which we are lead to seek in *Faust*. Perhaps I had better speak, in making my final point, not of truth, which relates to idea, but of wisdom, which is the product of experience. It is from experience that Faust, with Goethe, concludes about life, and we cannot appreciate the conclusions without having been witness to the struggle, without having read or

------

hero without irony, and to smile down upon his masterwork itself from his spiritual heights he is not wholly in earnest." On the subject of romantic irony see Hans Eichner, *Friedrich Schlegel*, especially pp. 56–59, 64–65, and 70–73, which deal with "The Theory of Romantic Poetry."

seen the work. Unlike the story, which fascinates, the conclusions, when simply stated, may in fact seem bland. They gain their significance, like all wisdom, only when their evolution has been shared. Yet no more than we can appreciate the wisdom *in* the poem, can we appreciate the wisdom *of* the poem, that is, the nature and necessity—and perhaps even chance element—of the form it took, unless we attempt to understand it in its full context, which is its evolution in relation to the development of the author. We must break down the work into its parts in order to describe the parts as actually developing from the whole, except that now the whole will include not just the work itself but also the growth of its author as thinker and writer. For the complete meaning of the poem is to be found not in its content alone, but also in its making.

If further justification is needed for approaching this unusual work in an unusual way, other than that it was often the way of Goethe, we may refer to another of his conversations with Eckermann, on this occasion containing praise as well as criticism of the manner in which his poetic writings were being received. The topic of the conversation, of May 3, 1827, was a French translation of his dramatic works and a review of the publication by J.-J. Ampère, a professor of modern literature at Marseilles. After having criticized what he imagined would have been a typical German review in similar circumstances, philosophical and comprehensible only to persons of the same school of philosophy, Goethe praised this interpreter for proceeding, according to Eckermann, "completely, practically and humanly. As one who is thoroughly acquainted with the métier, he shows the relationship between the product and the producer, and judges the different poetic productions as different fruits of different periods in the life of the poet."

It is just that *Faust,* though one work, is the product of different stages of development.

2

PREPARATION AND ANTICIPATION

I am a great fool, but also a good fellow.
  —The young Goethe to Behrisch, November 13, 1767

When Goethe was born on August 28, 1749, anything and
everything might have happened to him. His genius we must
take as given. But the world into which he was born, the city
of his childhood and youth, Frankfurt-am-Main, his family
circumstances, and the circumstance of his birth, together
suggest the possibilities of the best nurturing of that genius
and of equally great danger to it.

He himself in his autobiography speaks of the propitious
constellation of the planets at his birth, and whatever the
value of such astrological considerations, it is true that socially,
financially, and in terms of enlightenment and early environment his circumstances were fortunate. A grandfather was
mayor of Frankfurt; the father, himself a largely self-taught
man, undertook the early education of his children; and the
mother, who bathed the son in love, was so much a personality in her own right that we see her as exerting influence
on the boy while still giving him a sense of freedom and self.
Also, the city of Frankfurt at the time was just large enough
to encourage the ambition of a young and vital spirit in its
interests and concern; it had an important and praiseworthy
position in the history of the day; and Goethe, though he
later relinquished his rights as citizen of the city, remained
loyal to its memory and to the political and social ideals
it had bred in him. He mentioned these factors when he said
in later years that if asked "which place of birth I could
imagine more comfortable, more suitable to my sense of
society or more fitting my poetic approach,"[1] he could

1. Bettina von Arnim to Sophie Brentano; in the *Gespräche* under

name no other than Frankfurt. Moreover, the city had a
tradition of independence in politics, success in commerce,
advance in culture and in social reform, and it was well
designed in that sense to contain and encourage originality.
With this tradition, the old was recognizable in the new, so
that a sense of history and continuity, which fosters balance
and security, was as well an early experience for Goethe.[2]

It is also true that he was thought dead at birth, and had to
be brought to life with great difficulty, as the autobiography
notes. This has perhaps only symbolic value. Yet when we
attempt to account for the fact that the child of so well-
balanced circumstance was to become, at first opportunity,
as it were, the youth of mercurial temperament, of great
uncertainties and overcompensations, of extreme ups and
downs,[3] we begin to wonder whether that initial experience
did not also have real significance. It is the wondering, the
questioning, that is important, for it can provide the kind of
framework that will be needed time and again in interpreting
the man and his works. With Goethe, it was almost never
a matter of "either/or," but of "and/also." His comprehensive
view of life, his sense of a whole truth, was both a cause and
an effect of this attitude. If we can see already in his birth
an example of the perilous contained within the ultimately
secure, we have a beginning for understanding his further
development. Not that he made this point. In a fashion typical

----

October 19, 1824. A selection of Goethe's *Gespräche* is available in
English in *Goethe: Conversations and Encounters,* ed. and trans.
David Luke and Robert Pack (Chicago, 1966).

2. Of the French occupation of Frankfurt during the Seven Years
War (1756–63), he has only good to report. See *Poetry and Truth,*
Book Three, which covers the year 1759.

3. Not only psychologically, but scholastically. He ranked anywhere
from first to seventeenth in his class at any one time or in any one
subject. See *Der junge Goethe,* ed. Max Morris, 1:3ff. On the temperament of the young Goethe, see Barker Fairley, *A Study of Goethe,*
especially chapter 3, "Emotion Running Riot." In his introduction to
The Permanent Goethe (p. xvii), Thomas Mann speaks of "this rearing,
kicking thoroughbred colt."

of the positive tone of his autobiography, he referred only to
the stars that might have saved him and to the fact that
after the incident his grandfather, as mayor, instituted the
hiring of an obstetrician and better training for midwives so
that the same mistake might not be so easily made. Nor
can we make the point without noting, in addition, that of
six brothers and sisters, only he and one sister outlived
childhood.[4] As common an occurrence as early death may
have been for the times, still such experience, compounded
and confirmed, must leave its mark on the conscious or
unconscious mind.

What Goethe does cite as an early experience of the abrupt
taking away of what was thought secure is the catastrophe of
the year 1755 that befell a world lately used to peace and
quite—the earthquake in Lisbon. This impressed the child.
"God, the creator and preserver of heaven and earth, whom
the interpretation of the first article of faith presented to
him as so wise and merciful, since he sacrificed the just with
the unjust to the same ruin, had in no way shown himself
to be paternal." And since the scholars and wise men could
not agree on how such a phenomenon was to be regarded,
neither could the child make sense of his impressions, Goethe
says in *Poetry and Truth,* Book Seven.

But no more did Goethe, through his experiences with
death at birth and later, come to develop any inordinate
fear of the loss of life,[5] than did he come to regard nature,
whose destructive powers he early recognized and in detail
described, with any abhorrence or distrust. The concept of a
ruler of nature whom he had been taught to trust may have
suffered irreparable damage, but nature itself continued to
provide him with a fascination and an outward identification
that were to make it the one great concern, and perhaps the

4. A circumstance that brought him close to his sister; some say
too close. See the index under Cornelia Goethe in K. R. Eisler, *Goethe:
A Psychoanalytical Study, 1775-1786,* but especially pp. 32-131.

5. He abhorred funerals, however. See the index to Eisler, *s.v.*
"*Death.*" Also, Gerhard Schmidt, *Die Krankheit zum Tode: Goethes
Todesneurose* (Stuttgart, 1968).

only true faith, in his life. What happened to Goethe, in
short, happened to him as genius, we might say, or simply as
character or personality, but with the difference that that
genius or character or personality was such that even in
hindsight it is difficult to assess what influenced its development or how its very nature ultimately determined its course.
Goethe, with an eighteenth-century sense of realism and
enlightenment, believed that an answer could be found if
only all the facts were known. "But that," he said in the
preface to his autobiography, "demands something hardly
attainable, namely, that the individual know himself and
his century, himself to the extent that it has remained the
same under all circumstances, and the century, which as such
carries with it, determines and forms the willing as well as
the unwilling, in such a way that one can probably say, anyone born only ten years earlier or later might, as far as his
own development and his effect outwardly are concerned,
have become a quite different person."

He could also believe, with a more nineteenth-century
romantic or poetic sense of self, virtually the opposite. In
response to the assumption by Eckermann that *Faust* reflects
a knowledge of the world that must have been gained
through broad experience, Goethe replied: "It may be, but
had I not through anticipation already carried the world
within me, with seeing eyes I would have remained blind, and
all exploration and experience would have been nothing but
a totally dead and vain endeavor" (to Eckermann, February
26, 1824). If for Goethe the experience of the objective
world served only to confirm inner knowledge, the whole
matter of environment would seem irrelevant. Surely it was
not; but because the events in his life were never determining
factors in the same way that they might have been for a
lesser personality, we rarely can be certain about what was
given and what was gained. And it is interesting to note that
literary historians, faced with the problem of placing the
man and his works in their times, have recently chosen instead to place the times in them and to call the period
the "Age of Goethe." We will sometimes have to follow

a similar course in attempting to understand *Faust* within the
context of Goethe's development, and when we cannot find
Goethe in *Faust* look for *Faust* in Goethe—that is, in his
thought and works which surrounded and accompanied the
poem through its long history. Our question of early environment and subsequent development in fact best resolves itself in that fashion. We cannot claim from the evidence that
the environment was essentially favorable or unfavorable to
his genius, or indeed of discernible importance in that regard,
but we soon recognize that no environment could have wholly contained Goethe. Thus his environment, in being containing (in the sense of structured), might be positive, and yet
in its containment as such, restrictive. That proved to be a
central theme in *Faust,* though it may not have begun as a recognition on the part of the author when he first conceived
the work. It is also a further example of paradox, on "and/
also."

We must let Goethe be. What is thereby lost in immediate
clarity is gained in openness, which is the more essential element in understanding a personality of which we know not too
little but too much. We know too much, even about the
young Goethe before he became famous, because as soon as
he began to express himself both as person and as poet, he
expressed not only what he thought to be true, not only
what might befit his sense of self, but also simply what occurred to his mind and to his person. Everything is there, and
the question is how to regard it. To say, as is sometimes said
in an attempt to bring Goethe down from the Olympian
heights on which he is often placed and to make him more
real, that his protean nature of itself accounts for his change-
ableness, his scope and variety of expression and concerns,
may be true, but it only substitutes one generalization about
genius for another.[6] What is unusual in Goethe, and already
and especially in the young Goethe, is not that he experienced

6. In that this view implies the extraordinary already in the potential,
whereas the classical view sees the truly extraordinary in the accomplishment.

inwardly many moods and played outwardly many parts, but
that he possessed the confidence or sense of freedom to express the moods without hesitation and to play the parts with
all their consequences.[7] He may have been psychologically
brave, and to others may have seemed willful, but in his own
eyes he was being candid and acting in ways which initially
he had no reason to believe would be rejected. If in a letter he
found himself making little sense, and twisting and turning in
thought and emotion like a weathervane in the wind, as he
put it, he would not only write the letter (as, for example, to
Behrisch, November 2, 1767) and send it, but would also refer back to earlier correspondence of a different state of
mind as an illustration of his true feelings, and say amid all
the logical confusion: "But God understands me." If in looking objectively at his actions he could only regard them as
foolish, he would not couple the recognition with a resolve
to change but with an appeal for understanding of his
basically good intentions: "I am a great fool, but also a good
fellow," he wrote at age eighteen.

He was impatient, and as aggressive as he was likeable, as
allusions to and descriptions of him from his first year as a
student at Leipzig indicate, but as we also gather simply from
reading his early letters. Older people tended to like him, as
he as a boy liked, and learned from, older people. The same
confidence and lack of inhibition were reflected in his man-
ners and dress, which a friend, in contrasting him to the
Goethe he used to know, said would make one rage with anger or burst into laughter, though neither would seem to affect Goethe. With his slightly younger sister he was the
pedagogue and moralist, writing to her in prose and in verse,
and in French and in English as well, for their mutual education: "French enough! Let us write English! I shall become

7. There are similarities in the behavior of the young Goethe and
the young Byron. See, for example, E. M. Butler, *Byron and Goethe.*
Goethe knew Byron only through his works, but greatly admired the
poet. Byron is the model for the figure of Euphorion in *Faust, Part II*
(see Eckermann, July 5, 1827).

haughty, sister, if thou doest praise me in like manner. True-
ly, my English knowledge is very little, but I'll gather all my
forces, to perfection it. Visiting my letters, ye shall have
found many faults, ye may pardon . . ." (October 12, 1766).
He advised her to read certain authors, with the teachings of
not all of whom, we note, his own attitudes and behavior
would have corresponded. Sometimes he wrote, though not
to his sister, when he was intoxicated.[8]

Yet little of this verbal and emotional effusion was unmotivated or undirected. Most of it centered on a jealous love
affair in which Goethe's reactions seem typical enough—
unique only in the fact that he so readily received the contradictory feelings that arose in him and immediately transmitted them to others. The flesh became word. Not that there
was a lack of sensibility. With his father, for example, who
had been his taskmaster, he was less than free; he knew it was
better, as he said to his sister, in English, to "turn my bab-
bling to those I am so fond of" ("Ce 13 d'Octobre '67," since
the letter ends in French). But freedom of expression, found
even in his earliest poetry, was the rule. There was not as yet
the breakthrough to an original voice, which came somewhat later, but at least we see that Goethe easily used the
many forms and styles that were available, in French, in English, and in German, and wrote his verse as it came to him,
in letters or as verse as such. This was an open, in essence
noncritical, approach to life and to art, and it persisted in
him—one wonders whether, in his capacity as literary genius,
it did not begin with him, for he carried it through.[9]

8. ". . . besoffen wie eine Bestie," in a letter to Behrisch, October
16, 1767 (included in Morris, *Der junge Goethe*, but not in all collec-
tions of Goethe's letters).

9. Speaking of his preference for some of the early poems of Klopstock which the author later rejected, Goethe says in *Poetry and
Truth*, Book Twelve: "This much is true, that a life pressing forth
from a beautiful spirit makes just that much more free an impression
the less it appears to have invaded the realm of art through criticism."
On the creative process in general, we find some pages later: "Since,
amid this distraction, I could succeed in no artistic projects, I lost myself again and again in artistic speculation—as, then, all theorizing suggests lack or failure of productive energy."

These considerations have a special relation to *Faust*. Otherwise it would have been unnecessary to demonstrate an early talent and need for expression in one who was to become a great poet, the more so when the poet is Goethe, part of whose greatness lay in his natural ability to express a variety of experiences in different forms. But if expression was natural to Goethe, why did *Faust,* which was conceived in the next stage of his development, once begun, not simply get written? This was the period, after his return from university, in which Goethe created his early great works and poems. Ostensibly, he was practicing law, the profession of his father. But he found no lack of time to complete, in the relatively short period between 1772 and 1774, a drama in the historical manner of Shakespeare, *Götz von Berlichingen,* a novel in the romantic vein, *The Sorrows of Young Werther,* and a number of cycles of poems reflecting a newly found sense of nature and of poetry. He also wrote two important essays, one on Shakespeare and the other on Gothic architecture, which reveal a conscious artistic direction accompanying his spontaneous creativity. "Nature! Nothing more like nature than Shakespeare's figures," he said. Of the unfinished Gothic cathedral at Strassburg—which, however, he preferred to call German in order to avoid the derogatory connotations of the other adjective—he said, "Art is long developing before it is beautiful, and yet here is such true, great art, yes, often truer and greater than beautiful art itself." Much of this urge to express the natural in art, and the implied faith in its results, are directly attributable to the influences of Herder, whom Goethe had met in Strassburg while completing his law studies and to whose view of poetry as the truest expression of the spirit and character of a nation he had immediately responded. "Poetry is the mother tongue of man," stated the new position, though it was a doctrine that came from Hamann,[10] the northern mystic

10. "Poesie ist die Muttersprache des menschlichen Geschlechts." See, for example, James C. O'Flaherty, *Unity and Language: A Study in the Philosophy of Johann Georg Hamann,* pp. 10–32; William M. Alexander, *J. G. Hamann,* with selections and translations from the *Fragments,* pp. 85–87.

philosopher, as did most of the English influences on the young
Goethe, via Herder. But whereas Herder soon felt that
Goethe had gone too far in his artistic freedom in search of
the true ("Shakespeare has completely corrupted you,"
Goethe quoted him from a letter of July 10, 1772), Goethe
himself continued to believe in the basic rightness of his own
instincts. In later years he could cite *Götz von Berlichingen,*
to which Herder referred, as an example of great objectivity
and truth gained through intuition, as Eckermann reported,
February 26, 1824.

It was not a question of corruption but of inspiration, a
realizing of what Lessing had anticipated when he pointed to
Shakespeare, and away from the French, as the model for a
future great German dramatist, and said: "For a genius can
only be inspired by a genius." He made the remark in introducing the fragment of a *Faust* which he himself had written,
but which he attributed to an anonymous writer. But Lessing,
on his own admission, did not feel "the spark of genius,"[11]
and perhaps knew from the beginning that he would be unable to complete the work. In any event, the few scenes from
his *Faust* reflected the highly literate, epigrammatic, and
anything but spontaneous style of the eighteenth century, in
which as writer and thinker he still stood. With Goethe, however, everything would appear to have been ready for the
writing of a great German *Faust:* the writer, a new literary
climate that encouraged indigenous themes, and a developing
style that could absorb the "monstrous" nature, as Schiller

On Herder and Goethe, see Alexander Gillies under that title in
German Studies: Presented to Leonard Ashley Willoughby, pp. 82–97;
also his "Herder and Faust," *Publications of the English Goethe Society,* n.s. 16 (1947): 90–111.

11. "Ich fühle die lebendige Quelle nicht in mir . . ." (*Hamburg-
ische Dramaturgie,* Nos. 101-04). See the English translation, *Hamburg
Dramaturgy,* ed. Victor Lange (New York, 1962), which is reprinted
from *Selected Prose Works of G. E. Lessing,* trans. Helen Zimmern,
circa 1890. An English translation of his *Faust* fragment is included
in Arndt/Hamlin.

termed it in a letter of September 13, 1800, of the material the legend presented.

Time and energy were not factors. The works cited above were meant to illustrate the greatness, not the quantity, of achievement of which Goethe was capable even at this early stage. The quantity would have had to include much more, in drama, in the epic, in satire and farce, and in verse, in his earlier manner and in some new styles. Not to mention the fact that for a large part of this time Goethe thought of himself as a draughtsman and an artist as well as a poet. Loss of interest, with which, if it is true, there is no arguing, may have played a part in his initial failure to complete *Faust*. Yet when we know that he was to return to the work eventually, and then continually, until it became toward the end of his life "the main order of business,"[12] we suspect that loss of interest, should he have experienced it at all, would have been simply the conscious reason he might have given himself for problems from a different source. He himself made no allusions to such a question. One thing Goethe, like his hero Faust, seems never to have known was want of interest.[13] That, too, seems related to the essentially noncritical nature of his approach to life. One thinks, in contrast, of Valéry, who in *Mon Faust* made ennui the central issue.[14] And Goethe

12. "Das Hauptgeschäft"—so called for the first time in a diary entry for February 11, 1826.

13. On the other hand, we find in *Maxims und Reflections:* "If the apes could get to the point where they would sense boredom, they could become human beings." For an excellent selection of the maxims and reflections, see *Goethe's Wisdom and Experience*, translated, edited, and with an introduction by Hermann Weigand. Walter Brednow, in "Goethe und die Langeweile" (*Neue Sammlung* 4 [1964] : 1-9), emphasizes the positive and productive aspects of boredom and idleness for Goethe. Goethe to Mayer, Spring 1814: "The day is so long that it sometimes gets boring and that, you know, is favorable to invention—'der Erfindung günstig.'"

14. Also, Valéry's Faust becomes the spirit who negates: "Tu ne sais que nier." For a comparison with Goethe's *Faust*, see Kurt Weinberg, *The Figure of Faust in Valéry and Goethe* (Princeton, 1976), pp. 50ff.

did in a sense complete a *Faust* in this period, in that, as I
mentioned earlier, his original version carried out the dramatic
action to an end rather than remaining totally fragmentary.

But the action that is completed does not relate to the
essential Faust theme. It is concerned with a motif current
in the age of Storm and Stress, that of the unwed mother.
The version as it stands could be called "An Episode from the
Life of Faust," though it is generally thought of as the
"Gretchen Episode," after the tragic heroine. This is the
earlier mentioned *Urfaust.*[15] But it should not surprise us
that Goethe was able to complete such a version at the time,
especially when we know that the immediate inspiration for
writing came from the trial and execution, in Frankfurt in
1772, of a girl who had killed her illegitimate child. What is
surprising, or at least leads to questions, is that Goethe himself did not see fit to publish the work, and that when he
did publish the *Fragment,* some fifteen years later, it proved
to offer less, not more, than had initially been written. It
is truly a fragment. Had he published the original version, as
one interpreter has suggested, the play, coming after *Götz
von Berlichingen* and *Werther,* would surely have been a
success.[16] For the character of Faust and of the Devil are
palpably there, and if certain motifs, such as the pact and the
rejuvenation of the hero, are missing, they could have been
extrapolated from the legend or might have gone unnoticed
under the dramatic impact of the whole. The play is still
today regularly performed. It is also the part of the plot from
Faust on which Gounod based his opera. Yet something
made Goethe hesitate with the work.

He hesitated with, and failed ever to complete, certain of
his other writings of the time. The most important are the
projected poetic dramas, or dramatic poems, *Prometheus* and
Mahomet.[17] Again, the precise nature of their form is in

15. *Ur* meaning "original." The manuscript was first discovered in
1887.

16. Barker Fairley, *Goethe's Faust: Six Essays,* p. 66.

17. Goethe says of another major project, "The Eternal Jew," that

question, and that is the immediate relation they bear to
Faust. We tend to assume from *Urfaust* that Goethe from the
very beginning intended the work to be a drama, if a drama
that was to include fantastic elements and, as with Shakespeare,
verse as well as prose, tragedy as well as comedy. But there is
no reason to believe, especially in the light of the product
that was later to emerge, that that was actually the case.
Goethe might already have envisioned for *Faust,* as he had
for *Prometheus* and *Mahomet,* a totally new form,[18] a form
that would grow naturally out of the spirit of the theme as
he conceived it; he might have envisioned the form, and then,
as with the other fragments, though here only temporarily,
no longer seen clear to its realization. Not that these three
projects are similar in form. It is their originality, or freedom
of artistic expression, that connects them. *Prometheus* is
written in the freest of free rhythms, a kind of prose broken
up into lines of varying length, almost always short, yet
continually varying, to suggest directness and spontaneity.
Mahomet, though it begins in prose and shows only a fragment of the lyric or choral portion to come, where characters
speak in unison, begins in a prose that likewise suggests
feelings springing to life in words. Goethe even broke up the
opening monologue of *Mahomet* into short paragraphs of
equal length, as though now they were stanzas of verse. If
he could write prose in stanzas and poetry without meter
and rhyme, he could also, in *Urfaust,* conceive of drama without acts, but simply as a series of changing scenes. One of the
scenes is only four lines long, another six, and both require
a change of setting.[19] Whatever the advantage in terms of

---

it was ended but not completed—"Geendigt, aber nicht abgeschlossen"
—in *Poetry and Truth,* Book Fifteen, where he recounts the story in
the poem.

18. See again Fairley, *Goethe's Faust: Six Essays,* the second essay.

19. *Faust* keeps alive the Storm and Stress drama of the day, few
specimens of which, with the exception of the early Schiller plays, are
regularly performed. See Roy Pascal, *The German Sturm und Drang,*
pp. 300–13.

dramatic effect (and with *Urfaust* it proved great), and whatever the difficulties in terms of staging, the very freedom
of form in the original version implies an initial conception
that, potentially at least, might have included many more and
different things. If Goethe did not publish *Urfaust,* it may
have been that he felt that its present form and content would
give no real indication of what he had in mind for the
finished product.

He published neither of the other fragments, but he did
salvage—and this is the second, more important relation they
have to *Faust*—a great lyric poem from each. The *Prometheus*
poem, a monologue (or "mono-poem," for it is not reflective
but direct),[20] recreates the essence of the Promethean spirit
in its defiance of the gods and its assertive individuality. The
poem ends, after a series of challenges and assertions, with
the simplest, strongest, most appropriate and yet syntactically
unusual final word, the first person singular, I.[21] Faust will
say to the Earth Spirit: "It is I, I am Faust, am your equal."
And the "Song of Mahomet," if different—almost opposite—
in theme, in that it expresses a pure acceptance of God
(though now it is the pantheistic god of nature), conceives
of the prophet, like Prometheus, as the leader and former of
a new race of men. Faust, in the final, highest moment before
his death, will envision himself in a similar role, and from the
beginning he shares the pantheistic belief. The first of these
poems was composed out of separate lines and motifs from

20. The completed opening monologue of *Faust* has been likened to
the monodrama which was popular at the time. Goethe thought of the
monologue as a monodrama (in a conversation with Graf Brühl, May 1,
1815). See, further, *Goethe's Faust,* ed. R-M. S. Heffner, Helmut
Rehder, and W. F. Twadell, 1:60–61; also, Atkins, *Faust,* p. 26.

21. "Hier sitz ich, forme Menschen / Nach meinem Bilde, / Ein Gesch-
lecht, das mir gleich sei: / Zu leiden, zu weinen, / Zu genießen und zu
freuen sich— / Und dein nicht zu achten, / Wie ich: / . . . Here I sit, and
frame / Men after mine own image / A race that may be like unto myself /
To suffer, weep, enjoy and have delights, / And take not heed of thee. /
As I do!" (Trans. Theodore Martin, included in *The Permanent Goethe,*
ed. Thomas Mann).

the fragment and the second was taken over whole, with only the designation of choral voices removed.

But there is no lyric *Faust* poem from the period. Nor would there have been, for the still more important relation these fragments bear to *Faust* is not that they reveal parallels in theme and form—we may add that in the midst of the predominant verse style of *Urfaust,* Faust expresses his pantheistic view in a freer form—but that Goethe seems to have kept and incorporated in the latter what he had partly abandoned in the former. It was as if he did not need to complete *Mahomet* and *Prometheus* is he completed *Faust.* But what was he to do at this stage with the secular Mahomet or the modern, self-conscious, philosophical Prometheus he would then have inherited in Faust?[22] For Faust is all these things already in *Urfaust.* It was one thing to extract from myth and legend the essence of figures whose fate and significance were known, and quite another to resolve the conflict between the new elements he had introduced in the character of Faust and the legend he was drawing upon.[23] Not that the larger question of the condemnation or salvation of the hero need have arisen at this point. But the simple fact of the treatment that Gretchen receives at his hand would be irreconcilable with any concept of a noble Faust, whether damned or saved, unless the whole were reconceived in a much larger context. We are greatly anticipating, to be sure. We do not know for certain that Goethe initially saw Faust as the prophet of a new age or the symbol of modern man, which he only clearly becomes—in terms of composition, sixty years later—at the end of Part II, and even then, one may add, as much in his own mind as ever in the eyes of others. The tragic irony in his mistaking the digging of his own grave for the breaking of ground for a great social project that will bring him the "highest moment" is lost on no one.

22. The projected Mahomet drama is described in *Poetry and Truth,* Book Fourteen, the last pages.

23. A version of the legend has been translated by H. G. Haile as *The History of Doctor Johann Faustus.*

This accounts in part for the paradoxical fact that the work could be called a tragedy and also end with the assumption of the hero into heaven.

But even the lesser anticipation of fifteen years to the *Fragment* can throw light on the problem. It is what Goethe left out—and now we have the surer comparison with *Urfaust,* since both are fragmentary—that is important. He added substance and more direction to the character of Faust through dialogues with Mephistopheles which hint at, but do not include, a pact, and introduced the motif of rejuvenation in the "Witches' Kitchen" scene, but he left out the whole of the dramatic end to the action, the very part in which Faust so badly inculpates himself by his abandonment of the heroine. This implies an awareness of inherent contradiction. And when Goethe finally did restore the whole of *Urfaust* to *Faust* with the publication of Part I in 1808, it was only after he had conceived the "Prologue in Heaven," the section of the poem that provides the broader perspective of the action, defines the role of Faust and virtually guarantees his salvation, so that whatever his actions, we now judge them in a new light. By that time, Goethe had even added a further death for which Faust is partly responsible (that of the heroine's brother), as if he meant to press rather than deemphasize his point that living includes sinning. And since the "Prologue in Heaven" is based on the Book of Job, we come to see, beside the profane prophet and the modern Prometheus we glimpse in Faust, the new figure of a Job in an active role, thus an erring Job. At this point, any contradiction between the actions and the idea of Faust has been resolved in a reconception of the theme. But in the early period it would appear that Goethe, though he was able clearly to conceive and create the character of his hero, as yet was unable or unwilling to assign him a fate. Hence the want of a pact with the Devil, even in the fragment of 1790, which would have sealed his fate; hence, ultimately, the device of a wager instead of a pact, which was designed precisely to keep the question open. We surmise from the "Prologue in Heaven" that Faust will be saved, but we do

not know how and why. Nor did Goethe then need to know,
but could go on to write Part II, with his hero, as it were,
still in moral receivership.

The question of assigning a fate now relates *Urfaust,* by
contrast, to the major works that Goethe did complete at
the time. We cannot say that *Götz von Berlichingen* and
Werther were completed simply because the author could
foresee the destiny of their heroes; he knew the destiny of
Prometheus and of Mahomet. Moreover, Götz was a historical
figure whose fate had been described.[24] Werther also had a
model in the unfortunate Councillor Jerusalem, whom Goethe
had met at the embassy in Wetzlar where his law profession
for a short time had taken him and the report of whose suicide prompted the writing of the novel. But, as Goethe wrote
in *Poetry and Truth,* Book Thirteen, the idea for the work
had already been taking shape in his mind. He, too, had contemplated suicide, not with intention, but philosophically,
and yet with enough personal involvement to carry for a while
a dagger and to wonder seriously at times whether he could
accomplish the act. In fact, it was in order to rid himself of
this morbid speculation that he pressed the issue in his imagination—unlike others of his circle who, as he claimed,
merely indulged the thought and paraded its manifestations.
This was the period of fashionable melancholy when the
youth read Young's *Night Thoughts* and the dark bardic
poems attributed to Ossian. And when, in Wetzlar, Goethe
found himself in a relationship, with the fiancée of a friend,
that could only end unhappily, he was well on the way to
forming the plot of his novel and needed only an assurance
from experience to know its certain end.

This came, after his return to Frankfurt, with the report of
the suicide of Jerusalem, who had also been tragically involved with the wife of a friend. Goethe wrote the novel in
four weeks. For what was clear to him from his knowledge
of the unfortunate man and from his own experience was that

24. Although Goethe altered history, for example in having Götz
die in battle rather than in prison.

the tragic love was the occasion and not the cause for suicide.
Jerusalem also had pondered the great questions of life, with
sensitivity and direct concern, as had Goethe and would
Werther. But unlike Goethe, though like Werther, he seems to
have shared no equally profoundly concern with outward
action or expression, or a purpose or belief. It was Werther
who could say, in the letter of May 10 of the first part of
the novel, "I could not, right now, draw, not a line, and I
have never been a greater painter than in these moments."
We think of him as the Hamlet bound in a nutshell and counting himself king of infinite space, but without the bad
dreams, which, as it is said, are ambition (act II, scene ii).
And the author who could have him make that statement,
like so many others that ring psychologically true, must
have known the sentiments behind it, perhaps from his own
frustrated attempts at painting.[25] So directly, in fact, is the
whole taken from personal experience, down to the detail
of the name of the heroine, Lotte, who is the Lotte Buff
with whom Goethe had been in love in Wetzlar, that we can
say that it was, above all, his ability to express himself
creatively, to tell the story of Werther that was his story,
that saved him from its worst consequences. Werther attempts three times to paint Lotte's portrait, and three times,
as he says, he "prostituted" himself. Goethe succeeded so
well with his portrayal of Werther that for a long time the
novel was thought to be an apology for suicide and was imitated, unfortunately, in real life.[26]

But that Goethe typically, and specifically with *Werther*,
used writing for therapeutic reasons, we know from his own

25. See *Poetry and Truth*, Book Nineteen, where he spoke of how
the writer in him often took over from the artist when the latter
faltered. On the artist, see, for example, Naomi Jackson, "Goethe's
Drawings," *Harvard Germanic Museum Bulletin 1*, nos. 7 and 8 (1938);
also Johannes Urzidil, "Goethe and Art," *Germanic Review* 24 (1949):
184-99.
26. See Stuart Atkins, *The Testament of Werther in Poetry and
Drama.*

admission, and mentioned the fact at the outset. The question now is what with *Faust,* or in *Faust,* would not lend
itself to the same process. Of all the characters in the early
major works, Faust is most strikingly like Werther—most
strikingly, but not totally, which could not be said of a figure
we have just compared with Prometheus. The new internal
elements—not those expressed through action but those of
temperament—that Goethe introduced in the character of the
early Faust brought him farthest away from the legend and
closest to the romantically tragic hero of his novel. Also, the
modern Promethean or Renaissance man in Faust seemed
almost a prerequisite of the theme after the treatment by
Marlowe.[27] (The mundane culpability in his actions, if original
with Goethe, came into being with the conception of the
Gretchen eipsode.) But nothing in the legend or in the
Gretchen episode or in Marlowe suggested what today we
could most easily call the manic-depressive workings of
the mind that are reflected in the opening monologue of
Urfaust. That psychic rhythm, once the work has evolved
to the stage of Part I, will serve as a prelude or accom-
paniment to the attempt at suicide that Faust will make.
It is the same rhythm, marked by the beginnings and endings
of the letters, that Goethe had Werther write to reflect the
workings of *his* mind. Even some of the motifs are the same.
We will have the opportunity to point out particular similarities when we discuss *Urfaust* in its own context. But it
is clear that the experience of the fragility and changeability
of consciousness in the extreme is not peculiar to these

27. Goethe probably did not know *Doctor Faustus* when he began
his own *Faust*; he makes no mention of Marlowe in *Poetry and Truth,*
but does praise the poet later (in a conversation of August 13, 1829)
and is known to have read *Faustus* in 1818. But the Faust puppet plays,
which he did know as a boy and which much impressed him, had
absorbed much of Marlowe either directly or through the versions of
the travelling players. See Otto Heller, *Faust and Faustus,* pp. 91–100;
see also the interesting comparison of the major Fausts by Erich Heller
in the essay "Faust's Damnation" in his *The Artist's Journey into the
Interior and Other Essays,* pp. 33ff.

figures, but is a characteristic of Goethe himself.[28] He was
well aware of the phenomenon in his own personality. More
important at this stage, he was concerned about it.[29] If it
was his practice, as he said, to write about whatever pleased
or pained or otherwise concerned him, then the extent of
his concern in this regard can be measured by the number of
figures in his writings of the period who partake of this experience.

There are many. It was as if Goethe drew the trait into any
character with which it would not be incompatible, as if,
one is tempted to say in current medical terms, he transplanted
such a heart into any body that would not reject it. When
the hero of a work could not serve the purpose, a secondary
character was created who would. It is here that *Götz von
Berlichingen* has bearing. The hero of the drama, the sixteenth-
century knight with the iron hand, is a figure in whom in-
constancy in any form would be unthinkable. The strength
and nobility of Götz, as well as his tragedy, derive from the
persistence and wholeness of his thoughts and actions,
which he refuses to alter in order to survive in a changing
world. He gains his sense of freedom: his last word in death
is "Freedom," from adherence to a constant ideal.

Into the figure of Weislingen, the pendant to Götz, went
the opposite ingredient and the problematical concern in
question. Weislingen has his being in fluctuation. He provides
much of the dramatic tension and most of the psychological
content of the play, by his shifting of loyalty from Götz, the
friend of his youth to whose sister he is betrothed, to the
imperial court of Bamberg, where his ambitions lie, and back
again. He knows the unworthiness of his actions, but he
follows his feelings where they lead him, and is a slave to
them. In that, he is like Werther, as he is like the hero in
Clavigo or in *Stella*, two plays from the period not as yet

28. See, again, the chapter "Emotion Running Riot," in Fairley's
A Study of Goethe.

29. A letter of March 10, 1775, is striking: "How can we talk of our
condition, since it changes from hour to hour"; "If I did not write
dramas now, I would perish."

mentioned. He shares with Clavigo the conflict between love and ambition and the resultant breach of promise, and with Fernando in *Stella* a love divided equally between two women of opposite nature, for ambition in Weislingen is identified with his fatal attraction to an influential lady at court.

All three share with Faust the guilt of abandonment of an innocent woman. The lowest common demoninator in these figures, of course, is weakness. But the characteristic is not depicted simply as such. It appears more as the symptom than as the cause of a particular mode of thought and action. The focus, in short, is psychological rather than moral. There is even a suggestion of progression toward acceptance in the lessening retribution for similar conduct: Weislingen is forgiven, if in death; Clavigo is punished only by a bad conscience; and in the strangest of the pieces, *Stella,* Goethe seems to be asking us to sympathize with the emotional plight of a man whose long-abandoned wife by chance arrives in a town where he himself has just come to visit his mistress. *Stella* is not a comedy.[30] Goethe apparently was aware of the discrepancy between situation and intended import when he entitled the piece "A Play for Those in Love." In other words, the reconception of morality in terms of psychology was leading him toward a limited rather than a broader view of human behavior, and while this view may have served the immediate purpose of relieving his own mind in regard to the subjective concerns he incorporated in his works,[31] it brought him no closer to a general resolve.

Not that the aim in the use of art as therapy need be re-

30. The title drew obvious attention to the Stella who had lived with Vanessa in the household of Jonathan Swift. Goethe devised a tragic ending for the play for the premiere in Weimar in 1806, after its performance in the original version had been prohibited in the Hamburg theater for moral reasons.

31. Although Goethe did not, most commentators do include Ferdinand with Weislingen and Clavigo as a figure in whom "might well" be reflected his regrettable behavior toward women he had loved (as Goethe said in *Poetry and Truth,* Book Twelve).

solved—at least not within the work of art itself. *Werther,*
for example, would have been a quite different product had
Goethe chosen to include in the novel what he had learned
through writing it. The supreme motivation to suicide and
the general psychological authenticity in the work derive
from the very fact that it recreates the emotionally true without reference to a standard of the objectively real. Hence the
first person singular, and the unanswered-letter form of the
epistolary novel. The great moment for Goethe as a novelist
came in *Werther,* not only because his close identification
with the hero could inspire his writing, but also because the
subject matter demanded precisely the kind of subjective
approach toward which the author at the time was inclined.
Suicide is a private thing.

But where does suicide lead? This is not a facetious question, but one meant to point up the difficulty Goethe was
bound to meet in treating any theme that did not so well
suit his instincts. It may seem strange to say of so versatile
a poet that his strengths could thus be his limitations. One
usually reserves such a remark for artists whose work is in
a single vein. With Goethe we do not see the limitations for
the sheer variety in his creations, of each of which we ask
only what is offered; I said at the outset, he has a way of inducing acceptance rather than provoking thought. But of
Faust we ask more. Into this work went collectively what
went only singly and separately into the other works, with
the result that its resolution, whatever form it was to take,
would have to be of a deeper, broader, or more complex
nature. This applies especially to the completed *Faust,* but
it is a problem already inherent in *Urfaust.* Its lines of
potential development are not clear. It presented neither the
possibility of evolving character to the point of internal conflict, as in *Werther,* nor the alternative of placing the hero
in an objective setting and resolving his fate in terms of character and circumstances, as in *Götz von Berlichingen.* For
in a work in which magic is an element or dimension, char-

acter and circumstance, together or separately, lose their usual significance as resolving factors and touchstones for meaning. Circumstance, which normally functions as an objective force, now becomes a matter of choice—Faust can bid the Devil do what he wishes—and thus a reflection of character, and character, in turn, which we generally think of as fixed and limited, becomes with this new "seventh" sense or power boundless, and thus the reflection of something beyond individual experience. The traditional modes of development of realism, whether the subjective realism of *Werther* or the objective realism of *Götz,* were blocked to *Faust* by the nature of the theme.

On the other hand, and for the same reason, the confessional or therapeutic urge could not further the work in the usual fashion. Where there is no realism there is no therapy. An objective world that can be altered at will no longer serves to test the validity of thought and feeling. Faust can indulge with impunity in the very fantasies and desires that destroy Werther. Nor are actions in this imaginary world subject to the discipline of reaction. The will that Faust exerts provokes no counter will of consequence, unless it be within himself. Where Götz is brought down for upholding his ideals, Faust can seek and realize the ideal, and in the moment of its conflict with reality can escape to a new ideal and a new reality. The point is not his apparent want of integrity in contrast to Götz, but the want of an objective frame of reference in the world he inhabits that could serve to measure his actions in the absence of other criteria. Where there is magic there is no morality. We can see from this how important were the clearly defined conditions of the pact with the Devil in the traditional treatment of the theme. The time limit and the irrevocable agreement to forfeit the soul illustrate and reaffirm in advance the existence of a higher order which can only be temporarily suspended, and at the greatest cost. We are not disturbed by the implication of magic in the sixteenth-century *Faustbuch* or in Marlowe, not because magic is assumed there to be simply evil but because we are reassured that for all it might change things for a time

below, it cannot change things above. Whatever its meaning,
its effects are defined.

But from the beginning in Goethe no provisions are made
for magic. It functions freely, and hence disturbingly, in its
artistic as well as its philosophical implications. It upsets the
preconditions of realism within a context which itself has
not been defined. There is no pact in the early versions. Any
presupposed moral or metaphysical restrictions on the
actions of Faust, if they were in the mind of the author,
were as yet not included in the work. The only hint we have
from *Urfaust* in this regard is to the contrary, namely, that
Faust is not bothered by religious scruple. And if we look outside the work to Goethe's thought at the time, we find that
far from holding the conventional view of magic, he was
actually experimenting in the occult and cabalistic. He tells
us in *Poetry and Truth,* Book Ten, that he kept his interest
in the Faust theme secret from Herder for fear that the latter,
with his focus upon the natural (to which he had just won
over the young Goethe), would disapprove. The world for
Faust and in *Faust* at this stage would appear to be a world
of the imagination, a world almost solely of the mind.

Yet from any point of view other than the logical or
speculative, *Urfaust* is realistic. We are repeating the observation that Schiller made in regard to the figure of Mephistopheles, that his character is real while his existence is ideal.
The character of *Urfaust* is real, in its effects and personages,
while its presuppositions are unreal or still undefined. I said
that in order to resolve the similar discrepancy between
the actual moral culpability of Faust and the ideal vision of
the hero as a representative man, Goethe had created, in the
"Prologue in Heaven," the new concept of Faust as an active
and thus erring Job. But I also said, on the evidence from the
works conceived in the same period as *Urfaust,* that the
question of the morality of actions was secondary to their
psychological causes. Whether Faust was to be condemned
or saved, he would have to be condemned or saved as a
psychological and not merely a moral being. This would

give Goethe pause. The decision that was so clear in the case
of Werther would be a problem in the case of Faust. Faust
was a composite figure. The practice of incorporating individual traits in individual characters had come together in him
and produced for the first time a hero who not only in one
way or another resembled, but inwardly came closest to
being, Goethe. There was no Goethe outside of Faust in the
way that there was an author outside of Werther, and this
had come to be, it would appear, by chance, or at least not
by deliberate design. We think of Goethe as having chosen
the Faust theme, as the great German poet having answered
the challenge of the great German legend, but the theme
seems also to have chosen him. For the point in which he
and his hero are most essentially one is not in the broadness
of their urges and concerns, not in the lyric voice they so
often share, not even in their psychology, though these are
the things that create the resemblance. Rather it is in a
simple fact of their existence that could seem almost coin-
cidental: they both create worlds and are not merely subject
to them, the one through magic and the other through art.

One wonders if this existential point of identification was
not in fact the starting point for the others. There is a short
piece from Goethe's early period that suggests itself as an Ur-
Urfaust, and its protagonist is an artist. "The Artist's Earthly
Pilgrimage"[32] only occasionally rises to the level of *Urfaust,*
and it is too scant and inconsequential to bear real comparison. But in its initial pattern and theme it is similar. The
artist in his studio before sunrise, dissatisfied with himself
and turning for inspiration to a picture of Venus Urania,
the goddess of the planets and the stars, only to be interrupted
by the coming of day and mundane duties, is the scholar
Faust in his study in the opening scene, likewise dissatisfied,

32. "Des Künstlers Erdewallen," which Goethe probably had in
mind along with other pieces and poems when he spoke in *Poetry and
Truth,* Book Fifteen, of the urges to create in words and in pictures
running parallel in his development in the early years. The Artemis edition of *Dichtung und Wahrheit* makes this assumption. See its index
under "Goethes Werke," "Künstlers Erdewallen."

and turning to books of magic to glimpse visions of the cosmos, only to be disturbed by his pedantic assistant and restored to his real surroundings. The Mephistophelian tone and manner are present in the gentleman and lady who visit the artist, and the spirit of their meeting is the spirit of the opening lines of the scene that will be called "Martha's Garden," where Mephistopheles does the honors. Peculiarly, a muse who appears and exhorts the artist to accept his earthly fate does so with the same observation that Gretchen will make in recounting the joys and sorrows of her lot, that sleeping and eating are better enjoyed for hard work.[33] There are other echoes and repetitions of phrases and motifs,[34] and since the piece is composed in the same distinctive *Knittelvers* form,[35] we can think we hear in it, as it were, the Faust song in Goethe's head just before it was written.

Not that there are not other fragmentary pieces from the time that could be said to vie with "The Artist's Earthly Pilgrimage" for the same position. The short drama about the false prophet of sentimentality, "Pater Brey," if it does not suggest *Urfaust* in tone, nevertheless treats a motif that had become attached to the legendary figure of Faust, charlatan-

33. *Urfaust:* "Da gehts mein Herr nicht immer mutig zu,/Doch schmeckt dafür das Essen und die Ruh" (Witkowski, ll. 999–1000). "Des Künstlers Erdewallen": "Wenn man muss eine Zeitlang haken und graben,/Wird man die Ruh erst willkommen haben."

34. Most strikingly from "Künstlers Abendlied," rather than the piece in point. Certain lines from this poem, which was written in 1774, immediately suggest *Faust*: "Ich fühle, ich kenne dich, Natur/Und so muß ich dich fassen. . . . Wie sehn ich mich, Natur, nach dir. . . . Wirst alle meine Kräfte mir/In meinem Sinn erheitern/Und dieses enge Dasein hier/Zur Ewigkeit erweitern." "I feel I know you, Nature, and so must I grasp you. . . . How I long, Nature, for you. . . . You will enliven all my powers in me/And broaden this narrow existence into Eternity" (trans. Sir Theodore Martin, *Poems and Ballads of Goethe,* 3rd ed. [New York, 1907]).

35. *Knittelvers,* rhymed-paired, four-stressed verse form popular since Hans Sachs, the meistersinger and contemporary (1494–1576) of the legendary Faust.

ism, and it is written in Knittelvers. As is the delightfully crude little—as Goethe called it—"microcosmic" drama, "Hanswurst's Wedding," which not only has as its central figure the clown that the young Goethe knew from the Faust puppet plays, but also begins with a set of lines so close syntactically and verbally to the opening lines of *Urfaust* as to seem a deliberate parody. The piece would then have been written after *Urfaust*.[36] But that would not alter, so much as add a dimension to my main point, and allow us to sense beside the various urges and ideas that seem to have been clamoring for expression in the work, a potential for complete reversal, an ability to see the high seriousness of the actions and sentiments of Faust in a devastatingly reductive manner.[37] But that will prove to be the manner of Mephistopheles, who in *Urfaust* emerges as the Hanswurst of the traditional plays transformed into a a sophisticated rogue, now a true rather than crude pendant to Faust.

It is as if Goethe wished to write a drama with the artist as protagonist, as he had wished to write a Prometheus and a Mahomet drama, had begun to write them all at once, and had come to write them all in one. This would have been in keeping with his spontaneous mode of creating. One is reminded of the advice he once gave in the matter of writing a trilogy, which was that the poet should not seek out a subject to be treated in that form, but should he discover among his writings pieces possessing latent similarity in conception or sentiment, there would be nothing simpler than to complete a third piece for the express purpose.[38] If *Urfaust* did not come into being precisely in that way, in that here

36. As is sometimes assumed, for example by Ernst Beutler in his introduction to vol. 4 of the Artemis edition, *Der junge Goethe*.

37. Just as Goethe could write a parody of *Werther*, "Anekdote zu den Freuden des jungen Werthers"—apparently for his own amusement, for the piece was never published.

38. In a letter of December 7, 1831, to Frédérich Soret, natural scientist and translator of "The Metamorphosis of Plants" into French, himself the composer of a verse trilogy.

we are assuming a totally unconscious and simultaneous
process, still the underlying principle may be said to be the
same. But only the Faust theme would have allowed such a
fusion of intents without inherent contraction. The Prometheus theme could have supplied the motifs of defiance and
will, but not those of philosophical speculation and intro-
spection, which are related to the hero of inner conflict but
not to the hero of resolve. The Mahomet theme encompassed
more. As Goethe describes his intentions with this work at
the end of Book Fourteen of his autobiography, we can see
it emerging on a scale with *Faust*. The drama was to describe
the conflict between the ideal and the real, the eternal and the
earthly, and was to exonerate the prophet, whom, as Goethe
tells us, he had never been able to see as anything but an im-
poster, by showing how inevitable is the erosion that takes
place in the higher being of man when he extends himself in
the real world. That surely is a major theme in *Faust*.

But the Mahomet drama was conceived objectively. Its
lyrical passages and the plan for a great hymn in the first act
may suggest the kind of immediate expression of emotion
that we look for in Goethe at this stage, but if we have Goethe
in the person of Mahomet, it is only in that one regard. There
is nothing in the fragment or the plan that would indicate
that the conflict which the author saw his hero undergoing
and exemplifying was a conflict of which the hero himself
was consciously or introspectively aware. Like Prometheus
and like Götz, Mahomet seems to have been intended as the
essentially "naive" protagonist, as profound as his visions
and sensitivity might have been.

The Faust theme did not demand the introspective hero,
but neither did it preclude the possibility of that element in
his character. The Faust of the legend was a scholar, but he
was not less but more than an artist: he was able to bring to
life what he imagined, not as art, but in the real world. He
was Werther unbound through magic, as Goethe was Werther
redeemed through art. In him the barrier between the inward
and outward world could be surmounted though he would
retain knowledge of and, so to speak, competence in both

worlds, but not because Goethe would choose to lend him this special characteristic, but because the special powers he possessed were by their nature designed, as is art, to make the imaginary real, to make idea into experience. That is one of the reasons Faust makes the wager with the Devil: "The god who throned within my breast resides . . . with sovereign sway my energies he guides [but] he cannot move external things" (ll. 1,556-59). If Faust is not the artist in fact, he is the artist in essence, or the artist unto himself. He reflects the creative process in his actions. In that he is different from Goethe's figures of the artist proper, whose creative powers are conceived as part of their nature or character but without extension in the objective world. An artist such as Tasso dreams of an ideal society; he does not, as will Faust, begin to execute plans for one. And if in this endeavor, as in others, Faust is aided by magic, that fact does not serve to dissociate him from reality but only allows him to penetrate and broaden experience in a way that would not be possible in a drama or poem of strict realism. For Goethe will not use magic simply to alter realities by a wave of the wand. Whatever the laws that will come to govern and delimit the powers of Faust —and it will be our task to identify them when and as Goethe himself uncovers and poetically incorporates them in the work—they will be fixed, and beyond magic. In Goethe all roads lead back to life and to experience. But with the element of magic, everything short of the immutable could be changed, and everything within could find palpable outward expression, with the result that both the figure of the hero and the form of the play could enjoy the ultimate freedom in development—the former limited only by the limits of human nature, not those of an individual, and the latter only by the creative and imaginative powers of the author, not by the formal concerns of art. All this is a natural outgrowth of the theme, which now appears not only to have chosen Goethe but also to have chosen him at the right time.

The period in which he conceived *Faust* was precisely the point in the development of German literature where the revolt against the norms of society and of art was gaining

momentum. The young Goethe may have been the foremost
poet of this Sturm und Drang movement, but still he was part
of it. There were many *Fausts* written at the time, in prose
or as drama, independently of his, not to mention the greater
number of what, since his *Faust* became famous, we now
call Faustian figures who populate the works of lesser-known
contemporaries. But if the Faust idea was in the air, it was,
like all ideas in their early stages, more attractive than in-
structive. Just as the Storm and Stress movement itself was
to remain for all but its leading representatives a beginning
without development, so its versions of the Faust theme
reflect the initial impulses of new feeling and vision but fail
to realize their potential. So, too, with Goethe, but with the
all-important difference that he, who did develop, took and
developed with him his initial version. His *Faust* as it stands,
or even Part I alone, which provides the design and broad
metaphors that serve to contain the unwieldy action, could
not have been completed at a time when Goethe was still
in, and not yet beyond, his own Storm and Stress period,
but he might not even have begun the work had the idea for
it presented itself to him only later. We have seen from some
of his remarks that his attraction to the theme could become
at times almost a revulsion, and so often was his engagement
with Faust broken that we wonder how (some still wonder
if)[39] the marriage of mind between author and work eventually did take place. However, coming to him at the right
time and providing a real—if as yet not fully recognized—
opportunity for the expression of his instincts as a poet and
a thinker, the Faust idea was as difficult to abandon as it
was to absorb. From such dynamics came development in
the true sense, or at least in the sense that Goethe himself,
as we have seen, conceived of development, as vital evolution
of parts in relation to a whole, rather than progressive fore-
seeable steps along a line from beginning to end.

But what happened to *Faust* from without was also to
happen from within. The idea of evolution, of organic growth,

39. The so-called fragmentarians noted above, chap. 1 n. 12.

proved to be more than simply an aspect of the work, a perspective we gain by knowing the manner in which it was composed. It was also to become the uppermost idea in Part II; as if, given a work which itself had gradually evolved in its continual attempts and failures at resolve, the only conclusion it could rightly reach was that evolution was the resolution, that the process was the purpose of life, as well as the true meaning in art. But since the idea of evolution grew out of the work as much as, later, the work out of the idea, we have in *Faust* not only the results but the display of development. It was not a matter of steps taken which were then reversed, nor of foundations deliberately laid which were then built upon, but a matter of impulses expressed which then had to be comprehended, of things having been done, the purpose and meaning of which would only gradually emerge. Like any phenomenon in the process of evolution, *Faust* includes much more than what from any point of view we may discern as essential to its development, and thus forces us constantly to alter our point of view in order to grasp its meaning. It was not much different for Goethe. Creating instinctively—he said to Schiller in a letter of June 22, 1797, that his approach to *Faust* was wholly subjective—he was forced to grasp the reasoning of his instincts and constantly to enlarge his poetic vision in order to account for them. "How do I know what I mean until I've heard what I've said?" is a remark, variously attributed, that peculiarly applies to the process of artistic creation in *Faust*. And since this process itself underwent an evolution extending over the many years it took to complete the work, each of its stages or aspects, and each of the meanings it lent to things that had come before, were at the same time anticipatory of what was to be, motifs in the development of further meaning.[40]

At some point, to be sure, *Faust* had to end. But it is

40. See the essay by Willoughby, "*Faust*: A Morphological Approach," in Wilkinson and Willoughby, *Goethe: Poet and Thinker;* further, Peter Salm, *The Poem as Plant: A Biological View of Goethe's Faust.*

fitting that the end came, both for the author and the hero,
not so much as a conclusion, which is not in the nature of
evolution, as from necessity. Faust dies naturally, of old age,
just before his author died. And further, since this process
of development was not an isolated phenomenon but occurred
within the active context of an age of change, *Faust* came
to reflect not just the development of its author but the
broader developments in German literature and thought as
a whole. Within his lifetime, Goethe anticipated, influenced,
and partook of what we now identify separately as the
Storm and Stress, the classical, and the romantic movements,
though in him, as in *Faust,* they were made to be one. Related to a single theme, in fact, these movements appear to
regain some of the vitality that they possessed in coming
into being, and which they so often lose when seen in retrospect, through the medium of a variety of authors and
individual works. Accomplishment impresses but does not
reveal. For that matter, we might say of the accomplishments of Goethe himself in his other works that although,
taken together, they give us the whole man and his thought,
it is we who make the fusion, whereas in *Faust* it is the
author who attempts it.[41]

In effect, we have now stated our problem in reverse. Instead of looking to the tendencies in the young Goethe for a
gauge of his preparedness to treat the Faust theme, we have
looked to the potentials of the theme itself in order to
anticipate the kind of development it might conceivably

41. The attempt was aided in the German world by the fact that his
other works were familiar to those who might read his *Faust,* with
the result that early interpreters could use his other dramas, poems, and
novels as frames of reference in their interpretation and appreciation
of the masterwork. The life and works by Albert Bielschowsky, first
published in 1896 (English trans., 3 vol., 1905 and following), which
has *Faust* as its centerpiece and constructs the life from the work and
vice versa, remains unsurpassed. Later interpreters, while allowing
Goethe's own contention that his writings were "part of a general confession," began to ask not only *what,* but *how,* he confessed in his art.

undergo. It almost goes without saying that had Goethe not completed the work, our anticipations would remain mere speculations, and wrong ones at that. He diverged so widely from the traditional treatment of the theme—one critic has made the point that his *Faust* is really the exception and that only some hundred years later did Thomas Mann in his *Doktor Faustus* revert to the rule[42] —that any presupposing of his intentions would be misled. It would be to put the theme before the poet, which in Goethe is rare. I quoted him in the preceding chapter in regard to his few works in which that might have been the case. On the other hand, he himself possessed such great potential for development in so many ways that to attempt to explain his difficulties and hesitations with *Faust* in its initial states, or even later, solely in terms of his actual accomplishments to date would be to put the poet before the theme, and equally wrong, as it is equally rare in Goethe.[43] He developed in developing *Faust*. It was a matter yet again of "and/also," and with the completed work before us we can see more clearly just how.

Once overcome, each apparent difficulty, in short, proved to be an opportunity, a directive for a new necessity. From the limitations of the urge to realism that had set the work in motion came the explorations of the unreal, or rather, the not yet real forces that underlie and motivate human thought and action and are only discernible and describable in the realm of fantasy. Much of the motivation in *Faust* shows the progression from unconscious anticipation (the dream stage) through conscious thought to deliberate action, although, in terms of composition, the order was reversed, the action having been described in *Urfaust,* the conscious motivation further supplied in the *Fragment,* and the anticipation eventually woven into the work through the various poetic devices of imagery, metaphor, or imaginary sequences of either the "low" order, such as the "Walpurgis Night," or

42. Erich Heller in *The Artist's Journey into the Interior,* p. 3.
43. See Wilkinson and Willoughby, *Goethe: Poet and Thinker,* especially the essay "The Poet as Thinker: On the Varying Modes of Goethe's Thought."

the higher, such as the "Prologue in Heaven." The whole of
Part II, in which Faust goes forward in his own development,
is at the same time an elaborate poetic anticipation of the
broadest conditions that formed contemporary man,[44] for
the action goes back in time through Western culture, first
to the medieval, then to the ancient world, and once again
forward to the present, the now, in terms of the poem. It
goes back even further in the creation of the figure of Homunculus, the spirit created in a test tube who in his search for
a body must return to the sea, the source of all life, in order
to come properly into being.

The fantastic, in other words, remains in the service of
a natural view. So does the subjective element in the poem,
which initially, in conjunction with the therapeutic urge,
may have been related to personal concerns, but gradually
freed itself from content and was brought to bear on form.
Goethe was as original and unhampered in Part II of *Faust* as
he was in the early conceived dramatic portions of Part I,
but whereas in the one case the spontaneity stemmed from a
closeness to the subject matter and to the inner world of the
hero, in the other it suggests artistic prerogative more than
personal need. So many levels of operation had accrued to
the work in its attempt to objectify the impulses of its author
and its hero that no conventional literary form could serve
as a guide to their development—and to what must one turn
in the default of tradition but to instinct? One of the few
ironies—there are many paradoxes—that attach to the composition of *Faust* is the fact that at the very time when
Goethe had overcome any tendency to conscious subjectivity
in his art, he was forced by this one work to resume his
original way and to create once again essentially out of his
own poetic being.[45] What are called for convenience sake the

44. European man, that is. Goethe is clear on the point. See Willoughby's essay on *Faust* in Wilkinson and Willoughby, p. 117.

45. ". . . to accomplish through purpose and character what really
should be the task of freely active nature alone," as he put it in a letter
to Wilhelm von Humboldt, March 17, 1832, his last. There is a full
discussion of this important letter in an article by Barker Fairley,

classical elements in Part II, as opposed to the Storm and
Stress or romantic elements in Part I, are an outgrowth of the
action as it proceeds into the ancient world and takes on the
guise and spirit of the surroundings. They are not a reflection
of a classical conception of the action or of any other readily
definable artistic focus, for the free factor of magic has
rendered the question of the form in the work as problematical or—as Goethe would have it—as incommensurable
as that of its meaning. The form itself remained poetical,
that is, associative more than logical in nature, and freely
associative.

It is just that the same factor of magic that was used in the
first part of the play to enhance the action—it was not
essential to the Gretchen tragedy, though it heightened the
drama, as magic heightens all that it touches—became in the
second part the lever to action, the necessary link between
the extensions into other times and places, with the result that
the more the work attempted to resolve itself in terms of
a natural view, the more dependent it became on the unnatural
element at its core. This paradox persists in the poem. Yet
if magic is poetical, and if poetry is magic in the sense that it
makes real and tangible in the mind what otherwise remains
only feeling and apprehension, then not only are the theme
and the mode of expression here related, as they might be
in any literary work, but they are one. It would be unrealistic
but not illogical to claim that magic is the only true subject
of poetry, in that it is the one subject that does not force the
ultimate compromise of accepting as actual what we know
in fact to be fiction. The suspension of disbelief in *Faust* is
not willing, but given, or obviated, by the content of the
work, thus freeing its form not only from the demands of
realism within a particular genre but also from the demands
of genre as such. Reality in *Faust* is at a remove. It is not
produced *by* the work so much as, through magic, *in* the

———
"Goethe's Last Letter," in *The University of Toronto Quarterly* 28
(1957-58): 1-9.

work. It has a life of its own. And while this recognition
solves neither the philosophical problem of the meaning of
magic within the poem, nor the aesthetic problem of the
form that a literary work dealing with magic should or could
take, it does suggest as imperative a point that might easily
be thought of as too obvious to consider. The point is that
we read the work as it was intended, as a product of the
imagination, since so much that occurs in it is a realization of
and a confrontation with things imagined and desired. *Faust*
is a work in the subjunctive, and the subjunctive knows no
bounds.

We need only add, finally, that *Faust,* whatever the form
it eventually took, had to be a total work more than a
masterwork. Conceived in a period of development, and
absorbing rather than resisting change, it had to grow larger
before it could be reduced to its just and natural size; it had
to be different in order to be itself.[46]

Yet the work began relatively simply, and it is to its actual
beginnings that we must now turn.

46. "You must assert the rule of the fist [*das Faustrecht*] everywhere in your Faust," Schiller wrote to Goethe (September 13, 1800).

3

URFAUST IN CONTEXT

Nothing is revealed that is not already anticipated, and only through the revelation does the anticipation become clear, like the prophecy through the fulfillment.
—Goethe speaking of the scientific writings of Carl Gustav Carus, in "Aphorisms and Fragments"

It is difficult to read *Urfaust* within its own context. Goethe took over the whole of the early version into Part I, extending and surrounding its scenes with new material but leaving the scenes themselves, the original lines, virtually intact. We tend to read these lines in the light of the finished product, and while they thereby gain in clarity and weight of meaning, they lose some of their immediate, and indeed transitory, truth. Not only which of these lines, or what in them, proved true, but also which or what proved false is the question to which in effect we address ourselves when we attempt to read *Urfaust* in its own right.[1]

For Goethe retained, as it were, the falsely as well as the truly prophetic or intuitive elements that went into the initial conception of his hero and the work. He did so, one begins to believe, not from simple fondness for his original creation, though the dedicatory poem written some twenty-five years later suggests this,[2] nor in order to obviate the

1. "As much true as false tendency"—"Eben soviel wahre als falsche Tendenz"—is a notation in one of Goethe's diaries which Ernst Beutler, in his introduction to the poet's autobiography, singles out as surprising in one whom we regard as having so well succeeded with life, not only *in* life. See the Artemis edition of *Dichtung und Wahrheit*, 10:884.

2. On the other hand, one of the related poems written upon the completion of Part I, and virtually stating with its title, "Leave-taking,"

the movement of the hero from darkness to light, though
that too, following the decision to save Faust, became a
matter of central importance, but from a sense that the false
is a part of the true, albeit the part that falls away, as the
true, like the piece of sculpture hewn from rock, gradually
comes into being. To have rewritten first impressions so that
they might better conform with eventual recognitions, to
have deleted what finally would come to be seen as tempo-
rary or fragmentary, would have been to deny the raw
material out of which the end product grew. Many a work
of art has this pretension to virgin birth. For that matter,
the sheer weight of traditional emphasis on purity of form
and consistency of purpose tends to put *Faust* in question
as a great work. By the same token, with its unique degree of
spontaneity and freedom of form—there is no work of
literature generally designated great that is quite as truly
free, only lesser ones—*Faust* puts in question, becomes
a critique of, artistic form itself, no matter how highly accomplished.[3] Of course, the simply bad is as easily recognizable as the formally, but only formally, good, and nothing
is furthered at this point by arguing the priority of freedom
or of order in great art, which often partakes interchangeably
of both. Nothing is freer than true form, and nothing more
self-controlled than true freedom, is perhaps all that one can

-----

the intent to go no further with the work, suggests the opposite by
asking, "Who would gladly describe the confusions of feeling who has
already been led to clarity?" (Witkowski, 2:511–12).

3. In the realm of humor, *Tristram Shandy* does the same, and may
be said to make questionable the distinction between humor and
gravity, which Goethe, in turn, himself no great humorist except in
his creation of Mephistopheles, somehow comes upon in his description of Part II as "serious joking." See William R. Pringer, *Laurence
Sterne and Goethe*, for the literary relation between the two authors.
On the subject of "serious joking" in Goethe, see Herman Meyer,
Diese sehr ernsten Scherze.

say in this matter in the abstract.[4] Practically, however, we
shall have much to do with the question as we go on.

Apparently, *Urfaust* (1772?) was written with a clear
purpose in mind. Goethe spoke of the conception of the
work as having been clearly before him from the outset; only
its development, its succession of ideas and scenes, remained
undefined. Also, as we have seen, he had good reason for
writing a *Faust*. The theme, its hero, and its setting in the
sixteenth century were related to the kind of problem,
personality, and milieu to which he was attracted at the time.
The work remained a fragment for many years, it is true,
but that may be attributable to the fact that the steps in its
progression were indeed unclear to the author and he chose
simply to give them more thought. This argument would
explain at least the initial delays with the project, although
the prolonged postponements, as I suggested earlier, must
have had more telling causes. As I also suggested in the same
context, *Urfaust* has the feel of a completed work.

On the other hand, if the motto to the present chapter is
appropriate, it throws a somewhat different light on the
question. We no longer see Goethe as knowing the full extent of his intentions before the fact, but rather as gradually
discovering his purposes, uncovering the potential of the
theme, recovering, often after long intervals, the impulses
that originally prompted his creativity. The "Dedication"
to Part I begins: "Dim forms, ye hover near . . . shall I strive
to hold you once again?" This fragmented and yet undeni-
able involvement with *Faust* may account for the seemingly
contradictory statements Goethe made concerning the work.

For what, we may justifiably ask in the light of the motto,

4. "Only when he must work within limitations does the master
show himself; the law alone can give us freedom" is a paraphrase of
"In der Beschränkung zeigt sich erst der Meister, und das Gesetz nur
kann uns Freiheit geben," from "Was wir bringen," written for the
opening of a theater in Lauchstädt.

is knowing, when the word is applied to the creative act? The
point where unconscious knowledge becomes conscious is
often difficult to determine from a subjective, let alone an
objective, point of view. We are just as wrong when we
attribute to the creative process the kind of cognitive functions dominant in the logical or critical mind as we are when
we forget that the imaginative faculty, for all its incom-
mensurate elements, has inner laws of its own. Goethe himself makes this distinction in his essay "On German
Architecture," when he speaks of the need for the artist to
resist the influence of "principles" and "models" and follow
the dictates of his genius. There is no rejection of law or
form or purpose in such a precept, but only a deepened,
and thus freeing, sense of the ultimate source of artistic guid-
ance, which is within the artist himself. "I shun no rule
which derives from observation of nature or from the character of a thing," the hero says in the early version of *Wilhelm
Meister,* Book Two. And since the essay was written in the
same period as *Urfaust,* we can imagine Goethe applying the
ideas of the former in the workshop of the latter and allowing an undefined inner purpose to shape his work, which he
then, in turn, in recalling the beginnings of the project,
would remember as clearly defined because it had in the
meantime become that, "like the prophecy through the
fulfillment."

In any event, nothing seems more natural than the way in
which the problems inherent in the first version were
absorbed and resolved in the finished work. Very often
Faust, like Nature, appears to have taken the path of least
resistance and to have made the problems themselves into
solutions, by restating them on higher levels, or reviewing
them in expanded circles of meaning. That was the case, as
we shall see later—for now we must remain within the limits
of meaning in *Urfaust*—with the problems that relate to the
character of the hero, the nature of evil, the terms of the compact with the Devil, and, most importantly, the form the
work was to assume in its final state. Faust became Faust,
that is, the hero became the hero and the work became the

work it is, by joining the forces they could not resist. The
phenomenon is best described by Mephistopheles, who in
climbing the mountain with Faust in the midst of a crowd,
in "Walpurgis Night," says: "You think you are pushing and
you are being pushed."[5]

The elements I have just mentioned are not the only, or
even the main ones that constitute *Urfaust*, but they are the
elements that proved the most problematical. In other regards and areas the original version is straightforward. Or perhaps I should say that it strikes us as straightforward, since
the impact rather than the formal presentation of its contents
is what first impresses. The psychological realism of the
prison scene, when Gretchen awaits her execution, or the
dignified pathos of her anxiety earlier in "Cathedral," or even
the relatively quaint tragedy of her encounter with public
opinion in "At the Well," are meant to move. It is a measure
of the genius that went into the composition of these and
other scenes related to the Gretchen episode that, despite the
indications of their genesis in the Storm and Stress movement, they are almost never overdone. What Goethe did with
complete freedom, apparently, he often did just right. Interpreters of *Faust* are agreed, for example, that in the instances
where he attempted to raise the formal artistic level of the
drama by later turning prose dialogue into verse, in the one
case, "Auerbach's Cellar," nothing essential was gained, and
in the other, the prison scene, something perhaps was lost.[6]
The thick-skinned atmosphere of the wine cellar, in the first
instance, was not to be sensitized with verse and, in the
second instance, the torment and confusion of the situation,
so directly reflected in unmeasured speech, could only be
compromised by meter and rhyme.

My point is not that Goethe should have left well enough
alone. The matter is not that simple. We soon see reason
and advantages in the change. Mephistopheles, whose role in

5. "Der ganze Strudel strebt nach oben;/Du glaubst zu schieben und
du wirst geschoben" (Witkowski, ll. 4116–17).
6. I discuss the changes in chapter 7, below.

"Auerbach's Cellar" is expanded in the later version, where
his character also is more clearly defined, is suited by temperament to doggerel, to mocking rhyme. Humor in general,
it may be said, is closer to verse than to prose. Likewise, the
compromise of tragedy in the final scene, though it is truly
a compromise, has an artistic justification. It makes easier the
transition from bleakness to hope which is given in the
changed version when a voice from Heaven answers "She is
saved" to Mephistopheles' condemnation of Gretchen,
"She is judged." In the original German, judged and saved,
gerichtet and *gerettet,* are themselves a virtual rhyme.

The point is rather that consistency of form, whether in
regard to detail or to larger questions of genre, was not to
be maintained in *Faust,* for reasons which multiply as one considers the drama from different points of view. Ultimately
the work, which begins by resisting, will come to accept in-
consistency, flux, and change as facts of existence, and it
will reflect these facts in its mode of being. That alone could
serve to rationalize its unrestricted form. Even in the minor
example of the transfer of prose to verse, which occurs relatively early, we can notice the process of growing with
change and changing with growth. But here we glimpse the
process in reverse, as it were. Where before we could speak
only abstractly of an urge to artistic freedom which Goethe
shared with his age and indulged in his youth, and where
we could see the urge reflected in the nonformalistic quality
of his early work, now, in a particular instance, we can see
freedom arising through an attempt at restraint. *Gerettet*
could never have been rhymed with *gerichtet* in a prose setting, especially since the word is elicited from a poetic, an
unreal, realm. Rhyme, so necessary at this one moment in
the play, makes prose now seem the luxury;[7] just as, conversely, the verse forms and motifs in Part II, so conventional
in antecedent, seem almost capricious when introduced in

---

7. T. S. Eliot has made the point that the advantage of verse drama
lay precisely in making available for use when necessary the lofty language of profound emotion or thought (in his essay *Poetry and Drama*
[Cambridge, Mass., 1951]).

the wake of the emotionally devastating tragedy in Part I. Again, the point is that something is lost with each gain. In this case, the something partakes of the spirit of immediate, real, and engaging experience that is the whole of life in *Urfaust* but which, as the work progresses, becomes, or at least seems, more and more only a part of an increasingly complex totality. The real is elevated, given a purpose beyond itself, and yet at the same time dissolved (the German would say *aufgehoben*)[8] in the greater idea. It is this kind of "loss" that I had in mind when I spoke of transitory truth in *Urfaust*.

Also straightforward are a number of scenes in the early version that suggest realism, but not of the sort we associate with the Storm and Stress—in its best, or worst, manner. The realism could be termed static, in order to contrast its tranquility with the volatility of certain other scenes, but is pehaps better described as genre realism.

The sixteenth-century setting of *Faust* and the familiar realistic painting of the same era are in this way joined in our mind. We know that at the time of the writing of *Urfaust* Goethe was deeply involved in the study of the Dutch masters, who satisfied his urge to "seek nature in art." Not that a passion for realism in painting, even if carried, as Goethe tells us was so in his case, to almost "insane" lengths,[9] need have

8. This Hegelian concept is not unrelated to Goethe's notion of "heightening": "Steigerung." Walter Kaufmann in his *Hegel: A Reinterpretation* quotes the remark by Goethe that I have used as motto for this study, and adds: "Hegel tried to show, beginning with his first book, that this same consideration applies to philosophy, as well" (p. xii). See further, Karl Löwith, *From Hegel to Nietzsche: The Revolution in Nineteenth-Century Thought* (trans. David E. Green), whose point of departure is the introductory "Goethe and Hegel," but who through comparison and contrast places Goethe in relation to later thinkers, including Nietzsche. See pp. 195-99.

9. "To see nature in art became with me a passion which in its highest moments had to appear to others, even the ardent lovers of art, almost an insanity; and how better to foster such an inclination than through the continual contemplation of the excellent works of the Dutch masters" (*Poetry and Truth,* Book Thirteen). My translation.

influenced his style in writing. Least of all are we thinking
of "painting with words." Yet many minor motifs, some simple stage directions, and, in a few instances, descriptive
passages emerging naturally from the dialogue, make us *see*
Faust's study or Gretchen's room, the wine cellar in Leipzig, or the soldier Valentin carousing with companions and
extolling the virtues of his sister, glass raised on high. The
visual factor, paradoxically, helps us to believe that we are
actually hearing rather than reading the words on the page, in
somewhat the way that the musician is said to see the notes
he composes. In production, of course, these realistic elements
in the drama are greatly reinforced. For that matter, much of
our sense of seeing while reading may itself derive from our
experience of the play in the theater (and today, on film, in
color). The costumes and settings, in turn, were derived from
the art of the appropriate period.

Yet the argument is not wholly circular. Goethe provided
not only an allusion to surrounding with each new setting,
but often, as well, a verbal *mis-en-scène*. We know the appearance of the study in which Faust sits at the beginning of the
play from his own description, and we know its atmosphere
from his reactions to what he describes. We know Gretchen's
room in the same way. It is fixed in our mind not by the
stage direction or design, which simply calls for a small, neat
room, but by Faust who, infatuated with Gretchen, evokes
for us the spirit of her room. In its simple goodness and order-
liness, he says, that spirit prompts her "even to curl the
strewn sand" under her feet.[10] Faust, we feel, can see better
than any stage designer. But it is not only Faust who describes
so well. Caught up in an emotion or engaged in immediate
experience, all the characters seem capable of seeing equally
clearly, as if what was claimed early in this play about

---

10. "Sogar den Sand zu deinen Füssen Kräuseln" (Witkowski, *Urfaust*, 1. 558.) Whereas I quote from the Anna Swanwick translation
of *Faust* in the body of this study, for *Urfaust* I have translated almost
literally, to keep better within my argument. Line numbers for *Urfaust*
refer to Witkowski.

rhetoric, that it cannot persuade unless it comes from the soul,[11] could be applied also to poetry, that it cannot envision unless it feels. This, again, is a Storm and Stress concept. Valentin is able to capture perfectly the mood of his drinking companions, for the aggressive good will they display is his kind of good will. He evokes it, cites it, in order to protest his normally humane attitude in contrast to the harshness toward his fallen sister he feels he must now manfully assert. Not perception or sensitivity, but self-defense makes him see so well. Even Gretchen in her deranged state of mind in prison does not lose her perceptive powers, and perhaps in insanity only truly gains them. She sees and relives her drowning of her child in a pond, and, fixed on a past that is her momentary present, she calls upon Faust, giving hectic directions (here the verse in the final version had to be allowed to break down), to save the child, which she sees as still wiggling. To be sure, this horrific vision has nothing to do with genre realism, any more than does another of her visions in which she sees her dead mother sitting on a rock, nodding her head as if feeling the effects of the lethal sleeping potion Mephistopheles had slyly administered. One whole scene, albeit of only six lines, "Night. Open Field," is given over entirely to the evocation of vague occurrences offstage, to the setting of mood, and has no dramaturgical function.

When *Faust* is described as epic rather than dramatic in essence, not only its length, the number of its characters, and the wanderings through space and time in its second part are taken into account, but also the envisioning, visualizing, objectifying tendency of its language. More is seen in the mind than in fact appears on the stage in this play. That applies as much to the limited, dramatic world of *Urfaust* as to the fantastic and panoramic world of the completed work. From the beginning, long before he consciously held the

11. "Und wenns euch Ernst ist was zu sagen/Ists nöthig Worten nachzujagen" (*Urfaust*, ll. 199–200). There is little punctuation in the manuscript.

belief that man can only truly measure and know himself in
relation to objective reality, Goethe was what the Germans
call an "Augenmensch." The fact that he continued for years
to think of himself as an artist while he was a most success-
ful writer is quite understandable when we keep this pre-
ternatural trait in mind. Only later, in Italy, when close to
the age of forty, did he seem to have abandoned the ambition
to draw and to paint, though he never really stopped sketch-
ing.[12] And it is illuminating to read of his habits in drawing.
On the one hand, he described in Book Nineteen of his autobiography how, when pressed for time, he would broadly
sketch a landscape or an object, set down at the side words
describing the details he was not able to include, and thus
gain "such a sound inner recollection of the subject that
should he wish to use it in a story of a poem it was at once
present in his mind and at his disposal." Sight could become
word. On the other hand, his imagination was so easily
fired by words that conversations about places could create
in him the strongest desire immediately to sketch them.
This he relates in his biographical records for 1810, where
he speaks of a journey on which the experience had so
noticeably occurred; the verbal became visual. But words
never failed him, as his drawing pen did.

The purpose in mentioning the plasticity of the poetry in
Urfaust is not to praise, so much as to anticipate, the function and importance of this element in the broader work.[13] It
will serve as an anchor. The more far-reaching and profound
the problem in *Faust* became, and had to become as the
work began to meet the modern ethical and metaphysical
demands on the legendary theme, the less dispensable were
its roots in tangible experience. The whole had to feel

12. After Italy, the year 1813 especially shows the renewed
interest. In the entry for December 1, 1787, of *The Italian Journey*,
Goethe notes that he sketched when he could not write.

13. In an article on "Torquato Tasso" in *Goethe: Poet and Thinker*,
Wilkinson speaks of the hero's being made not only to speak verse, as
do the other figures in the play, but to speak as a poet. Yet so does
Faust, albeit as a quite different kind of poet from Tasso.

true as well as be true, in the sense that logical and philosophical arguments may be said to be true. And feeling derives
from palpable sense, as Goethe said in objecting to the notion
that his *Faust* could be understood solely from the point of
view of its ideas. The very impact of the Gretchen episode,
and the all-leveling humor of Mephistopheles of which I shall
speak in a moment, as well as the quality of the language in
Faust, help to counterbalance the fantastic or incommensurable evolutions it describes in other respects. Part II will
make of the moment, of being, of immediacy, a focus and a
duty, but from the beginning there was an involuntary
commitment to objective reality. Goethe was almost never
abstract, but nowhere was he more concrete than in *Urfaust.*

That in itself is interesting. The hero and the theme
suggest the opposite. The striving and perceptions of the
work are romantic—wholly so in its early stages. We might
have expected *Götz von Berlichingen* or the soon-to-be-
completed *Egmont,* with their extroverted heroes and historical subject matter, to be encased in a vividly real world,
but not *Faust.* Yet we soon realize that this world too
abounds in image, for it is a product of the same mind
that created the other worlds. A theme does not change an
artist's instincts; rather, the artist's instincts change the
theme. In *Urfaust,* Goethe had merely—and justifiably, since
he was writing poetic drama—evoked his objective world
through words, as was his lyrical wont,[14] rather than through
the directly generic devices of stage production. And I was
perhaps being too philosophical when I said above that it was
from a faith in the rightness of things in their own time that
Goethe had retained the whole of his early version in the
finished work. Any number of practical reasons could have
prompted the same decision. It may have been the need for
immediacy and emotion in an increasingly ironic drama
(Goethe would come to refer to Part II as "these very serious
jokes") or the recognition of the advantages of the lyrical

---

14. The verbal mis-en-scène at the beginning of the "Classical Walpurgis Night" is striking.

approach in a work which, with magic as a factor in its
actions, could not remain long in the real world; or simply
the desire for plot. Yet here, too, we realize that what had
come from youth—the emotion and the immediacy, the
storm and the stress—is only, or best, given in youth. Not
that art is unable to recapture, to recollect. But then it partakes of re-creation, with concomitant new perspective,
and not of direct experience. Goethe *had* his Storm and Stress
and, in *Faust,* used it. And the more one views the work in
the light of its interrelating of personal experience and broadest intent, of apparent patchwork and freedom of form, the
more one is struck by the peculiarly organic nature of the
whole, though one may be hard put to name the organism
that has thus evolved.

Mephistopheles provides the humor in *Urfaust.* Where he
is, there is humor, and when humor is needed he is there.
This latter function is of some importance. For where in an
imaginative work with a basis in realism we might speak only
of the characteristics of an individual, as though he actually
existed to possess them, in a work predicated on freedom of
time, place, and action, which magic supplies, we can speak
also of the function of a character, as though the elements he
represents and provides alone have brought him into being.
Neither concept will account fully for Mephistopheles, to be
sure. A devil is as little or as much a reality as an idea. But it
is true that in *Urfaust,* at least, where his character is vivid
but his nature still undefined and his purpose wholly unclear,
we can see Mephistopheles, as it were, as a simple fact and
seek to define him by what he does. He counteracts. He does
not laugh, for all the humor he provides. To laugh is to react
and Mephistopheles acts upon. At best, he can produce a
forced laugh, an act upon himself. Why this should be so is
not explained in *Urfaust*; only the completed Part I, with
its "Prologue in Heaven" and the piecemeal apologetics the
Devil himself supplies, will suggest an answer. There, too,
he will be seen to function as a polar element, but with rami-
fications that go beyond humor and involve the very principle of polarity, in the universe as well as in the realms of
psychology and morality.

Faust has no humor, nor does Gretchen. The more important then that Mephistopheles provide the humor, not out of
himself, to be sure, as it does not lie in his nature as it does in
the nature of a Falstaff, but through his actions or, rather,
the way he is made to act or function. His first appearance in
Urfaust, unannounced and unexplained, comes precisely at
the moment when comic relief, or some other change, is
needed. This is after the weighty and distressed opening
monologue and the despondent conversation of Faust with
the pedantic Wagner. Mephistopheles comes unannounced,
but the play, and its content and tone at the moment, call
for him.[15] I am referring to the scene with the student, and
it could serve as illustration of my point, as could the action
in "Auerbach's Cellar." But the former, a mocking introduction of a student to university life, might have been conceived
by any upperclassman, if not carried out so brilliantly, and
the latter, with its magical pranks, is not on the level of the
true Mephistopheles. Neither has much to do with his essential nature. Goethe was here only beginning with his devil.

There is one scene in particular, however, that serves very
well to illustrate the function of humor, and of Mephistopheles, in the early version. It serves so well, by counterpoint
and through persistent counteraction, by identifying the
Devil with his mode of humor, by defining his character
through his instinctive actions, that one might easily read
through it amused and miss a point about Mephistopheles
that for the first time is being established. He negates
compulsively; he creates in order to negate. This is part of his
instinct to counteraction, an aspect of his polaric role in the
play. In the later version, when pressed, he will come out and
identify himself as the spirit that always denies or negates:
verneint. But already in "The Neighbor's House," he is doing,
if not saying, just that. In fact, since the doing comes before
the saying in the composition of the work, we suspect that
once again Goethe had relied on the intuition of a truth or
idea which he only afterward consciously recognized and

15. See Fairley, *Goethe's Faust: Six Essays,* the first essay.

could identify in abstract terms. His devil *was* before he
meant.

The scene in question involves Gretchen, her neighbor
Martha, and Mephistopheles, who has come to the house ostensibly to testify to the death of Martha's husband in
Padua. His story will be pure fiction: it is merely a part of
the scheme to introduce himself and Faust into the circle
and allow the seduction of Gretchen to occur in a more
proper, and thus surer, way.

What he tells cannot be of consequence. That the husband
should have died in Padua accommodates the fact that he
is a sailor and provides a remoteness that encourages belief,
for anything can happen if it happens far enough away.
Besides, the Devil *looks* foreign, and could easily be thought
of as having recently been in Padua.[16] But the way Mephistopheles tells his story is gratuitous and ultimately malicious.
We forgive him his malice and may not even notice it, for he
is diverting. Note both his opening announcement to Martha
that her "husband is dead and sends his regards" and the
veiled proposal of marriage on his own part, which he is then
afraid she might well accept: "She could hold the Devil
himself to his word."[17] Yet, at the risk of seeming pedantic—
one ought not explicate humor—it should be pointed out that
Martha is made not only to hear recriminations from her
husband, tales of his infidelity, and descriptions of his destitu-
tion, but to hear them immediately following, as if in one
breath, confessions of remorse, prayers for wife and children,
and a story of great, if illicit and short-lived, prosperity.
The hope precedes—in effect produces—the disappointment.
For it would not have been there had it not been just created.

And at the further risk of presuming to psychoanalyze a
devil, I repeat that the foregoing is totally fictitious, with no

16. On Mephistopheles' outward appearance, see, for example, Atkins, *Goethe's Faust: A Literary Analysis*, pp. 18, 43, 73.

17. "Ich hoff sie lässt nicht büsen: / Ihr Mann ist todt und lässt sie
grüsen. . . ." "Sie hielte wohl den Teufel selbst beym Wort" (*Urfaust*,
ll. 769–70 and 859).

factors determining its content or form other than the desires
or needs of the teller. Not that this example will prove
Mephistopheles compulsively destructive. Other, later examples, in which he clearly acts in his worst interest, will
better make the point. In the present example we might find
the destruction not only humorous but ineffective, since it
is practiced on Martha, a person who, being unable to find in
her husband, as she tells us, any fault other than his roaming,
wenching, drinking, and gambling, must be close to inde-
structible.[18] Our example shows, rather, that we understand
only after the fact, as we are assuming Goethe did. We
connect the humor with the destruction by experiencing
them as one, and then come to recognize their essential
affinity.

We also see the affinity between humor and contrast, and
contrast and negation, in the scene immediately following,
"Garden." Here, Faust with Gretchen, and Mephistopheles
with Martha, walk a circle that brings them alternately to
the fore, and we overhear their conversations. The contrasts
are endless, though we are hardly conscious of them, so
charming and natural is the situation, so in character are the
characters. That, in fact, is a not unimportant characteristic
of the work as a whole, namely that the naturalness of its
contents results not in a diminishing of the things contrasted
but in an enhancement of their respective qualities. Goethe
will discover later[19] that polarity produced heightening, and
will exemplify the phenomenon in his work. The sentiment
that surrounds Gretchen and Faust is not made to seem mere
sentimentality in its contrast to the implacable realism of
Martha and Mephisto—that is the way of satire—but to seem
what it is in a purer form. Conversely, we appreciate rather
than deprecate the unerring sense of the realities of existence

18. "Ihm fehlte nichts als allzugern zu wandern,/Und fremde
Weiber und der Wein,/Und das verfluchte Würfel Spiel" (*Urfaust*,
ll. 849–51).

19. Or, perhaps, had already learned in his alchemistic studies in the
early period, as Ronald Gray suggests (*Goethe, the Alchemist*), rather
than in his later scientific studies.

which the latter enjoy. The two souls that Faust will recognize
as inhabiting his own breast, the one reaching ever beyond
and above and the other holding fast to the earth, are an inward identification of what is here outwardly, dramaturgically, displayed. Yet just as we cautioned ourselves in regard
to the explication of humor, we must be wary of seeking
symbolic content in action easily explained in terms of character and circumstance, or artistic prerogative. Much occurs
in *Faust,* as Goethe warned, that cannot be "strung on the
thread of a single idea." Mephistopheles has sides to his character that *are,* and do not *mean.* At times he seems simply
evil, as Gretchen is the first to sense. But we are attempting
here to define only his function in the early version rather
than his total nature or character, which later will become
more evident.

Gretchen, on the other hand, cannot be said to have a
"function." Surely *she* does not mean. In fact, the difficulty
in speaking about her arises from the very completeness or
wholeness of her nature that is apparent from the beginning.
We ask no questions of her and therefore need no explana-
tions. Even our natural assumption that her wholeness, in
contrast to the dividedness of Faust and the destructiveness
of Mephistopheles, is her meaning, though true, partakes of
an order of abstract thinking in which Gretchen has no part.
At best, once Helen of Troy has appeared in a kind of
heightening of the female element in the play, and Gretchen
herself has *re*appeared among a heavenly host in the choral
finale, we may think of her more generally: as part of the
"Eternal Feminine" of which the Chorus Mysticus inscrutably
speaks. In *Urfaust,* she is wholly concrete. Her tragedy
would not be so poignant were she less so.

There is another reason for our difficulty in speaking
about Gretchen, and one that relates to her solely as a character. She has no significant past. Our knowledge of persons
in a play derives as often from what they have done as from
what they do and say. Our knowledge of Gretchen, for
all the poetry that is evoked by the mere mention of things

attached to her simple life—Faust imagines her childhood in
his rhapsodic description in "A Small Neat Room," and she
herself speaks of her daily chores and of her past in "Garden"
—remains meager as well as unimportant. She is too young
to have had a past, at least a past that could determine character. Her main characteristic is that in her wholeness and
completeness she seems to have no characteristics. She has
no edges, as it were. Not that she is meant to represent the
ineffably ideal, although one does suspect that her roots
lie in the Storm and Stress preconception of feminity as the
opposite of the tormented and divided male in revolt. In
any event, she is the perfect pendant to Faust.

But her want of a dramatic past is combined with the
want of a future, with the result that not only *may* we choose
to leave her unanalyzed and unexplained, we virtually *must*.
She will be lent no meaning in the sense that her tragedy will
be shown to have had purpose or her character revealed as
the cause of her fate. She will gain no new meaning in the way
that Mephistopheles and Faust, outgrowing the early version, gain in meaning as their author sees them anew and more
fully. Except for the minor details related to the transposing
of prose into verse in the dungeon scene, Goethe alters none
of her lines in the completed Part I. More significantly, he
adds none. Even the lesser figures Wagner and Valentin undergo further development, if not in character, at least in
extension. But no further mention is made of Gretchen until
the very end, as if she had been forgotten by Faust. But
not by Goethe. We assume that she had come to him poetically whole and he had produced and dispatched her immediately. She was not meant to transcend the world of *Urfaust*. She is thus the figure most easy to understand in
context, and Faust the least. She is most realized and he most
anticipated, as we shall see.

Gretchen is the product of Storm and Stress, as is *Urfaust*
as a whole. Her fate as an unwed mother has parallels in
the drama of the period as well as in its poetry and prose.
Lenz treats the theme specifically in *The Tutor* and partially,
through the motif of seduction, in *The Soldiers*. Heinrich

Leopold Wagner, like Goethe, presses the question to its logical end in *Infanticide*—the harshness of the laws against unwed motherhood typically led to that extreme. Infanticide forms the subject matter of long poems by Bürger and, later, Schiller. The motif occurs in ballads—Gretchen sings one in the dungeon scene[20] —and stories. In 1781 a prize was offered for the best essay on how infanticide might be checked, and there were four hundred entries.[21]

This concern suggests the acute consciousness of social injustice which is prelude to revolt. And the Storm and Stress was revolutionary, in thought if not in effect.[22] It also suggests an acute conscience. Not only Goethe, with his penchant for confessional writing and an ample number of liaisons outside his circle and class,[23] but any of the young intelligensia, barely out of university, could be expected to have written on the theme. The problem was in and of the social order of the day.[24] In a gesture reflecting more sen-

20. "Meine Mutter die Hur / Die mich umgebracht hat. . . ." It has been noted that the song closely resembles the song of a bird in a Grimm fairy tale which begins, "Meine Mutter, die mich umbracht':" It is possible that Goethe consciously altered the first line to fit his needs—the unwed mother regarding herself as a whore. See Heffner, Rehder, and Twadell, 1:429.

21. So notes Oscar H. Werner in *The Unmarried Mother in German Literature,* with special reference to the period 1770–1800, p. 4.

22. See Pascal, *Sturm und Drang.*

23. Apparently, the first was the so-called Frankfurt Gretchen, the relationship with whom Goethe describes in veiled terms in *Poetry and Truth,* Book Five.

24. Werner cites eighteenth-century humanitarianism as prompting concern over the matter, though he also allows actual experience to have played a part. In the case of Goethe, it is interesting to speculate "to what extent the Gretchen episode, in terms of biography, rests on Goethe's unhappy flight from Friedrike Brion (1771), or to what extent it was occasioned by the execution in Frankfurt, almost under Goethe's eyes, of an unfortunate unwed mother, Susanna Margretha Brandt, who in her desperation had killed her child (1772)," as Heffner, Rehder, and Twadell put the question (1:33).

sitivity than logic, the tutor in the drama we have just mentioned
castrates himself. Greater conscience hath no man. The
anguished guilt of the culprit, to be sure, is the best illustration of the innocence of the victim, and that innocence
was prerequisite to the point being made; Rousseau had his
influence upon the social thought of the Storm and Stress.
But whether this innocence had a basis in reality or was the
complicated projection of cultural and ethical forces is for
us less important than the fact of its general acceptance.
Gretchen shared, in other words, not only the fate but also
the attributes of her counterparts in life and in literature.
The Storm and Stress produced many Gretchens under different names. When Mephistopheles says in *Urfaust* "She
is not the first"—"*Sie ist die erste nicht*"—the remark is so
devastating because it is so true. Only the genius of Goethe
could make of the type an archetype, and only the setting
of his drama in the sixteenth century could produce both the
distance that makes poetry of tragedy and a milieu that
could render plausible what at a later date might appear extreme. For, unlike the heroine in the typical eighteenth-
century setting, his Gretchen is guilty not only in the eyes
of society but profoundly so in her own. She condemns
herself, not from overzealousness, but out of a piety as natural to her time and place as to her character. She will not—
psychologically cannot—take the step to escape that Faust
offers her. It is we who appreciate her innocence and she who
perceives her own guilt. The difference is important; it is the
same difference that characterizes all her virtues. As Faust
says: "Simplicity and innocence,/When will ye learn your
hallowed worth to know!"[25] However, in the interest of realism and the solid base of motivation in the play, it must be
noted that the recognition of guilt grows with the tragic action.
In the end, Gretchen has lost her innocence both in the
philosophical and the moral meaning of the word. In that sad
sense, she may be said to have developed.

---

25. "Ach dass die Einfalt dass die Unschuld nie/Sich selbst und
ihren heiligen Werth erkennt!" (*Urfaust*, ll. 954–55).

Goethe is deceptive. An author who could speak of his magnum opus as a serious frivolity cannot have been wholly without conscious guile. Moreover, as I mentioned earlier, at times he deliberately played hide-and-seek with his literary audience. The result for *Faust* was a number of passages, allusions, and motifs which found their way into the work for what appear to be private reasons, rather than higher reasons of art. The tendency became more pronounced as the work approached its end, and some commentators, presumptuously but perhaps correctly, have seen in this fact a reflection of senility.[26] The presumption, right or wrong, is highly illustrative of the problems created by the sheer uniqueness of *Faust* as a literary work. What *is* playful or willful in the realm of free form?

But there is a deceptiveness in Goethe neither willful nor playful, rather the contrary. His very naturalness tends to deceive. "At its highest peak, art appears wholly external," he wrote later in *Maxims and Reflections*, for in his mature years he regarded representation, externalization, as the task of poetry, and all internalizing as a symptom of decline.[27] Yet even in the period with which we are dealing, his instincts, if not his conscious views, led him always to create from with-

26. For example, Pniower in "Fausts zweiter Teil," *Dichtungen und Dichter, Essays und Studien,* p. 74.

27. Further: "The poet is bound to representation, the highest form of which is when it vies with reality, that is, when it depictions through imagination become so living that anyone could consider them as actual or present. . . . Those which describe the inner without embodying it in an outer, or without allowing the outer to become felt by the inner, are both in the last stages of the departure of poetry into common concerns." My translation, which is partially an interpretation. The original reads: "Der Dichter ist angewiesen auf Darstellung. Das Höchste derselben ist, wenn sie mit der Wirklichkeit wetteifert, das heißt, wenn ihre Schilderungen durch den Geist dergestalt lebendig sind, daß sie als gegenwärtig für jedermann gelten können. . . . Diejenige, die nur das Innere darstellt, ohne es durch ein Aeußeres zu verkörpern, oder das Aeußere durch das Innere durchfühlen zu lassen, sind beides die letzten Stufen, von welchen aus [die Poesie] ins gemeine Leben hineintritt" (Hamburg edition, 12:510–11).

in a context, to go out from experience rather than thought. I remarked on this quality in his art at the very outset, and throughout have noted the similar qualities of spontaneity, concreteness, and realism. But just as my original purpose in mentioning the quality was not for its own sake but in order to point out its special bearing on *Faust,* now my purpose is the same, but narrower. Earlier I asked whether spontaneous creativity, the quality we associate most with Goethe, might not have proved the wrong talent when brought to bear on material demanding or encouraging abstract organization and thought, such as the Faust theme. Here I ask whether what I am describing as externality might not have stood in the way of realizing the central figure, who is introspective. Gretchen as a personality is wholly external; even when she turns within, at the same time she reaches out, in that her monologues tend to take the form of song or prayer, that is, objective or given expression.[28] Mephistopheles has a private world, we suspect, but we shall never know of it. Faust has a world within him that must be revealed.

The question, here as there, needs raising, not answering. Of course the nature of Goethe's genius did not hamper him in the creation of his Faust, either the work or the character. But it proceeded to make both different: in the first regard, as we have seen, by developing a form to house its special needs, and in the second by persisting in its natural way and imperceptibly bending the hero to itself. Hence the deceptiveness. We expect from this Faust what we do not get and miss what we should receive.

The opening monologue sets the pattern. With its Knittelvers it suggests the puppet theater, but with its accumulating intensity of feeling it appears to be leading into a greater world, which, however, does not materialize. When we hear philosophy, law, medicine and theology spoken of, we anticipate that the conclusion to be reached upon rejecting these pursuits will itself be an intellectualization, something

28. Prayers, as well as song, are created, but one cannot sing an *individual* song.

that can be sought and put into words, and we are wrong.
Faust speaks of seeking the truth in magic, of *"beholding
with his own eyes* the innermost workings of the world."[29]
This is already less than abstract, as my italics are meant to
suggest. Moreover, the pursuit is aborted. *Urfaust* has little
to do with magic and its accoutrements of fantasy and
wonder, and even less to do with philosophy in its metaphysical form. The action is mainly psychological and
dramatic.

That is what we look for; what we miss is more important.
The lightness of the Knittelvers as verse, the meter, makes
us assume a lightness of content, an easiness of comprehension.
At the unconscious level, to be sure, something quite different may happen, and it will be to my point soon, as well
as later, to attempt to say just what might be the difference.
But now, with the rhyming of *philosophy* and *theology,*
the sardonic listing of titles of learning, and the direct expression, in the manner of the puppet theater, of impatience
and anger, we probably note only the main thrust of the
argument: in his disenchantment and frustration with knowledge, Faust has turned to magic.

What we most likely overlook is the necessity or the com-
pelling logic of the choice, which results not from the failure
of learning in itself—learning that included all the disciplines
of the day—but from the corollaries of the failure, and from
circumstance. This is not the Faust of the chapbook or of
Marlowe, or indeed, later, of Lessing, who has chosen to over-
step bounds within which he might reasonably live. Rather,
it is a Faust who, born into an age (I speak of Goethe's own
age) which for all its religious scepticism has not succeeded
in finding in philosophy a substitute guide to moral and
spiritual truth, nor for all its rationality an ideal way of life,
has been forced to look beyond these modes of thought
to a new manner of knowing. There is nothing in the chapbook—which, to be sure, is not on a high intellectual plane—

29. "Schau alle Würkungskrafft und Saamen / Und thu nicht mehr
in Worten kramen" (*Urfaust,* ll. 31–32). My italics.

to suggest that the religious or philosophical presuppositions
of its day required a revaluation of the kind that a Faust
might undertake. There is the suspicion in Marlowe that his
sympathies, born of his age, lie with his audacious hero and
that only reluctantly does he allow him condemned;[30]
but no order, religious, philosophical, or social, is thereby
seriously challenged, let alone upset. For that matter, the
twitting of Catholicism in the comical scene at the Vatican
would appear simply to reaffirm the Protestant position
of the time. Much later (1759) Lessing, though he would save
Faust, would save him not for pursuing his course despite
his essential blindness, his inability to know, but for defiantly
following the light wherever it might lead him. "If God held
in his right hand all truth and in his left the everlasting desire
for truth, although with the condition that I would continually and eternally err, and said to me: 'Choose!' I would
humbly grasp his left hand and say: 'This one, Father; the
pure truth is really only for you alone.'" This famous passage
appears in a polemic entitled "A Rejoinder," which Lessing
published during the time of the theological controversies in
which he was engaged in later years. We can imagine his
Faust pursuing truth in the same enlightened way, though
without the same humility.

Such optimism no longer accompanied the search for truth
toward the end of the Enlightenment, the period in which
Goethe conceived his *Faust.* The belief in a purposeful design
in the universe remained but had lost its logical demonstra-
bility. The result was a condition typical of ages of transition in which a principal belief in itself is retained and what
follows from it rejected. It is as if mankind cannot swallow
the pill at once and must first nibble on it. What followed
from the concept of demonstrable universal design was not
only the belief in God, which, as the deism of the times
shows, was not an essential in a purposeful life, and not only
the faith in the perfectibility of man, which if we read

30. See C. L. Barber, "The Form of Faustus' Fortunes Good or
Bad," in Paul E. Bates, ed., *Faust: Sources, Works, Criticism.*

Lessing correctly was not of pressing importance,[31] but the
relatively simple prospect of a realizable goal for an individual
life. It was not necessary to know the truth, but only to
know that there was a truth, in order to pursue with some
confidence any aim beyond the basic needs of survival. When
this structure of thought collapsed or appeared to collapse,
it was not its design but its spirit that suffered, or better,
changed. There was a sudden distaste for, rather than a considered rejection of, the principal modes of thought and
feeling it had produced. Goethe spoke of having been ready,
had he been able to get hold of the author, to strangle
Voltaire for his *Saul,* so great was his youthful distaste for
the tone of the play.[32] The same Goethe would never
abandon the belief in an ultimately ordered world, however,
nor, the trust in order in life; his differences with the Enlightenment would prove to be not in aim, but in method. His
task, like the task of his Faust, was to discover a viable way
of existence based on less than absolute knowledge of man's
place and purpose in the universe. It was essentially the
task of the humanist.

All this is implied in the opening lines of *Urfaust.* When
Faust speaks of the limitations of human understanding
(". . . and see that we can know nothing"),[33] in his disenchantment he states the position in the extreme. But he is
in no way suggesting the traditional belief that the awareness of ignorance is the beginning of knowledge. He is feeling,
with his times, barred from the essential truth. When he

31. Paragraphs 81–82 of *The Education of the Human Race* read:
"Or is the human race never to reach the highest levels of enlightenment and perfection? What? . . . Never? Do not let me think this blasphemy, all-gracious God.—Education has its *goal,* with the species no
less than the individual. What is educated is educated to something."
My translation.

32. In *Poetry and Truth,* Book Twelve. Goethe could, however,
admire Voltaire as a person "abstracted from his age," as a conversation with J. A. Leisewitz, August 14, 1780, suggests.

33. "Und seh daß wir nichts wissen *können*" (*Urfaust,* l. 11, my
italics). The precise wording is important.

professes his agnosticism ("I am plagued by no scruples nor doubts"),[34] his boldness is apparent, but his thinking is of his day and not merely of his character. If this is blasphemy, it is rather bland blasphemy, for Faust does not forget to add that his want of belief results in a new want: "But for that, all joy is taken from me."[35] And since he does not assume he knows the truth, either through religion or through learning, he cannot presume to teach the truth, either in the abstract for its own sake or for the purpose of effecting social good: "I do not pretend to any theories for changing and improving mankind."[36] This social corollary to the negative axiom, "We can know nothing," was the more disheartening in a context in which the higher endeavors were themselves being questioned. One might ignore social reform as one strove for the perfection of mankind, just as, earlier, one might deny this life in the hope of happiness in the next. But once "the view beyond" was lost, as Faust puts it in Part II, the want of knowing even the more immediate purposes of man became intolerable. (It is not surprising that the times soon found a new guide to truth that would serve these purposes: the voice of the majority of men.) And since, finally, Faust, from circumstance or as the result of a professional hazard, has not the "property nor money, honor nor worldly splendor"[37] that could make the purpose of life pleasant in the feeling, if hard in the knowing, he has turned to magic.

In its search for a new way to truth, the age as a whole turned to a mode of perception closely related to magic, that is, poetry. The philosopher king would be replaced by the poet as prophet. In general, poetry would guide where thought had stopped. Schiller would write on the "aesthetic" education of man, while Lessing had seen mankind as trained on

---

34. "Mich plagen keine Skrupel noch Zweifel" (*Urfaust*, l. 15).

35. "Dafür ist mir auch all Freud entrissen" (*Urfaust*, l. 17).

36. "Bild mir nicht ein ich könnt was lehren / Die Menschen zu bessern und zu bekehren" (*Urfaust*, ll. 19–20).

37. "Auch hab ich weder Gut noch Geld / Noch Ehr und Herrlichkeit der Welt" (*Urfaust*, ll. 21–22).

the Bible in childhood, the philosophers in youth, and on
something which we can, but he could not as yet, see as the
philosophy of science, in maturity.[38] But Schiller and
Goethe both would look for truth through the arts, through
a means of knowing that partook of the senses as much as
the mind.

But here we speak of the age in Goethe. Following the lead
he gives us in his own biography, we must also speak of him
in his age. Goethe initiated, as well as exemplified, or better,
he exemplified as he initiated. That is why he was inimitable.
Not only did he do so many things in poetry, he did them so
completely that they begged not to be redone. He appears
to have shared this feeling, in that he virtually never repeated
or imitated himself stylistically or thematically. The number
of fragments among his writings, especially in the early period,
peculiarly attests to this fact. They represent not abandoned
material so much as themes or motifs being concurrently
treated in other projects.

There were those who did not sense the completeness, as
there are always those who will not leave well enough alone.
Werther,[39] for example, which marked for Goethe an end no
less than an onset of a sentimental phase, obviously seemed
to others a mere beginning. The novel spawned enough imitations among lesser writers to merit a generic classification,
"Wertheriade." A later work such as *Wilhelm Meister* had so
measurable an influence as to initiate a form (one might
almost say *the* form) of the German novel, the "Bildungs-
roman," that has persisted into the present day. The example
of *Wilhelm Meister,* however, is much more to our point.
Its influence is reflected less in imitation than in *imitatio,*
which is an imitating in spirit but in an independent context
and with independent means. Goethe's influence on his age
generally was of this indirect nature. He inspired in others, at

38. In his essay *Die Erziehung des Menschengeschlechts,* first published in 1780, English translation, *The Education of the Human
Race,* by F. W. Robertson (London, 1896).
39. See Atkins, *The Testament of Werther.*

least in the best, a will to their own independence and individuality, and hoped to foster these qualities through his
art. He wished, we recall, that the Germans would have
the "courage" to let themselves be moved by his *Faust,* instead of searching always for abstract thought and defini-
tions. His contemporaries almost without exception felt the
effect of his spirit, but rarely did they attempt to define its
nature. "Only a genius can inspire a genius," Lessing had
said. But only a genius might resist the inspiration. Thus the
case of Schiller. The young poet who had declared, "Goethe
is simply in my way," and on reading *Iphigenia* felt dejected
by the thought that he himself could not create a work of
this kind, came in writing the treatise "On Naive and Sentimental Poetry" to an understanding and acceptance of the
difference between himself and his great contemporary and
could then assert the validity of his own conscious, less
spontaneous form of creativity. Schiller, we might say for
our purposes here, had defined Goethe and was free to
be himself. Others, more in the spirit of Goethe, omitted the
intermediate step.[40]

Goethe, we said, initiated; he did not merely exemplify.
For all that he was a product of his age, he was no mere
reflection. The ideas inherent in his writings, though they
clearly partook of the spirit of his times, were no more
received into his art in conscious awareness than they emerged
from it in logical sequence or perspective. A more disorderly
process took place, as art is disorderly in the making if it
dare not be so in the end result. When I connected the ideas
implicit in the opening monologue with prevalent ideas
of the day, my purpose was not to suggest that Goethe was
deliberately expressing through Faust the thought and
spirit of the times. The free-associative quality of the monologue speaks against deliberation. The ideas in question, for

40. In his essay on Heine, Matthew Arnold sees the later poet as
assuming the role of Goethe rather than following him in thought or
style. But Heine (1797–1856) was of a distinctly separate generation
and did not require the imaginary confrontation in order to justify
his own position.

that matter, were being born *into* the age; they were not yet there for the taking and explicating. Goethe was among the chief bearers. Hence the sense of unrehearsed thinking in the opening lines, hence the impression of psychology, as what is said is being felt and what is felt is being said, and hence the anticipation, the embryonic form, of ideas and attitudes to life which only later were to come fully into being. But hence also the scrambled logic, the carrying of the extraneous and false along with the essential and true insight, and the ultimate inconclusiveness in most regards.

I speak of the monologue only as it appears in *Urfaust*. Later, when Goethe had more clearly separated himself and his thinking from his central figure and, through the device of a prologue in Heaven and the motif of attempted suicide and miraculous rebirth placed these early words and thoughts in a broader context, they appeared more errant than misconceived, more like tentative beginnings (despite their Storm and Stress bravado) than aborted ends. And if we ask yet again why Goethe, having come to understand more, retained his earlier version rather than begin wholly anew, we now find a further reason. Virtually everything he appears to have introduced instinctively into the concept of Faust as hero and theme he might well have retained on rational grounds. Faust sounds like Goethe in his lyric poetry of the time. There is the same associative as opposed to logical quality of thought, and a strength that derives from dynamics rather than coherence. When Faust, having informed us in his function as dramatis persona of his reasons for turning to magic, awakes from his musings and, glimpsing the reflection of the moon, forgets his thoughts and indulges his feelings, he may be inconsistent but he seems the more human. Soon he is speaking what sounds like a poem to the moon but which in fact is a dramatically justified as well as lyrically beautiful set of lines. Faust is seeking escape from thought in an envisioned death, or passage of the soul, in which he moves in moonlight with spirits over mountain tops and caves and meadows until, free from the weight of all his thinking, he is reborn to health and life. These are lines of the kind that truly should not be translated, for it is their musical quality—for Faust and not merely for the reader—rather than their content, that renders them effective. They have to do with seeking and longing, as music so often does. In short, the lines are "romantic," though Goethe would not have had that word to describe them when first they were written.[41]

The next major motif, which again is advanced without notice, also partakes of a development in thought which we in retrospect readily identify but which Goethe himself at the time was barely on the verge of exploring. It is the idea of *Naturphilosophie* which we associate with the name of the most prominent of the romantic philosophers in Germany, Schelling.[42] Goethe comes to the idea without Schelling, as

41. For the history and definition of the concept "romantic," see Hans Eichner, ed., *"Romantic" and Its Cognates;* also René Wellek, "The Concept of Romanticism in Literary History," *Comparative Literature* 1 (1949).

42. The influence of Schelling (1775-1854) becomes more apparent as *Faust* progresses. Witkowski (2:421) notes that the abstract outline, or schema, for Part II seems, in part, literally transcribed from a passage in Schelling's *Entwurf eines Systems der Naturphilosophie* (1799), which suggests that Goethe might have found in the philosopher systematic formulations of what he himself as a poet had known only intuitively and separately. There is an English translation of the schema in Thomas, 2:vi; also in Arndt/Hamlin.

In *Ideen zu einer Philosophie der Natur* (2nd ed., 1803, p. 5), Schelling claimed ". . . das Wesen des Menschen ist Handeln"; i.e., human beings realize themselves in action, which is what Goethe implies both at the beginning of *Faust* ("Im Anfang war die Tat" [l. 1237]) and at the end ("Nur der verdient sich Freiheit wie das Leben,/Der täglich sie erobern muß " [ll. 11,575-76]). The *Ideen* contains chapters on light, air, electricity, chemistry, and on attraction and repulsion as a basic principle in the system of nature. Schelling would not have formed Goethe's view of life, but one wonders whether this example of systematization of knowledge did not force the poet finally to express his own position in full, which is *Faust*. Goethe is said to have thought of entrusting the composition of an epic poem on nature to Schelling (Richard Friedenthal, *Goethe: His Life and Times*, p. 372), which is a sure indication of an affinity of views. We know from

he predates him, and seems to have been influenced, if that was at all necessary, by the views of Herder and the style of Hamann, though the visions in the opening monologue are transmitted by means clearly intended to evoke an earlier age and manner of thinking, the age of mystical and alchemistic thought in which the theme is set. That mode of thought, in a sense, formed an historical antecedent to the as-yet-to-be-defined philosophical presuppositions (they were still only feelings) of the late eighteenth and early nineteenth century. Neither was subjected to the predominant rationalism of the intervening era. Faust, again as dramatis persona, could come to the idea without Goethe. That is, his suprarational approach, whether it is seen in terms of the theme as a symptom of his presumptousness or in terms of literary history as a sign of the Storm and Stress, would of itself force him to seek an alternative to rationalism, whatever form that alternative might take. In fact, the scene calls for Faust, having sought the escape I just mentioned, to become again aware of his immediate surroundings and, once more denouncing all that relates to learning and science, to seek a new escape, in nature: "Flee! Out into the open land."[43] On this journey of the mind he will take as companion a book by Nostradamus, a name which suggests the occult and, at the same time, adds an element of historical plausibility to what in essence is simply poetical. No more than the important events in

his notebooks that he had read the introduction to the "Entwurf einer Naturphilosophie," as he called it, which Schelling had "friendlily shared" with him in 1799, the year in which there was much new activity with *Faust,* though the activity may have begun earlier. (Schiller, June 23, 1797: "If you really get to work on Faust I have no doubt that it will be completely carried out." The place of first importance in influencing Goethe to complete the work must continue to go to Schiller, whose proddings and incisive, but constructive, criticism are clearly documented in their correspondence. But since the proddings produced no immediate, and the criticism no real, results, a second place may be made for the views of Schelling, having come at the right time and led to production through thought, not mere motivation.

43. "Flieh! Auf! hinaus in's weite Land!" (*Urfaust,* l. 65).

Urfaust need magic, as I said, to cause their occurrence do
the visions require cabalistic signs for their inspiration. In
the garden scene with Gretchen, Faust will speak inspired
lines evoking the spirit of the Almighty in nature with
no recourse other than to his own verbal powers;[44] later, in
the scene "Forest and Cavern," first introduced in the
Fragment, he will evoke a spirit apparently from his own
private world or inner life, though it will resemble closely
those he now summons through magic.

Gradually, the poem in general will free itself from the
restrictions of realism and become more admittedly poetical.
Paradoxically, the motif of magic in *Urfaust,* except where it
takes the form of pure hocus-pocus, as in "Auerbach's
Cellar," seems to have its source in that same urge to realism
which we saw reflected in so many other aspects of the
original drama. The poetic instinct that created the descriptive, the social, and the psychological realism of the early
version also put an occult book of a contemporary in Faust's
hand.[45] Poetry and magic are joined. What now occurs,
however strange, seems perfectly natural in its context.
Moreover, so closely are they joined in the completed *Faust,*
with its imaginative and fantastic second part, that when it
comes time, at the end, to separate them, we almost think
that the rejection or overcoming of the one implies a rejection or transcendence of the other. As I said in an earlier
chapter, poetry produces in the world of mind what magic
apparently or professedly produces in reality: Faust has the

44. In the pantheistic hymn which begins "Who dare name him?/
And who claim,/I believe in him!?" and which is retained unaltered,
except for punctuation, in the final version. The passage ends with the
lines that literary history has made almost programmatic in its description of the Storm and Stress: "I have no name for it. Feeling is all!"—
"Gefühl ist alles/Nahme Schall und Rauch" (*Urfaust,* ll. 1048–49).

45. Nothing reverberates more as fact in fiction than this, or than
the later minor action where Faust makes a contemporaneous attempt
to translate the Bible into German, which was about to be done by
Luther. The "mysterious book from Nostradamus' own hand" has
never been identified.

privilege to realize his fantasies. Yet in the end, in one of the
final scenes, he will say: "If I could only clear magic from my
way, unlearn the dark liturgy and stand face to face with
nature as a man. . . ."[46] This may not be intended as a rejection of the imaginative faculty, but it is clearly in line with
a development in thought which from the beginning of the
work has been emphasizing action over thinking, life over
poetry or art. Not to think, but to be, will come to claim
priority.[47] It is also in keeping with the experience from history, intellectual or real, that all great ideas, themes, or
movements contain within them the potential for their own
negation, as if to complete themselves they must come full
circle and, like the symbolical snake of alchemy, feed on
their own tails. As the world is round, so are the things of
mankind. In any event, magic does no harm in *Faust,* and if
the devil who is the custodian of this magic does, it is only, as
we will be told in the "Prologue in Heaven," ultimately to
produce good. We shall have to return to this question, also.

For the equation of magic and poetry, like that of form
and freedom, is important to our understanding of the
making of the work. We will see that the equations are
related to each other, and related in turn to the broader concept of romantic irony which, with the completion of Part
I, will be seen to have had a direct bearing on the composition of *Faust.* The prefatory poem and the two prologues,
the one in the theater and the other in Heaven, take the
drama (and the illusion of it as independent reality) and show
the relation, respectively, of the drama to its author, of
its author to the public, and of its action to the viewpoint of
eternity. Not to mention the interruptions in the action
proper, which show the relation of the work to other works
of literature, and to the theater in which it is being performed, as in "Walpurgis Night's Dream." All this goes toward

46. I give this line (Witkowski, l. 11,404) from the prose translation by Barker Fairley (Toronto, 1970).
47. "Dasein ist Pflicht, und wär's ein Augenblick" (Witkowski, l.
9418), i.e., to *be* is our duty, even if we exist only for a moment.

detaching art from life, in that it exposes art as fabrication, while at the same time relating it in a new way to life, that is, by making us aware again of the inevitable presence of man in everything that is done or thought. But such concerns have little to do with our discussion of the work in its present stage of development. The Storm and Stress had no relationship to irony.

Faust opens the book of Nostradamus and contemplates the sign of the macrocosm. The sign evokes in him a vision of universal harmony and a sense of elation: "Am I a god? Everything is so clear to me."[48] Indeed, the vision would seem to satisfy the desire for ultimate knowledge which Faust has stated as his goal and purpose in turning to magic.[49] Yet it is a vision only, a spectacle, as he calls it, and his deeper need is for a living experience of truth, a palpable, sensory, even sensual, grasping of reality: "Where can I grasp you, Nature? Your breasts, where?"[50] The Earth Spirit, which he now calls up, better provides that kind of knowing. Rather than the harmonious interrelation of cosmic forces, this sign suggests activity in proximity and incites to action. The very violence that surrounds and informs the spirit reminds one of the paroxysms of dreaming and contrasts with the previous vision as experience contrasts with thought. But the contrast is more felt than real. The first vision also revolves around the perception of living truth, but at such a great remove that its harmonies mute its tremors, just as the tremors of activity emanating from the Earth Spirit

48. "Bin ich ein Gott? Mir wird so licht!" (*Urfaust,* 1. 86).

49. For he sees in its design the reflection of living nature, and uses much the same words to describe his vision as he did his hope; in the present instance: "Wie alles sich zum Ganzen webt / Eins in dem andern würkt und lebt. . . ." "Ich schau in deisen reinen Zügen / Die würckende Natur vor meiner Seele liegen," and in the earlier: "Schau alle Würkungskrafft und Saamen" (*Urfaust,* ll. 94–95, 87–88, l. 31).

50. "Wo fass ich dich unendliche Natur! / Euch Brüste wo!" (*Urfaust,* ll. 102–03) is an appositive, not a possessive, relation between nature and breasts, and for all its Storm and Stress spirit is retained in the final version.

distract from its essentially ordered nature. This spirit may
be one of restless change and whirling energy, and might well
appear to Faust in "repugnant form" as a "frightful image,"
but it is the spirit which through ebb and flow, birth and
death, and the many other balancing tendencies in nature
"weaves the living raiment of the godhead on the loom of
time."[51] The two visions are almost one image seen from
opposite ends of the telescope, in proximity formidable and
at a distance serene. I am not extrapolating; in what came
to stand as the opening lines of the drama Goethe has a
chorus of archangels view Earth from the vantage point of
eternity and see, in the panorama they deem as "beautiful
as on the first day of creation," an "incomprehensibly rapid"
interaction of opposing, indeed "devastating," forces.[52]
If the archangels in their reading of the universe cannot
ignore the apparently essential negative element in the composition of reality, though they choose to praise the "gentle"
side of the process, how much less so can Faust? The very
thing which by its nature attracts him to the Earth Spirit, its
vitality, by its degree repels him: "You who roam the wide
world, active spirit, how close I feel to you." And when the
Spirit in reply appears to relegate Faust to a different order
of knowing and of being ("You are like the spirit you comprehend, not me"), still there is no clear implication, as
Faust himself would believe, that that order is of a lesser ("I
who was made in the image of God am not even equal to
you!")[53] and not merely a separate domain. The position of the observer does not change the nature but only the

51. ". . . in wiederlicher Gestallt" . . . "Schröckliches Gesicht" . . .
"So schaff ich am sausenden Webstuhl der Zeit / Und würke der Gottheit lebendiges Kleid" (*Urfaust*, ll. 129–156).

52. ". . . herrlich wie am ersten Tag" . . . "schnell und unbegreiflich
schnelle" . . . "ein blitzendes Verheeren" (Witkowski, ll. 250–63).

53. "Der du die weite Welt umschweiffst / Geschäftiger Geist wie
nah fühl' ich mich dir" . . . "Du gleichst dem Geist den du begreiffst, /
Nicht mir!" . . . "Ich Ebenbild der Gottheit! / Und nicht einmal dir!"
(*Urfaust*, ll. 157–63). The verb *gleichen* means both to resemble and to
be equal to.

aspect of the observed, as witness the view from eternity.

Yet Faust cannot make this distinction for the reason that, unlike the reader, he has no means of contrast. Although he may desire to take upon himself "everything that falls to humanity,"[54] as he will say in the *Fragment,* and for all that Goethe will supply him with a poetic realization of his wish, yet his experience and knowledge will be experience and knowledge from his own point of view, which is human. If he is Everyman, still he is a man. Even the whole of Part II, which will take him beyond the time and space limits of a human life, will restrict itself to a sphere of natural and historical antecedents that in a non-fantasy world would have had their effect through culture, that is, would have been experienced in the mind. If Faust is a Superman, as the Earth Spirit calls him already in *Urfaust,* he is also a European. For that matter, the significant breakthrough in point of view occurs neither with the perspective from eternity, where the archangels avow the "unfathomable" nature of the universe, nor with the extension of experience afforded Faust in Part II, but at the point where, before entering the "great world" of cultural and historical change, he himself comes to the recognition that he must "let the sun remain behind me,"[55] in order that he perceive by its reflection and not be blinded by its light. The brilliance of the sun may here be related to the frightful aspect of the Earth Spirit.

But Faust at the beginning is as unable in his absolutism to accept conditions as he is unlikely in his urgency to put a measure to truth. He cannot help but see a formidable hierarchy in what is in essence only a concentricity of relations and being.[56] As will the reader of *Urfaust,* who has not as yet been taken outside the action and provided with an alternate perspective.

54. "Und was der ganzen Menschheit zugetheilt ist . . ." (Witkowski, "Faust: Ein Fragment," l. 249).

55. "So bleibe denn die Sonne mir im Rücken!" (Witkowski, l. 4715).

56. "Harmonic correspondence" it is called in Jantz, *Goethe's Faust as a Renaissance Man,* p. vii.

And Goethe's perspective at the time? This is a question
we must ask in regard to *Urfaust*. For if I am correct in the
assumption that the meaning of the work grew as its author
grew, I must attempt to show in just which fashion this was
possible, perhaps even inevitable, at any one point in its
development. Up until now the question has been brought to
bear only on lesser figures and matters in the work. In fact,
the discussion of the opening monologue was postponed to
the latter part of this chapter mainly to allow the introduction of the philosophical content of *Urfaust* to come last,
as most significant. And the Gretchen episode does follow
the opening monologue like the tail of a meteor, being of
greater effect but less importance. Except for the hymn to
God in nature, and perhaps the sceptical remarks on the
uses of history which are directed at Wagner,[57] Faust after
the beginning lines delivers himself of little for thought in
contrast to his great effusions of feeling. I am not arguing
a supremacy of the rational over the emotional, which obviously would be contrary to the spirit of Goethe at the time
in which he wrote. The intent is to show that an element
other than rational or conscious is present even in what would
appear to be the most objective or speculative relation between author and hero, the realm of ideas.

Not that no conscious relation existed between author and
hero. Goethe was expressing ideas *in* Faust as well as through
him. The notion of universal concentricity, for example,
is central in alchemistic-cabalistic thought, the circle itself
being a sign of this mode of thinking.[58] That Faust, who
has just turned to magic, should continue in a rounded world
to think in terms of squares, while his author knows better,
seems convincingly appropriate. Goethe was intently studying
magic at the time he conceived *Urfaust,* as we know from
his autobiography. And if one doubts the likelihood that a
poet disinclined to metaphysical speculation, especially in the

57. *Urfaust,* ll. 201–48. We leave the discussion of Wagner to Part II,
where his anticipated significance is fully realized. He, too, will appear
in "heightened form" (*gesteigert*), albeit negatively.

58. Gray, *Goethe, the Alchemist,* p. 182.

early years, should be drawing important parallels and distinctions between the spiritual and the natural worlds, there is evidence to lessen the doubt. The "Letter from the Vicar of **** to the New Vicar of ****,"[59] for instance, written before *Werther* and possibly before *Urfaust,* in 1772, though not metaphysically oriented, is so mature, wise, and redounding in humanity, that one is tempted to say that genius simply has a way of knowing without knowing, at least without actual experience. Further, and again in the spirit of the motto to this chapter, it should be repeated that the attempt to distinguish between the conscious and unconscious in the creative process may in any event be unproductive, and perhaps naive.

But the point in seeking an intuitive, or less than conscious, factor in any work of art is generally to account for its form rather than its content. The opening monologue, from its beginning lines to the point where Faust feels rejected by the Earth Spirit (later, the point will be extended to his attempted suicide) is a series of acceptings and rejectings, illusions and disillusionment, ups and downs. This rhythm is present in the fictional letters which comprise *Werther,* as well as in many actual letters of the young Goethe. "Rejoicing to the heavens/Troubled unto death," perhaps best describes the phenomenon in its extreme form.[60] The same rhythm, we cannot help recall, informed the song of the Earth Spirit, as it would later the hymn of the archangels. It is the rhythm of the scenes in which Mephistopheles appears, though there without its emotional content.

This leads finally to my main point. The fact that the moods and instincts of the creator can be related to his creation in a way in which he himself might well be unaware is of itself not notable. A work of genius is almost by definition the product of more than only conscious forces,

59. See the comments on this piece by Ernst Beutler in the Artemis edition of the works, 4:1054.

60. "Himmelhoch jauchzend/Zum Tode betrübt," from Klärchen's song in *Egmont* (III,ii), which Fairley (*A Study of Goethe*) quotes in his chapter "Emotion Running Riot," p. 23.

and may be said to represent precisely the coming into consciousness of urges as yet not identified by the artist or
the age. An age, it seems, gives rise to the ideas which, when
formulated, help us to define the age. But the nature of
this process is rarely apparent. Hence the special importance
of *Urfaust,* which reflects the process as no other work of
the era, including the completed *Faust, Part I.*

I must recapitulate somewhat in attempting to make a
final point. I spoke of a disorderly or freely associative
quality in the opening monologue that seemed symptomatic
of a particular mode of creating, though hardly foreign to the
restless nature of a Faust. I may speak now of an order underlying the spontaneity. The changes in mood and thought
and vision, if not deliberately introduced, are nevertheless
governed by a certain principle. That principle is the principle
informing the whole of the work, at least at this stage of
its development. That is why we find a concentricity of
design not only in the relation between author and hero, hero
and nature, nature and the universe—in a sort of extension
of the micro-macrocosmic identification[61] —but also in the
relation of art to thought in general. Experience and idea are
here indeed one. For example, what appears, and is in fact, a
simple reaction of Faust to the aridity of his life, namely,
the impulse to "bathe himself in the dawn", what appears,
and is, a natural desire to escape his confines (which are
marked spiritually by his critical thinking and physically by
his high, narrow study) and lose himself among "spirits
that hover over meadows in moonlight,"[62] are at the same
time projections of broader forces at work in the age. Romanticism had a natural birth, as does perhaps any movement
that will prove productive. Likewise the rival of romanticism
in the urge to deed and action which is the Storm and Stress:

61. See Jantz, *Goethe's Faust as a Renaissance Man,* extensively;
the Index lists the references under "macrocosm/microcosm, harmonic
correspondence"; see further his article "Patterns and Structures in
Faust" (*Modern Language Notes* 83 [1968]: 359–87).

62. "In deinem Thau gesund mich baden" . . . "Auf Wiesen in deinem Dämmer weben" (*Urfaust,* ll. 44, 41).

"Restless spirit, how near I feel to thee!" Quite concretely, in other words, through the medium of poetry, or if we will, through the person of a representative man, the ideas of the age would come into being.[63]

The process seems to have been not only natural, but overdetermined, as are natural phenomena. Who better than the young Goethe, with his still unbridled temperament— "Goethe lives in a constant inner war and tumult" was the first impression of an observer who would become a lifelong friend[64] —to conceive a Faust, the modern symbol of rebellious man? What better time than the end of an era to rebel successfully, for the old had best be rejected at that point? What better medium than poetry to express what is only becoming true and has not yet reached the level of abstraction? Even the genre, poetic drama—the Greek word *drama* meaning "to do"—seems suited to express new truth, which must be experienced and not merely perceived, as are older, given perceptions of reality. When Goethe comes to formulate the pact with the Devil, he will have to make the conditions subjective on that very account.

Indeed, if one asks at this point whether Goethe was mainly following his hero through the intellectual and emotional crux of the age, a paradoxical answer immediately suggests itself. To the extent that he was furnishing Faust with ideas the implications of which he himself fully recognized, to

63. The literary development in Germany at the time is complex. The Storm and Stress movement is the cradle both for early romanticism and for classicism. Thus, in the view of the outside world, Goethe and Schiller in all their phases may well seem romanticists—a not misleading concept, since "romantic" and "classic" may not have the same mutually exclusive implications in German as in other European literatures, as Walter Silz points out in *Early German Romanticism: Its Founders and Heinrich von Kleist.* For a definition of these terms as they apply to German literature, see *The Oxford Companion to German Literature.*

64. Karl Ludwig von Knebel, who mediated the invitation of Goethe to the Court of Weimar, in a letter of December 23, 1774 (sometimes dated earlier, December 11 or 14).

that extent his thought was limited. Conversely, the most productive insights he lent to Faust were those that only approximated the typical or characteristic of the period, and were thus free to develop independently. The romantic elements in *Urfaust,* examined in context, prove to be not of the essence of that movement, but rather a stage or phase in a similar but separate development. So also the Storm and Stress elements. For Goethe did not go beyond the trends in his times so much as he never fully entered into them. We tend to forget, reading on the one hand *Werther,* let us say, and on the other the Prometheus poem and *Götz von Berlichingen,* that the sense of life reflected in these individual works is not totally that of the author, so natural, and thus persuasive, is the reality that each suggests. In reading *Urfaust,* however, the precise nature of a motif or idea is immediately established by the context. The romantic tendencies are the less insinuating, the Storm and Stress tendencies the less powerful for having been conceived in reaction to each other, and both in response to the common antagonism of a rigid, rational approach to life. These tendencies represent live options rather than assumed positions (the dispatch with which Faust changes his mind is remarkable), and better mirror the dynamics of creation and the freedom in thought and sensibility that the young Goethe exemplified. Not only does *Urfaust* reveal the ideas of the age coming naturally into being, as we said; it also presents their immediate development in a natural way, that is, in conflict. Out of the conflict comes both the resolution to the work itself and the culmination of the literary tendencies of the period, in the view of man and life we associate with German classicism.[65] *Faust,* like the works generally of the mature Goethe and Schiller, finds its balance in the play of oppositions. But the young Goethe did not anticipate this eventual Hegelian resolution.

65. More broadly, perhaps, *Faust* may be seen as "the culminating expression and summation of an entire era, which we are (or were) accustomed to call the Renaissance" (Jantz, *Goethe's Faust as a Renaissance Man,* p. ix).

4

FRAGMENT AND TRANSITION

Goethe goes the way of nature, and good fortune comes to meet him.
—Herder in a letter to Knebel, November 6, 1784

It is not what was happening to *Faust,* but all around the work, that is of interest to us in the next phase of its development, from 1775 to 1790, the year in which *Faust: Ein Fragment* first appeared. Little was added to the manuscript during these fifteen years. It was enjoying, as Goethe once remarked of the manuscript of *Wilhelm Meister* as it lay for a time untouched in his desk, "an afternoon nap," albeit here of Rip van Winklean proportions.[1]

It was as well the work was not completed in the early period. Goethe had taken a deep purchase on the theme, more likely instinctively than with a conscious desire to create a great poem. He had not chosen the episodic-anecdotal approach which the legendary material suggested and the chapbooks and puppet plays had followed.[2] Even Marlowe shows traces of this development. Instead, he had heightened one episode to the point of intensified drama. But the Gretchen tragedy thus committed him to an undertaking the scope of which can only be appreciated in the end product, for by its very length and intensity the episode affected the basic conception of the work. There was no continuing in the same vein. A Faust play with a series of episodes with

1. "About the novel there is nothing to say; it is having a nap and I hope it will awaken all the more refreshed" (to Schiller, July 1796).
2. In German, see Karl Georg Wendriner, ed., *Die Faustdichtung, vor, neben und nach Goethe;* in English, the already-mentioned Bates, and Palmer and More, *The Sources of the Faust Tradition.*

some semblance of equal purport would spring the limits of
the dramatic form.[3] The one episode was after all a drama
in itself. Moreover, any stipulation of time (let alone that of
twenty-four years) in the compact with the Devil would
only encourage the epic linearity of the theme, to which as
a theme of quest it was naturally disposed and traditionally
fixed. Thomas Mann, in the only truly remarkable modern
literary treatment of the theme, chose as his medium the
novel. But Goethe chose the drama, again surely instinctively.[4]
    Likewise any further realism would only encourage the

3. As Schiller was the first to note. He speaks of the theme's "too
great circumstantiality and breadth" in a letter to Goethe, June 26,
1797.

4. We noted earlier his predilection for the dramatic form. His own
specific remarks on the subject are also interesting. In *Poetry and Truth*,
Book Thirteen, he says: "Those [subjects] that were to be treated in
dramatic form had the privilege of being treated most often and brought
closer to completion. Yet at the same time a transition to a different
mode of creating [*Darstellungsart*] was developing which is usually not
considered dramatic yet is closely related to that form. The change
occurred mainly as a result of a trait in the author [that is, Goethe him-
self] . . . . He was in the habit, namely, when he found himself alone,
of calling up in spirit one or another person of his acquaintance. He
would ask them to sit down, would pace back and forth before them,
stand still, and discuss with them the subject that happened to be on
his mind. Occasionally, they answered or gave their assent or dissent to
be known through the usual gestures. . . . Then the speaker would continue, further developing what seemed to please the visitor or qualify-
ing, more closely defining what the latter disapproved, and might well
yield his point in a friendly manner. The strangest thing was that he
never chose persons of his closer acquaintance but those whom he only
seldom saw; indeed, several who lived far away. . . yet mostly persons
of a receptive rather than outgoing nature. [They were] persons of
both sexes, every age and status. . . ." He goes on to speak of the clear
connection between such dialogue in the mind and letter writing, but
points out the difference between presupposing, as does the latter, a
single, trusted recipient and having an always changing, silent listener. He
attributes the special attraction of the letters that make up *The Sorrows
of Young Werther* to the fact that, while written ostensibly to one
person, they were composed in the imaginary presence of many.

epic linearity, since realism takes up time in the theater and
space in the imagination. A work of symbolism, a drama of
the mind, if not for the mind, was henceforth in the making.
The transition brought difficulties. The movement from the
"little" to the "great" world, so simple as a concept and so
readily rhymed—the lines are among the lightest in the work[5]
—presented problems dramaturgically. Goethe discovered
that he could not go "there from here" within the system he
had created, and must begin again from the beginning. And
Part II in fact envelops rather than develops Part I; it goes
forward by going back in time; in the mode of modern art,
it breaks up the surface of experience in order to see beyond
to its "inner workings."[6]

Goethe claimed, as I mentioned, to have foreseen the
development of his *Faust* in broad outline from the
beginning, and my intent here is not to raise or add to our
doubts and speculation in that regard.[7] My intent, rather, is
to take him at his word and attempt to show how, even with
foreknowledge and anticipation, his creation was not likely
to go forward in a period of transition. His not working on
his work thus has its bearing.

The year 1775 marked the move to Weimar and the assumption of responsibilities at the Court.[8] In his capacity

5. Faust: "Wohin soll es nun gehn?" Mephistopheles: "Wohin es dir
gefällt./Wir sehn die kleine, dann die große Welt" (Witkowski, ll. 2051–52).

6. I shall discuss this unique development under the head of literary
cubism in a second part to this study. See below the discussion of
"Walpurgis Night," which anticipates the development.

7. A most thorough study of the composition of *Faust* is provided
by Eudo Mason, *Goethe's Faust: Its Genesis and Purport,* which I follow in all important matters.

8. Goethe was to receive 1200 Thaler yearly. When the request for
2000 for the art historian Winckelmann had been made a decade
earlier, Frederick the Great, who had invited Voltaire to his court but
ignored Lessing, is said to have replied: "For a German, 1000 is sufficient." Wolfgang Leppmann, *Winckelmann* (New York, 1970), repeats
the anecdote (pp. 247–48).

as privy councillor to the Duke of Weimar, Goethe, within
the years in question, took charge in turn of such varying
duties as mines and recruitment, the education of young
Fritz von Stein, and the direction of the Weimar theater,
and took serious interest in other matters too numerous to
be mentioned. That he was concerned in human affairs is
the simplest way to describe the activity. Far from distracting
him from what we might believe to be the first allegiance of
a poet—that is, the cultivation of his talent and sensibility—
these matters seem to have fed his energies and abilities. To be
sure, there are only so many hours in a day, so many years
in a life. Yet the impression one gains on glancing at a simple
list of events and facts in this life is one of an ability to add
without the necessity of taking away. The supervision of
mines, if not the financial success it was intended to be,[9]
planted an abiding interest in Goethe for the things of natural
science, or better, fostered a curiosity about nature more
related to the scientific than the poetic view of what "holds
the world together at the core." He had already grown
curious about nature, as about so many other things, as a
youth; now he studied, and wrote treatises on, geology and
mineralogy ("On Granite," 1784; "On Rock Stratification,"
1785), anatomy (discovery of the intermaxillary bone,
1784), botany ("The Metamorphosis of Plants," 1790), and
began experiments in a number of other areas, again too
numerous to be mentioned, among them optics, the field in
which he was to produce his most contentious work, "On
the Theory of Color" (1791 ff.)[10] What perhaps best suggests
the scope and continuity of these undertakings is a visit to
a weather observatory on May 26, 1784, which culminated in
a meteorological essay, "Toward a Theory of Storms," written
in 1825. Violence in nature had always fascinated Goethe,

9. Friedenthal, *Goethe,* makes a great deal of this shortcoming
(pp. 188ff.).

10. See, for example, J. R. Kantor, "Goethe's Place in Modern
Science," *Goethe Bicentennial Studies,* ed. Hubert J. Meessen. Heinrich Henel, "Type and Proto-phenomenon in Goethe's Science" (*PMLA*
72 [1956]:651–68), contains many further references.

the more so as his own philosophy began to stress the essential harmony in the universe and he had the more to contend
with its ever-present opposite.

The recruitment of soldiers I mention in order to illustrate
the variety, not the importance, of these many activities.
Goethe accompanied Karl August on his military expedition
into France, 1792–93, and the journey can be regarded as an
outgrowth of his official functions, though it is true that he
often accompanied the Duke unofficially, out of friendship,
and in the early years, for pleasure. The memoir describing
the campaign, though it contains the famous pronouncement
at the battle of Valmy, on September 20, 1792 ("Here, today, a new epoch in world history begins"), contains little
else of high import and is hardly more than an indifferent
diary of events. Goethe took along his materials on the theory
of color, and even when the tides of war had turned, as at
Mainz, he sat out the siege with this work and the beginnings
of an epic poem in the classical vein, *Reineke Fuchs*. In
contrast, one thinks of the descriptions of the later Napoleonic
wars in Stendhal and Tolstoi. I cite these latter facts as
evidence of that supreme objectivity or Olympian overview
which was soon reflected in much of Goethe's behavior and
virtually all his poetical works, to the very end. This is in
contrast to the personality and poet we knew in his period
of Storm and Stress. But the objectivity was not callous or
cynical, and the Olympian attitude was not without concern.
Both were related to the position he came to hold in the view
of the world, in his more immediate surroundings, and in his
own eyes. He had his objectivity thrust upon him. He was
born too early to have been importantly affected by the
drastic occurrences of his age, being forty years old and
having behind him the most formative experience in his
development, the journey to Italy, when the French Revolution broke out in 1789. He lived too long not to strike
some balance with the forceful extremes of his youth, in
art as well as in thought and politics. The poet, the literary
being who coined the term world literature,[11] viewed things

11. ". . . poetry is cosmopolitan [*weltbürgerlich*], and the more

from the same perspective as the privy councillor, the political
being who regarded his interviews with Napoleon as more
important then any loss or gain of national territory in war.
To Goethe, Napolean was "beyond good and evil."[12]

These perceptions, though modern, looked not forward,
but back upon a time when it was still possible to conceive
of events in history, whether literary or world, as the product
of individuals rather than the conglomerate we call a nation,
a people, or a time. Goethe as a German still without a nation,
just as Goethe as a poet still without a national literature,[13]
might have been more inclined to adopt this view of a com-
munity of genius serving the interests of no man, only mankind. That could explain his indifference toward the immediate
public reaction to his work, which grew cooler the broader he
became, and the less interested the more he refused to repeat
himself. Schiller, just ten years his junior, felt compelled to
make the effect of art in the real world the touchstone of his
aesthetics.[14] and Heine, who succeeded Goethe as the German poet of world fame, was directly torn between the
demands he felt upon him as an intelligent, responsible

---

interesting the more it shows its nationality" (in a conversation with
Count Stolberg, between June 11 and June 19, 1827). To Eckermann,
January 31, 1827: "National literature is now of little importance; it
is the time for world literature. . . ."

12. Napoleon is a "daemonic" force, in the remarks to Eckermann,
March 2, 1831.

13. How can the Germans hope for a national theater when they are
not yet a nation, Lessing had in effect asked in his *Hamburg Dramaturgy*
(1767–69); later, Schiller in effect asks how the Germans could hope
to become a nation except through a national theater. See his *Aesthetic
Education of Man,* ed. and trans., E. M. Wilkinson and L. A. Willoughby
(Oxford, 1968), especially its excellent introduction. Goethe on the
question: "Only insofar as a people has its own literature can it judge
and understand the past as well as the present world" (under "Eur-
opäische Literatur" in the Artemis edition, 14:782).

14. See, again, the introduction by Wilkinson and Willoughby to
their *Aesthetic Education of Man.*

member of society and his elitist instinct for beauty.[15] Heine
went so far as to claim he had come into the world at precisely midnight of the new year 1800 and thus had been born
with one foot in the aristocratic eighteenth century and the
other in the democratic nineteenth. Independently of his
irresistible urge to humor, and with perhaps a modicum of
envy, he could say with some truth of his predecessor:
"[Goethe's works] embellish our beloved nation as beautiful
statues embellish a garden. But they are statues. One can
fall in love with them, but they are sterile. . . . The deed is
the child of the word, and the beautiful words of Goethe are
childless. That is the curse of everything that is the product
merely of art. The statue that Pygmalion made was a beautiful woman; the master himself fell in love with her; she came
to life under his caresses. But as far as we know she bore no
children."[16] There was also an inveterate abhorrence of death
in Goethe[17] which might equally account for his (apparent)
detachment in the face of war. He destroyed his notes and
diaries from the French war after the campaign, and wrote
his account from memory in 1822. There is no other example
of his having willfully destroyed written material, except
some letters from his early period in Leipzig.

Strict chronology would not have allowed the inclusion of
some of the activities we mention, such as the directorship of
the Weimar theater, which Goethe assumed only after the
publication of the *Fragment.* But we are not concerned with
measuring precise influences upon the work, at this stage
or later. The influences will reveal themselves. The science
Goethe absorbed surfaced as grand poetry, or wit, or as profound vision, as in the image of the rainbow, on which he

15. See my essay on Heine in John Gearey and Willy Schumann,
eds., *Einführung in die deutsche Literatur* (New York, 1964).

16. My translation, from *Die romantische Schule* (Paris, 1835), bk.
1. See Helen M. Mustard, trans. and ed., *Heinrich Heine: Selected Works*
(New York, 1973).

17. That he did not attend his mother's funeral or visit her grave
attests to the fact.

also composed a treatise, albeit after the composition of the famous passage in *Faust*.[18] His background in theater came to the fore: obviously when he introduced a scene in which an audience that could only be the Weimar audience was directly addressed, and with genius, when he succeeded in reducing to drama the unwieldy combination of imaginative playfulness and high purpose which is Part II. For all its playhouse unmanageability, this latter part is theatrically conceived, if one thinks of theater as masque, as figures in a setting, as art rather than life. The Weimar theater had been an amateur theater, a *Liebhabertheater*, before Goethe took charge, and his early years as author and actor in this inbred ensemble (many court personages took part) left as much a mark on his own work as he left on its further development.[19] The instruction of young Fritz von Stein, in itself not telling (though it may again reflect Goethe as dilettante),[20] provided the connection with Frau von Stein, whose influence was pervasive and, together with the Italian journey, almost definitive for the approach and tone that emerged in the period in question.

But influences do not often have the direct bearing that the mere mention of the word suggests, especially upon an unreflective poet. Goethe went the way of nature, and the way of nature is both simple and complex. It is simple when

18. The treatise is part of the "Theory of Color" (1832). The scene in which the passage occurs, the first scene of Part II, is sometimes dated as early as 1797. The pertinent lines are: "[Der Regenbogen] spiegelt ab das menschliche Bestreben./Ihm sinne nach, und du begreifst genauer: /Am farbigen Abganz haben wir das Leben," i.e., the rainbow is the mirror of human striving . . . we experience life as colorful reflection (Witkowski, ll. 4725-27).

19. See Walter H. Bruford, *Theatre, Drama, and Audience in Goethe's Germany;* Marvin Carlson, *Goethe and the Weimar Theater.*

20. See Hans Rudolf Vaget, *Dilettantismus und Meisterschaft,* which has an extensive bibliography in English and in German on Goethe's relationship to the arts, for example, Frederick Sternfeld, *Goethe and Music* (New York, 1954); Johannes Urzidil, "Goethe and Art," mentioned above.

one thinks of it as the path of least resistance, and complex when one remembers that that path is rarely a straight line. The numerous activities of these years may have distracted Goethe from his work on *Faust,* but his poetic production in other regards seems hardly to have suffered. The beginnings of new and different works abounded in the Weimar years prior to the sojourn in Italy, and the majority were duly, if only slowly, completed. Only *Faust* remained substantially unfurthered.

Moreover, the works at its periphery seem to have exerted, if not a negative influence, an influence by default. Goethe's practice of rarely repeating himself now resulted in his treating in other works motifs and concerns that would never be recovered for *Faust.* The effect of the relationship with Frau von Stein was immediately perceptible in the atmosphere of *Iphigenia in Tauris,* as was that of the court of Weimar as a whole in *Torquato Tasso.* Both plays further reflected the trip to Italy. Similarly, but in the realm of the problematical, the character study of Orestes in the former and of the hero in the latter joined with that of Werther to form a trilogy of analysis of the morbid, or romantic, personality. Goethe was coming to equate the romantic with the sick, the classical with the healthy in art.[21] For that matter, he was already pointing a remedy, in the ameliorative and purifying effect of the feminine, but asexual, influence. Though his own relations with Frau von Stein may not have remained platonic throughout, he recognized the significance of their encounter in the statement, "In another existence you were my sister or my wife."[22] Yet these recognitions and experiences prompted no immediate furtherance of *Faust,*

21. So he says in a conversation with Eckermann, April 2, 1829. The precise wording is important, for the remark is meant as metaphor, not definition: "'Mir ist ein neuer Ausdruck eingefallen,' sagte Goethe, 'der das Verhältnis nicht übel bezeichnet. Das Klassische nenne ich das Gesunde und das Romantische das Kranke.'"

22. "Ach, du warst in abgelebten Zeiten/Meine Schwester oder meine Frau" are lines from the poem that begins: "Warum gabst du uns die tiefen Blicke?"

as much as the comprehensive nature of its theme could have
absorbed them.

But as there was loss, there was gain, and by the same
design. The subjective, therapeutic, and by extension, "occasional"[23] approach to poetry, to the extent that it
succeeded in defining, also exhausted experience. The objectivity Goethe acquired so quickly in his art was as much the
result of a natural development out of his earlier subjective
position as it was the product of new insight gained in Italy;
both *Iphigenia* and *Tasso* were conceived before the Italian
journey. Thus *Faust,* to repeat my analogy of the statue
wrought from stone, came to exist by virtue of what was
taken away. This is not entirely true, to be sure. It is not at
all true of *Urfaust,* which corporeally remained. One may
also as justly see the experience that went into other works
as preparatory to *Faust,* through distillation.[24] Thus Goethe's
women, in his life and his works, seem comprehended in the
ultimate, incommensurable image of the Eternal Feminine
(*Das Ewig-Weibliche*) with which he chose to conclude the
poem. Again problematical, the morbid tendencies in himself
and his characters seem finally resolved in the classical confrontation between life and death in which the indomitable
spirit of man prevails. Faust is saved from suicide, not by way
of depth psychology, as in the case of Orestes, nor the
therapy of art, as with the poet Tasso, both of which means

23. ". . . occasional poems are among the best poems, when the
poet takes care to retain all the spirit of the occasion," Goethe is quoted
as saying to an English acquaintance, Henry Crabb Robinson, in a conversation of August 13, 1829. The report continues: "It is this which
has made Goethe a real poet, as opposed to the idealism of such poetry
as Wordsworth's. . . . [Goethe] repeated the remark, which is one of
his fixed ideas, that it is by the most laborious collection of facts that
even a poetical view of nature is to be corrected and as it were authen-
ticated." Goethe to Schiller, December 27, 1797: ". . . the specific
requirements should, if I am not wrong, actually come from outside,
and the occasion form [*determinieren*] the talent." See Ernst M.
Oppenheimer, *Goethe's Poetry for Occasions.*

24. As does Fairley, *Goethe's Faust: Six Essays,* p. 14.

of resolution apply in the particular; he is saved by the life
force itself, the generalized will to live. Goethe grew ever
more basic, not abstract; though we should remember that
Werther too, as the author recognized, died from an equally
generalized will to death, if not every reader so understood
it.[25]

We note, however, that the insights into life born of the
scientific study of nature did not immediately find their way
into the poetical works. Perhaps it was too early, Goethe
having come to science later than to poetry. Yet scientific
insight is opposed to poetic insight as the visual is opposed
to the verbal. One can describe what one sees, but the task of
art is to recreate, through form, the system within which the
observed subsists. The more radical the insights into the
system, the greater the demands upon the form. Thus *Faust,*
again paradoxically, while obviously making the greatest
demands in this regard, continued to be the one vehicle suf-
ficiently indeterminate or original in form to convey increasingly complex ideas. That the work did not immediately
go forward suggests not want of purpose, but clarity of
thought in one medium being transferred to—or better, reborn—in another. That this medium was drama made the
task the more formidable, since drama is the least speculative
of genres. And Goethe remained true to the form in the
sense that he avoided the kind of outright philosophical disputation that had attached to the theme since the *Magician*
of Calderon, and had become virtually requisite in the puppet
plays, usually in mock fashion.[26] In Goethe, thought becomes not words but vision, as in poetry; and argument, not
debate but confrontation, as in life or drama, where no
ideas exist independently of the persons who hold them. The
ease and art with which Goethe eventually presented his
incommensurable theme was bought at the price of maturation.

25. Death was already in him, Goethe says in *Poetry and Truth,*
Book Thirteen ". . . als vom tödlichen Wurm gestochen."

26. See the number of actual or virtual such scenes in Wendriner,
ed., *Die Faustdichtung, vor, neben und nach Goethe.* They are in the
majority.

The truly surprising thing about *Faust,* on second thought, is not the time it took to complete, but that such a project was ever ended. And when one hears of the difficulties attending an understanding of this masterpiece, one is tempted to paraphrase Kant in his introduction to the *Critique of Pure Reason* and say: The work would be easier if it had not been made so easy. Kant had said that many a book would be much clearer if it had not been intended to be so clear.[27]

In any event, as we survey the literary works from this period of transition for *Faust,* we should look to the limits of their form as well as subject matter. They remain traditional in form. A discussion of the scientific ideas as they relate to the poetical works we shall postpone to the point where they specifically find artistic expression, notably in Part II. The didactic poems on the metamorphosis of plants and of animals from the somewhat later years of 1798 and 1806 are descriptions in verse, not evocations or imitations, of natural phenomena scientifically observed. They also remain traditional rather than creative in form, as does the novel of bizarre content, *The Elective Affinities,* in which an analogy of chemical processes and human relationships is drawn with subtle irony that derives in no small part from the conservative dignity of the narration. The exception that interestingly proves the rule is the fragment "On Nature," a rhapsodic prose piece from the period in question (1781). The fragment so obviously reflects the combination of intense feeling

27. The passage reads, in the J. M. D. Meiklejohn translation (New York, n.d.): "Abbé Terasson remarks with great justice, that if we estimate the size of a work, not from the number of its pages, but from the time which we require to make ourselves master of it, it may be said of many a book—*that it would be much shorter, if it were not so short.* On the other hand, as regards the comprehensibility of a system of speculative cognition, connected under a single principle, we may say with equal justice—many a book would have been much clearer, if it had not been intended to be so very clear. . . . [Helps] to intelligibility aid us in the comprehension of parts, but they distract the attention, dissipate the mental power of the reader, and stand in the way of his forming a clear conception of the whole . . ." (p. xxii).

and clarity of observation we associate with the younger
Goethe that it was long attributed to him without hesitation.
That the piece was in fact written by an acquaintance "after
conversations with Goethe"[28] suggests both the naivety of the
actual writer and the instinct of the true author in com-
mitting to print what was not wholly formed. The example
goes to the heart of my contention that the sporadic development of *Faust* resulted generally from the conjunction and
disjunction of forces rather than from dint or want of purpose
or time. Conjoining in this period were the natural urge to
moderation, in life and in art, after the storm and stress of
the earlier years, and the support for that urge: in life, through
the demands of newly assumed responsibilities and, in art,
through the experience of the classical world in Italy. The
dramas we are about to examine show a remarkable progression precisely in this regard. Disjoined, as yet, were the
awareness of the inner workings of nature and the where-
withal artistically to represent them. This the tradition had
not supplied, from want of need. But what presented itself
to the older view as complete and whole now had to be seen
in parts, from many sides, and yet at once, as through the
prism of science, as through the mind when it thinks and does
not merely perceive.[29]

Egmont, the first of the dramas of rank from this period of
transition, was itself a transitional work. Begun in Frankfurt,
it showed traces of its origin and, completed considerably
later (in Rome, 1787), bore witness to what was to come.
In that, it resembles *Faust.* In addition, the kind of development it underwent parallels *Faust* in its progression from the
subjective, through the characteristic, to an objective point
of view.

28. Georg Christoph Tobler, the Swiss theologian (1757–1812), who
had visited Goethe at the time. The fragment is still regularly included
in editions of Goethe's works, for example, the Artemis edition, 16:921–
22. See p. 978, where the editor notes the lack of form in the piece.
29. See the discussion of "Walpurgis Night" below, chapter 6.

Egmont is the daemonic figure. Of the daemonic, Goethe wrote in Book Nineteen of his autobiography: "[I] thought I perceived in nature, organic and inorganic, animate and inanimate, something that manifested itself only in contractions and therefore could not be described under one concept, still much less by one word. It was not godly, for it seemed irrational, not human, as it had no understanding; not diabolical, for it was benevolent; not angelic, for it often betrayed malicious humor. It was like chance, for it had no consequence, but resembled providence, for it suggested design. All that limits us seemed, for it, unrestricting; it appeared to deal at will with the laws that govern our existence: it contracted time and expanded space. It seemed to content itself only with the impossible and to reject the possible with contempt. This force, which seemed to intervene with all others and both to separate and join them, I call daemonic. . . . I sought to save myself from this frightful phenomenon by taking refuge, as was my habit, behind an imaginary creation."[30]

The product of this creative imagining was *Egmont,* in whose central figure Goethe saw the daemonic as exemplified in man. Animals, he had noted, strikingly represent the force, but the daemonic appears almost frightening when dominant in a human being. A strange power emanates from such persons, who are not always exceptional in terms of intellect or talent, rarely so in terms of human qualities. Their strength lies in the incredible influence they exert upon others; the masses will stand in awe of them despite any attempt on the part of moral or intellectual authority to work their discredit. As there is seldom a contemporary who is their equal, they are to be overcome by nothing short of the universe itself, with which they have begun the battle. At this point Goethe quoted the dictum: *Nemo contra deum nise ipse.*[31]

The statement is extreme and its relation to *Egmont* unclear. There is little in the play to suggest a theme of such

30. In the last phrase of this passage I follow the translation by Oxenford. The German reads: ". . . indem ich mich, nach meiner Gewohnheit, hinter ein Bild flüchtete."

31. Apparently his own—"No one against God except God himself."

formidable dimensions. Goethe admitted that the concept of
the daemonic took true shape in his mind only much later,
and that in introducing the subject at this point in his autobiography, he was anticipating. Yet even the figure in whom
the phenomenon is to be observed seems too light for its
weighty implications and too happy for its sinister trappings.
Beyond the reaction of the people and the *Lebenslust* of
Egmont himself, few events or motifs seem specifically designed
to evoke a sense of primordial forces in action and at odds.
A *vivat*! from the people and a visit to a mistress on the eve
of an all-important political confrontation are the stuff of
historical rather than existential drama. It is as if Goethe had
chosen the wrong form for the deeper reaches of his theme
and had had gradually to modify the latter in order to create
a reasonable example of the former. He had difficulties with
the work, especially Act IV, as he confessed to Frau von Stein,
December 12-13, 1781. And when Schiller, who in a review
had found the play wanting in true tragic import, and its hero
in demonstrable stature—we are told about his greatness,
we do not see it, he had said—subsequently prepared a version
for the Weimar stage, he immediately moved to clarify and
intensify the main conflict. His solution was too theatrical,
too much in his own vein, yet effective. It consisted largely
in broadening the historical background and then, in the final
scene, bringing together protagonist and masked antagonist,
with the former literally tearing the disguise from the latter,
who retreats, exposed. Goethe had ended the play with only
the suggestion of the victory of freedom over tyranny in the
real world and, in a dream sequence, confirmed the victory
allegorically. The piece closes with a "triumphal symphony":
"eine Siegessymphonie."

Our task is not to interpret *Egmont* but to relate the play
to *Faust*. If we are right in assuming that Goethe chose the
wrong form for his initial concept of the play, the relation
is indeed important, by sheer contrast. For we may then contend that the two works, conceived at approximately the
same time, underwent precisely the opposite development.
The one, in adapting a traditional theme to a contemporary

consciousness, proved to point structurally and morally to
the future. The other, in subjecting an original insight to the
demands of verisimilitude in history and the theater, took
final shape under influences from the past. Realism was the
death of the daemonic in *Egmont*. And while Schiller was
hardly wrong in his hesitations about the play, he was not
wholly justified in his specific criticism.[32] The want of
stature in the hero is less directly the result of an artistic than
a conceptional failing. An inward quality of being such as
the daemonic is not readily demonstrable in the objective form
that is drama. Its rhetorical display is empty and its physical
display, given the normal confines of the stage, improbable.
Goethe attempted neither. In the first regard, he was guided
by his innate sense for the natural, and in the second, perhaps, by his memory of the criticism that Herder had leveled
at his unwieldly *Götz von Berlichingen*: Shakespeare has
completely corrupted you. His new close association with the
theater also played a part in keeping *Egmont* within sound
formal limits, as it did in the very conception of the so-called
classical dramas that were to follow—*Iphigenia, Tasso,* and
The Natural Daughter. Faust absorbed and then transcended
this influence.

More important is the nature of the content that Goethe
introduced into *Egmont* as the play evolved. We do not know
with this work, as we more readily do with *Faust,* just how
it developed; we know only that it underwent development
sporadically in the years between 1775 and 1787, when it
was finally completed in Rome. But it is generally assumed
that it was transformed from an initially conceived character

32. The 1791 performance was unsuccessful. It is in Schiller's
version that the play was performed for a long time. (See A. G. Blunden,
"Schiller's *Egmont,*" *Seminar* 14 [1978]:31–44). Later, in a conversation with Eckermann, February 19, 1829, Goethe said that it was a
consolation to him that there were theaters that would perform the
play as it was written. For Schiller's view, see K. R. Mandelkow, *Goethe
im Urteil seiner Kritiker,* pp. 105f., which reproduces the original
review of *Egmont* in *Allgemeine Literatur-Zeitung,* September 20,
1788.

drama to a historical drama with contemporary relevance.[33]
Chance even played into its hands, in that the year of its
completion saw a new revolt against outside authority in
Brussels, the parallels to which in earlier times were not lost
on the present day. Not contemporaneity, however, but an
objective world of persons and events in the play itself came
to dominate *Egmont* and proportionately diminished its
hero. Egmont blends into the background. Until *Egmont,* the
central figures in Goethe tended to be distinctive, partly
through contrast with a quality either of indeterminateness
or of flexibility in their surroundings which allowed them
better to be seen as themselves. Werther best exemplifies the
one contrast, Götz von Berlichingen the other, and Faust
in *Urfaust* both, in that the element of magic renders the reality
in the play ambiguous. Here a kind of mutable realism ob-
tained. This is not to say that the objective world played no
important part in these and other works from the early
period. On the contrary, the inability of Werther to contend
with reality in the form both of persons and events is a
direct cause of his downfall. He succumbs to his own subjec-
tiveness. Götz von Berlichingen is a victim of that most
formidable objective opponent, the change wrought by the
forces of history. And Faust, though he may have the power
to alter the world around him, responds to its offerings in
a manner that suggests their palpable existence and importance. He proves by his passionate action what Werther
proved by his inaction.

But it is to say that the objective world in Goethe existed
only equally and separately. It contained but did not determine individual fate, like the macrocosm the microcosm,
to continue in the vein of *Faust.* And Egmont, in the passage
most commonly quoted from the play, makes a statement
that parallels this concept when he says: "Man thinks he
guides his life and leads himself, and his inner being irresistibly
draws him toward his fate." But our question concerns

33. See Kurt May's introduction to the play in vol. 6 of the Artemis
edition.

development, not concept or intent. These words are spoken
in Act V, in the scene "Prison," after a fourth act that has
laid bare the conflict in such a way—the usually apolitical
Goethe surprises us with the acuteness of his analysis here—
that the tragic outcome can only be seen in terms of power
and the search for advantage, not in abstract terms of fate,
inwardly or outwardly ordained. The fourth act was also the
act that had given Goethe the most difficulty.[34]

Yet the daemonic is the theme of *Egmont* in intent, and
that alone relates the play to *Faust*. The works overlap
thematically, although most noticeably in their motif of
tragic love. Klärchen and Gretchen are variations on a theme.
Faust himself as a character is not general enough and too
introspective to fit the description of the daemonic that
Goethe first tendered. Goethe mentions only Egmont, not
Faust, in this regard, though *Faust,* Part I, was published
before the description was written. Euphorion, in Part II,
would better qualify, if only because Goethe associated this
symbolic figure with the daemonic person of Lord Byron.[35]
Faust might represent rather the daemonic in man, not in
an individual. "Two souls" inhabit his breast, not one "inner
law," as the poem "Daemon" later will describe the determining factor in the course of an individual life. For Goethe
did extend his concept of the daemonic to include all, not

34. The above-mentioned letter to Frau von Stein speaks of the
"annoying"—*"fatale"*—fourth act. The difficulty that Goethe had with
the work in general is reflected in a remark in a letter of September 5,
1787, the day of its completion: "Today *Egmont* was actually truly
completely finished"—"eingentlich recht völlig fertig geworden."

35. It is interesting that Goethe mentions the Duke of Weimar, along
with Napoleon, in his conversation about the daemonic with Eckermann (February 3, 1831). We better realize how complex, no less than
natural, a personality Goethe was when we hear him speak of others as
possessing unerring instinct, or wholeness—qualities we generally attribute to him. As he said of Gretchen in *Urfaust,* that innocence does
not recognize itself, and that is its beauty, we may say of him that
genius experiences itself as human, not exceptional, and in that lies its
humanity.

merely the exceptional individual in whom the force is most
clearly pronounced. In including all, he would include mankind, whose inner law, it seems, entails duality. Thus, again,
a particular concept from another work appears to be absorbed and transcended in *Faust,* or, to think in terms of
concentration rather than cumulation, refined and heightened.
One might even speak of diastole and systole in the process
that created the poem. This "eternal formula of life," as
Goethe called it,[36] may also apply to art.

But the *Fragment* makes no allusion to "two souls." At
this stage, as we shall see, Faust still appears as a figure
willfully, that is, individually not generically, overreaching
himself, with no prospect of salvation. But first *Iphigenia*
and *Tasso.*

Iphigenia is as little like *Egmont* as a Greek temple a Dutch
painting. The play is full of light. And were we to address
ourselves to the work on its own terms rather than in relation
to *Faust,* we would emphasize that fact. We would begin with
the heroine, her relation to a figure in real life, Frau von
Stein, and stress the influence of the latter upon Goethe and
the influence of the play in projecting a new ideal of human
behavior. But our attention will have to be given to the dark
element in the play, which is the exception; it exists only
within, in the mind or soul of the hero, and is soon expelled.

Goethe himself played the part of Orestes in the first
production of *Iphigenia,* in 1779. Having written the work,
he would appreciate the part, but also, having written
Werther and begun *Faust,* he would be no stranger in the
realm of the dark and vague: *das Trübe,* as he began to call
it after embarking upon his "Theory of Color." (*Trübsinn*
is melancholy.) What was new in *Iphigenia* was the need for an
escape from that realm. Werther had gone the way of death,
and Faust, as we just said, seemed likewise doomed. Orestes'
first words in the play are: "We walk the path of death" (II,i).

36. In using these terms, I have in mind Gray, *Goethe, the Alchemist;*
also Salm, *The Poem as Plant.* "Es ist die ewige Formel des Lebens,"
in the *Farbenlehre.*

The solution Goethe found is striking. His task was to modernize the ancient theme, and he seems to have made a virtue of the necessity. His internalizing of the Furies and his substituting of monologue for chorus, and imagery for rhapsody, might have been expected, after the example of French classical drama. For that matter, Euripides himself had all but modernized the theme. But the expelling of the internal by internal means, the use of monologue for what can only be accomplished subjectively, and the raising in turn of monologue to the level of chorus, all with logical as well as artistic purpose, are Goethe.

In their search for a statue of Diana which the oracle of Apollo has bade them restore to Delphi—"If you bring the sister . . . back to Greece, the curse will be lifted" (V, vi)— Orestes and Pylades arrive on the island of Tauris, where human sacrifice is practiced; they are captured and sentenced to death. Iphigenia, high priestess of the island, had until now succeeded in foregoing the barbarous rite, but she has incurred the displeasure of the king, who expresses his displeasure by reinstating the older practice. The two strangers will be the first victims, and the high priestess, of course, the performer of the ceremony. Orestes immediately perceives the morbid irony: the son who has killed his mother will now in retribution be killed by his sister, neither having willed the deed. The recognition scene is thus traumatic. What little emotional balance Orestes has managed to maintain is upset, and he collapses. Iphigenia seeks help, and the occasion for the monologue is created.

Orestes' psychological deliverance begins, as, half revived, and rising, he has a unfolding vision of his departed cursed family, from the oldest to the last generation. He sees them as reconciled, the enemy brothers, Thyestes and Atreus, walking in friendly conversation, their children in tow, and his own mother, Clytemnestra, on the arm of Agamemnon, his father. For the vision is born at once from the desire for peace, which is his persistent, conscious thought, and the need to make moral recompense, which is his natural ethos. But the desire and the need can only be joined in death,

so Orestes believes; and so he believes himself in this moment
to be in the underworld, having died, not merely fallen faint.
He asks his parents to bid him welcome, to say, "This is my
son." But after the family has bid him welcome, and he
believes he has joined them, he asks to be taken to the family
patriarch, Tantalus. The figures hesitate and turn away, and
Orestes has a final awesome vision of the great ancestor bound
in unbreakable chains.

The psychology here seems so modern that one is inclined
to speak of it in contemporary psychological terms. Such
terms would not be inappropriate, but it would be unwise for
us to begin with them. Freud was the first to point out that
the psychologist learns from the poets, not the reverse.[37] Moreover, the idea of redemption through death is as old as that
of death and resurrection, which is reflected in the biblical-
sounding words, "Behold your son"—"Sieh deinen Sohn"
(III, iii). The connection between physical and psychological death—i.e., the faint—is not difficult to make, especially
in poetry. The religious interpretation coincides with the
idea of spiritual death and rebirth so prominent in the mystical and cabalistic thought with which Goethe by this time
was well acquainted.[38] "Die and be reborn," he will say outright in a later poem, which we shall have cause to discuss
in direct relation to *Faust*.[39] More practically, one may speak
simply of the regenerative powers of sleep, and of the return
to the unconscious, and make the same point. Faust will
"sleep off" the whole tragedy of Part I and reawake to begin
Part II.

If we regard the matter from the viewpoint of theater
rather than thought, the result will be much the same, and,
interestingly, make the better connection with contemporary psychology. Goethe again has on stage a figure who

37. In the preface to *Psychopathology of Everyday Life*, first
published in 1904.

38. See again, Gray, *Goethe, the Alchemist*, p. 187.

39. "Stirb und werde!" from the poem "Selige Sehnsucht." See
below, chapter 5, n. 84.

must suggest an inner process by outward means. While
words might suffice to describe the process (*I feel* . . . , etc.),
vision externalizes it, both for the audience and the actor.
We imagine we experience what he imagines he experiences.
If the vision itself is unfolding (that is, dramatic), and it is
here, the result is theater within theater or, more accurately,
theater of the mind occurring within the actual playhouse.
But this high dramatic moment, which occurs precisely in the
middle of the play,[40] could as well be the reflection of a
psychological as an artistic need or urge to make what takes
place within to appear to be happening without. Goethe
knew both urges as they related to himself, as his early recognition of the therapeutic function of art suggests. Here,
surely, he employs them intentionally. A few years later, in
1782, in the poem "Der Erlkönig," he will cause the dying
child who rides through the night in his father's arms to see
and hear fantasy figures and voices in the dark surroundings.
The imaginings may have more of a base in reality in the
poem than in our present example, in that the trees and wind
become the figures and voices, and a wisp of fog the train of
the elf king's mantle, but the principle is the same. Orestes'
vision is as much a natural product of his tormented mind
as are the fantasies in the fevered consciousness of the child
who, as death strikes, says, "The elf king has hurt me."[41]
In fact, the poem helps us directly in interpreting the vision.
We see how the will or need to die expresses itself in positive
or attractive projections and the will to live in negative or
repulsive. Reconciliation, peace, and welcome in the vision
parallel the seductive images in the poem as expressions of
the desire for death as an escape from pain. But as Orestes'
imagined death brings with it a sense of redemption, his will
to live revives. He forgets his longing to forget (". . . pass

40. In III, ii, there being three scenes in the third act of this five-
act play. This is of course an unreal gauge of importance, but irresistible
in its neatness.

41. "Erlkönig hat mir ein Leids getan!"—"ein Leids" is child's
speech.

me the last cool cup from Lethe's stream" [III, ii]) and
confronts reality, seeks out the final truth, which repulses
him. Repulsion in the realm of death is an affirmation of
life. The hurt that the child experiences may be seen as the
last remnant of life before death, in which no pain can be
felt.

But we have come full circle. The ultimate vision of Tantalus suffering in death raises questions beyond psychology
which are not directly to our purpose to discuss. Perhaps the
intent was to suggest that the original sinner must atone
further for the greater depth of his transgression: Tantalus,
like Lucifer, sinned directly against the gods, not alone
against men as did his progeny, at what they believed to be
the behest of the gods. That might be too modern an interpretation for the ancient setting, but not for the moral
order implicit in the play itself. More likely, the meaning is
broader. The ultimate truth or principle in any order, moral,
philosophical, or aesthetic, is not to be fathomed by man,
though he must live within these orders. The legend is vague
on the crimes, if not the punishment, of Tantalus. The final
image in the monologue may have been dictated by poetry
rather than conscious thought. Art was regarded by Goethe
as incommensurable.

I have said almost nothing of Iphigenia to this point. And
her influence is to be understood as indirect. Goethe was
too much the writer from experience to have assumed that
the spirit of light in Iphigenia would dispel forthwith the
darkness in Orestes. There are few straight lines in the psychological world. Rather, Iphigenia causes an initially negative
response in her brother which only later will have its positive
result. Her presence, the atmosphere surrounding her being,
as Goethe might have thought of it,[42] at first does not inspire,
but unsettles Orestes. Her very being will not allow of irony.
Her presence denies him his will to negate, which, as attack,
has apparently served him as the best defense against his inner

---

42. "Alles Lebendige bildet eine Atmosphäre um sich her" (*Maxims and Reflections* [# 435 in the Artemis edition]).

grief. This negating spirit that Pylades has patiently tolerated
in his friend becomes, however, wholly unreal, becomes
shrill, in the presence of Iphigenia. Without this defense,
Orestes succumbs, and falls into the trance I have just described. When the others return, he believes them also to have
died and come to the underworld, and he welcomes them,
but with no trace of irony, in a rather childlike way. The
motif represents a dramaturgical, not a spiritual, transition
back to the real world. Orestes is willing now "for the first
time with a free heart to experience pure joy" in embracing
his sister (III, iii).

If it were our task to praise this work, we would note that
Orestes' psychological redemption is only one step in the
establishing of a new moral order which began at the outset
of the play with the abolishing of human sacrifice and ends
with the implied censure of inhumanity in any form. Goethe
does not have brother and sister simply flee the island by
deceiving the king, as legend required. Rather he has Iphigenia
beg leave, and the blessing, of a man who has acted toward
her not unkindly. Thaos's conciliatory response, "Lebt wohl!,"
seems, in its context as the last word of the play, a wish that
not only these, but all humans, should "fare well." For
Goethe succeeds, in a single dramatic action, in creating a
vision that parallels that of the great original treatment of
the theme in the trilogy by Aeschylus. The *Oresteia* celebrated the coming of an order that would prohibit the horrors
its story depicts by establishing the process of democracy
and the rule of law; appropriately, it is the patron of Athens,
the goddess Athena, who casts the deciding vote that saves
Orestes and both creates and exemplifies these new principles.
Iphigenia celebrates an equally profound change, that is,
the transition from a morality based upon religious custom
on the one hand and the rule of reason on the other, to a
morality stemming first from within, from a sense of the common humanity in all human beings which may not be vio-
lated. The play was of its age. Lessing, with his pioneering
religious tolerance, and Kant, with his concept of an inner

voice that dictates our moral precepts,[43] anticipate the ideal
of *Humanität* which Goethe projected in *Iphigenia.*

But even in our proper task of relating the individual
works to *Faust,* we find that *Iphigenia* only gains in significance by the comparison. It is a work of culmination, not
transition. The lines of development in Goethe seem to tran-
sect in it, with the freer forms of the earlier period gaining
in concentration and the freer thought, by virtue of its better
defined context, in clarity of purpose. There are no physical
walls in *Iphigenia,* since the play is set in nature, nor are
there spiritual walls, yet one senses that the action is contained
within a presupposed harmony. No world that Goethe had
created thus far both held and did not restrain its central figure. Werther, on the one hand, succumbed from sheer want
of context, Götz, on the other, from the opposite, the intract-
ability of his surroundings. Faust in the early version knows
no restraint, but also no broader purpose. Even Tasso, as we
shall see in a moment, though he lives in the sane and cultured climate of a fine Renaissance court, finds his environment lacking in a spirit which would more truly profit his
genius and his art. Our ultimate interpretation of the play
hinges on whether we consider this exacting demand neurotic
or merely utopian. *Tasso,* like *Iphigenia,* is titled "a play,"
Ein Schauspiel, not a tragedy, so that the unresolved friction
in its world is not to be seen as a requisite of form. Not that
the difference is more than incidentally one of spirit as
opposed to letter in the established orders of the two works.
The spirit in *Iphigenia* does not merely inform the order,
but creates it, much as Kant would have an inner voice or

43. Lessing with his parable of the rings, which makes all religions
equal but gives each a reason to excel, in *Nathan der Weise;* Kant with
the formulation of his categorical imperative in *The Critique of Practical Reason,* which in the original is worded: "Handle so, daß die Max-
ime deines Willens jederzeit als Princip einer allgemeinen Gesetzgebung
gelten könne." See Allan P. Cottrell, "On Speaking the Good: Goethe's
Iphigenie as 'Moralisches Urphänomen,'" *Modern Language Quarterly*
41 (1980): 162-80.

spirit create the moral law. Significantly, Goethe did not derive this concept from the *Critique of Practical Reason,* which appeared after his play, in 1786, but apparently from life, in his relationship with Frau von Stein.[44] He drew upon personal experience in formulating precepts that would be valid for a whole age. *Iphigenia* is thus the embodiment of Weimar classicism. And finally, since the work in its genesis manifested the same principle of willing restraint that it avowed in its contents, we may note a further sign of its classical character in the fusion of matter and form. The play was originally completed in prose and later rendered into blank verse, as if to pay due to its beliefs through action.

Indeed, when we claimed as a generality that the works from the successive periods were steps forward that at the same time entailed loss, we did not have before us the work that best substantiates the claim, *Iphigenia.* One wondered what could follow this accomplishment that would not be repetitious and yet not represent a falling-off. Art is true long before it is beautiful, Goethe claimed in the essay on Gothic architecture. But *Iphigenia* seems both true in its parts and ideal as a whole; and short rather than long would seem the time it took to produce its artful balance out of the intense and sometimes coarse realism of *Urfaust* and *Götz von Berlichingen.* For that matter, *Iphigenia* and the dramas in general from the present period[45] already imply the further question of what art becomes after it has attained beauty. And *Faust* in its completed form, though not at this stage, suggests an answer: it again becomes free. This freedom is the result of choice, not of revolt or want of discipline.

Of the works under discussion, *Torquato Tasso* is the most difficult to relate to *Faust. Iphigenia* provided contrasts in form, as just suggested, but also in content. Read in

44. On Goethe's relationship with Frau von Stein, see Fairley, *A Study of Goethe.*
45. Including quite a number of fragments in the classical vein. See the Artemis or the Hamburger edition of the works.

anticipation of the final scenes of *Faust*, where irony and evil
still hold sway, its "good ending" appears not only ideal,
but almost unreal.[46] I do not mean that one work is truer
than the other, more reflective of the view that Goethe held,
only that the dynamics of each is such as to require quite
opposite resolutions. The different resolutions to the attempts
at suicide by Orestes and Faust are likewise telling, in that
the subjective—or as Goethe might still have called it at the
time, "characteristic"—element in the former contrasts with
the symbolic or generic element in the latter, both marking
distinct phases of development. Faust recoils from suicide
when, with poison raised to his lips, he hears the bells chime
for Easter morning, the day symbolic of return from death,
and of rebirth in nature and in the moral world.

To be sure, *Tasso* supplies a contrast in form, and one
pehaps the more striking for the work having been conceived
after *Iphigenia* and thus modelled on a norm. *Iphigenia,*
after all, was begun in prose. In *Tasso* there are walls, physical
and spiritual, the struggle of the hero against the latter being
a main theme of the play. Had Goethe chosen to approach
his subject in a different way, and presumed these walls the
bane of true development, we would have had a drama not
unlike *Faust* in its concern with the limits set upon man, if a
drama still highly dissimilar in form. Form in Goethe rarely
functions independently, however, and to suppose a different
Tasso in an unaltered format would be to ignore the important part that conscious restraint and objectivity play in the
work. That the hero, fraught with inner conflict, speaks in the
same measured lines as those who do not share his anguish is
literary convention, yet a convention that here proves to have
further purpose. We come to sense in Tasso's strained conforming to verse—his excitements almost spring the meter, and he
speaks more than the others—the will and reluctance he shows

46. "Verteufelt human"—"hellishly humane," Goethe himself said
of the work in a letter to Schiller, January 19, 1802. See, for example,
Oskar Seidlin, "Goethe's *Iphigenia* and the Humane Ideal," in *Goethe:
A Collection of Critical Essays,* ed. Victor Lange.

in conforming to his surroundings as a whole. Language itself
is a product and reflection of conformity. Werther, who in the
extended monologue that is the novel would seem to enjoy
the privilege of expressing himself when and as he will, in fact
falls prey to his self-appropriated freedom, in that it creates
the vacuum in which he perishes. Through magic, as we noted
earlier, Faust remains immune to the law that requires that
freedom exist within a context, though this immunity is ultimately rejected in favor of an existence in which "freedom . . . must be regained each day" (Part II, v).

Goethe had a number of reasons for creating the *Tasso* he
did. The historical figure demanded sympathetic treatment, if
only as from one poet to another, and sympathy at the level
of art is objectivity. There could be no simple disparaging of
the surroundings in order to enhance the image of the hero,
which was the impression, though not the intent, of *Werther.*
Tasso is the true artist, and his surroundings as fine an example of a cultured milieu as history had produced to
Goethe's time.[47] Yet this refinement of the problem seems
less the product of a deliberate than a natural development.
When authors go back, they are usually unconsciously going
forward, in the sense that the return suggests disquiet with an
original position or conception as a lever to new creativity,
which in turn produces new problems requiring new solutions.
If *Tasso* is a "heightened" *Werther,* as Goethe accepted it to
be,[48] it is not a fully resolved treatment of the theme. The relation of author to hero remains unclear to the end. Indeed,
the public's initial misunderstanding of *Werther* may also
have been caused by a confusion or ambivalence in the mind
of the author and not solely by the fact that the action is
seen exclusively through the eyes of the protagonist. But in
Tasso the action is seen through the balancing view of other
participants, including ourselves as audience, with the result

47. See the section on "The Este in Ferrara" in Jacob Burckhardt,
The Civilization of the Renaissance in Italy (first published in 1860),
which does not ignore the harsh realities, either.

48. See E. M. Wilkinson, *"Tasso—ein gesteigerter Werther," Modern
Language Review* 24 (1949):305-28.

that any uncertainty has to be with the author. *Tasso* advances; it does not, like *Iphigenia,* come to an apparent conclusion. In that it is in the vein of *Faust.*

Goethe had also to motivate the mental imbalance which tradition had attached to the poet. Apparently instinctively, yet wholly in keeping with the spirit of his day, he made mental into emotional instability and created a viable dramatic tension. There is no writing plays about insanity,[49] and surely the historical Tasso was not deranged. But the positive aspect of the environment is less the reflection of this concern to illustrate the unreality of inner fear or despondency by contrast with a true outer reality as it is the direct expression of a special purpose, at least at the beginning of the play. *Tasso,* like *Iphigenia,* was written for Weimar. Goethe, by his own admission, had the court of Weimar in mind when he placed his setting in an earlier period. No one at court missed that point, though some stretched it to particulars of personality and relationships that the author would have had no intelligent reason to include.[50] Tasso is not Goethe, least conceivably the Goethe who completed the play in 1789 (albeit conceivably the former inner self who wrote *Werther*). In his first years in Weimar, Goethe was known for a quality virtually the opposite of the hypersensitivity we find in his Tasso, a certain *Grobheit*—coarseness.[51] In no way was he helpless in practical matters, as is the poet he created.

But that the court of the time in general was being addressed indirectly in this play seems certain. When Tasso praises his benefactors and says that the work he has just presented to them, his *Jerusalem Delivered,* belongs less

49. Since drama devolves upon character, a play abandons a hero or heroine, and so must do, at the point where he or she can no longer carry its weight.

50. See E. L. Stahl's edition of *Tasso* in the Blackwell series (Oxford, 1962).

51. Even Frau von Stein had difficulties with his behavior; so much more did those at court who were seeking to find fault. The letters from the first years in Weimar reflect the difficulties, as do the *Gespräche.*

to himself, whose talent and efforts may have formed its
outer beauty, and more truly to them, who in lending him
support and freedom made possible what "inner worth and
dignity" the poem might possess (I, iii), it is Goethe praising
his benefactors at court, chiefly the Duke of Weimar in his
counterpart the Duke of Ferrara, but not lastly the Duchess
Anna Amalia who, like the Princess Leonore in the play,
is the articulate supporter of the cause.[52] There are similar
examples of tribute to the nobility for its fostering of the
arts, some of them suggesting an exhortation in company
with commendations more suited to the actual situation in
Germany than to that great period for the arts in Italy when
court vied with court for the presence of talented man.
Yet Goethe had succeeded by this time in bringing Herder to
Weimar and would later in arranging substantial assistance
for Schiller; Wieland was there when Goethe arrived. The concept of Weimar as a Court of the Muses, a *Musenhof,* which
is attributed to the Duchess, was not a mere self-congratula-
tory provincialism, and its basis in reality grew in proportion
to the influence its members exerted, and continue to exert,[53]
on intellectual life. When one is aware, further, that *Tasso*
itself was a product of the special support and freedom from
practical affairs that was granted Goethe for his journey to
Italy, one can imagine the work being received in Weimar as
was *Jerusalem Delivered* in Ferrara, and the words of grati-
tude in its text being read—the play was not performed until
much later, in 1807—with a sense of life imitating art.[54]

   In any event, the point that leisure has essential fruits to
bear, which is a basic tenet of humanism and lay at the core

52. See Bruford, *Theatre, Drama, and Audience in Goethe's Germany,* under "Musenhof"; also Carlson, *Goethe and the Weimar
Theater,* pp. 161-224.

53. See Wilkinson and Willoughby, eds., *The Aesthetic Education of
Man,* who recognize the relevance of the Weimar philosophy to the concerns of the present day, in the notes as well as the introduction. This
in contrast to the above-mentioned essay by Oskar Seidlin on *Iphigenia.*

54. At the performance of *Tasso* on March 22, 1823, Goethe's bust
was crowned with a laurel wreath, as is Tasso in the play (I, iii).

of the new theory of art emerging from Weimar, was being
made, and before a tribunal who would have the power to
effect its acceptance. In addition, the art of life, as well as
art in life, is a theme in the play. To Tasso, who longs for the
that golden era when man in a more natural state knew that
what pleased him was right ("Erlaubt ist, was gefällt"), the
Princess makes the civilized response that if there once was
such a time, it is a time that can be regained, but now
through an understanding among equals of what is fitting,
not merely what pleases: "Erlaubt ist, was sich ziemt."[55]
To the logical, but here regarded clearly as sophistical, argument that the mighty and the clever have always seen as
fitting what is to their taste, she replies, in effect, look to
noble women: "So frage nur bei edlen Frauen an."[56] For
they subsist, and have their reason for being, in a naturally
moral order. These words seem a bow in the direction of
Frau von Stein, who tamed the younger and unruly Goethe
who first came to Weimar, but they are not empty flattery.
The whole of *Iphigenia* attests to the same belief.[57]

   This done, as it were, Goethe turned to his central theme,
which he described as the "disproportion of talent to life."[58]
Whether he intended the remark to include only Tasso or the
condition of the artist as such is a question both difficult and
necessary to answer. Let us make the former assumption.
Thus, again, Goethe was not Tasso. The separate entities of
sensitive poet and practical man of affairs who are so greatly
at odds in his play, who are "enemies because nature did not

   55. "That is permitted which pleases"—"That is permitted which is
proper" (II, i).
   56. "If you wish to know clearly what is proper,/Inquire of noble
women" (II, i).
   57. As does a late poem, "Zwischen beiden Welten"—"Between
Two Worlds" (1820), in which Goethe offered thanks to her, and to
Shakespeare, for making him what he was: "Euch verdank ich, was ich
bin."
   58. Caroline Herder, in a letter to her husband, March 20, 1789,
quoted Goethe as characterizing the theme of the work as "die Disproportion des Talents mit dem Leben."

form a single man from the two of them" (III, ii), are one in
himself. He had simply projected these selves into the imaginary realm of art where, cut off from nature, they tended
toward extremes. Hence the compulsive, and therefore often
seemingly unmotivated, antagonisms in the play. In reality,
life and talent in himself were so little at odds that in the same
period in which he wrote *Tasso,* Goethe conceived the
"Roman Elegies" (1789–90), the fifth poem of which contains the celebrated motif of the poet composing verse in
his mistress's arms, counting the hexameters on her spine.[59]
The problem was of art, not experience. The classical dramatic form, which demanded conflict without and not
merely within, seems to have compelled friction in the objective world that did not accurately reflect either the nature
or priority of the inner issue. Not only the central figure
but also the play itself seems to suffer a breakdown, and end
too abruptly and unresolved.

Let us make the latter assumption, again not on its full
merits but for our own purposes.[60] Tasso is still not Goethe
in this representation. Still he is a part of him, sorely, and not
entirely consciously, in conflict with his chosen environment.
The time was appropriate. Goethe had often enough com-
plained of the demands made upon him in Weimar; now, free
in Italy, he both better understood the nature of his conflict
and was more fearful lest it remain unresolved on his return.
Here lay the opportunity for therapy through writing, which
so often had a part to play, and the truth in his remark (to

59. "Oftmals hab ich auch schon in ihren Armen gedichtet/Und
des Hexameters Maß leise mit fingernder Hand/Ihr auf den Rücken
gezählt."

60. The full merits would necessitate a discussion of the conflict of
the artist with society, which is often said to emerge for the first time
clearly in *Tasso.* See the *Tasso* articles by Wilkinson mentioned above;
also her "Goethe's *Tasso:* The Tragedy of the Creative Artist," *Publications of the English Goethe Society,* n.s. 15 (1946): 96–127; or the
essay on *Tasso* in *Goethe: Poet and Thinker;* further, Stahl's introduction to his edition of *Tasso.*

Eckermann, quoted earlier) that the play was of his very
flesh and bones. The antagonist, Antonio, in this way comes
to incorporate the many forces in the environment that were
not likely to be found in one individual and which were truly
less antagonistic than simply antithetical to the interests of
the artist and art. Hence the apparently personally rooted
clashes in the play, which are better explained sociologically.[61]
There was no visible antagonist in *Werther.* The age was
forming a new image of the poet in his relation to society,
and to the extent that Goethe was a product of the age, he
contributed to the image, in *Tasso,* in *Werther,* and in a
number of poems, as if by instinct. Tasso himself provides
a classical formulation of the internal function of creativity
when he says, "And where other men fall silent in their
pain/A god gave me to tell how I suffer" (V, v). But to the
extent that Goethe was able to reconcile differences within
himself, and had early insight into the phenomenon of
polarity in the moral and the real world, he was wary of any
extreme as position, though he recognized its validity as
process. Tasso was Goethe in motion, as was Werther. Fifty
years after the publication of *Werther,* Goethe wrote a poem
to which he affixed as motto the lines from *Tasso* here
quoted, changing the one word *how* to *what* in ". . . to tell
what I suffer." The suffering in the poem is real, the result
of a serious attraction of a much older man to a young girl.[62]

Yet Goethe seems at the same time to identify with and
dissociate himself from the image of the poet that the original
lines conveyed. *What* he suffers is for the classical, *how* he
suffers for the romantic poet to say, the change seems to
suggest, with the emphasis upon their affinity rather than the

61. Caroline Herder, in the letter cited above, drew the distinction
between what a poet envisions in his work and what he has in fact
experienced: "The poet depicts a whole character, as it appeared to
him in his soul; such a complete character no single person possesses
alone."

62. Ulrike von Levetzow was seventeen when Goethe, at seventy-
two, first met her. Two years later he proposed marriage. The poem,
the second of the trilogy, is called "Elegie."

subtle difference evoked by the substituted word. If this is
true, we can sense an irrepressible romantic strain in Goethe
running parallel with the daemonic strain we recognize in
Faust, as if the one were merely the passive, the other the
active expression of his spirit, and as if both were in opposition to his classicism, his will to order. He could no more
resolve the question of the relation of art to life in *Tasso*
than he could that of man to nature in *Faust* without either
ignoring the complexity of the tensions involved, which
would contraidct his own experience, or bringing them into
an imagined harmony, while in reality they remained opposed,
the one defining the other. The only resolve could be that
there was no permanent resolve. The reason we might find
the conclusion of *Tasso* disturbing is that Goethe, in creating
the conflict, had gone so intuitively deep into its nature, its
pathology, one would have to say, that we are surprised when
presented with the final, somewhat perfunctory image of the
poet clinging to a reconciled and resolute Antonio, "like
the mariner to the rock which he thought would destroy
him." These are the last lines of the play. Earlier lines anticipate and help to counteract the imbalance, but the image is
stronger than the words. Goethe, we feel, would have more
to say outside the play, as in the motto just mentioned, and
elsewhere.[63]

In other words, where under my first assumption I argued
that the conflict seemed willful and unreal, now we may see
in its impulsive and unpredictable course precisely the sign
to betray its inner workings, and wish these workings projected
further, not resolved. In either case, form seems to have
played its part in determining content. The classical drama
which tradition came to regard as the vehicle for the timeless
was becoming unsuited to express the problems of an age
that had begun to conceive of time, evolution, and change

63. Namely, in the first poem of "Trilogie der Leidenschaft," titled
"An Werther," written fifty years after the publication of the novel.
Goethe now saw Werther as mired in torment, himself half to blame,
and wished a god would give him the power to express what he en-
dured: "Geb ihm ein Gott, zu sagen, was er duldet."

as synonymous with life. "Alles Vergängliche/Ist nur ein Gleichnis"—"Everything transitory is only a symbol"—Goethe says at the end of *Faust,* as if regaining a classical insight, but he says it from the viewpoint of eternity, through the mouth of the Chorus Mysticus, not that of life.[64] This is not to say that *Tasso* suffered a distortion of meaning in its adjustment to form, for the historical motif of emotional imbalance in the hero may account for more discrepancies than some of our higher arguments. Nor is it to imply that *Faust* by its very freedom of form achieved the consummate expression of its theme, though both may be true. But to the extent that *Tasso* labors, or simply controls, inner conflict or chaos beneath its ordered surface, to that extent it provides inverted insight into *Faust,* in which Goethe chose conversely to express all in the search for deeper truth and harmony, as if the one were the contractive, the other the expansive, movement of the same creative force. Neither *Iphigenia,* which seems wholly to have succeeded in its purpose and to be one with itself, nor *The Natural Daughter,* which as a finely balanced classical play treating the (for it) incongruous subject of the French Revolution seems wholly to have failed, affords as meaningful a contrast.[65] But we must return to *Faust* itself and to the development, though limited, it underwent in this period.

> *Faust:* . . . to know in my
> Heart's core all human weal and woe,
> To grasp in thought the lofty and the deep,
> Men's various fortunes on my breast to heap,

64. What he learns from Helen of Troy, that in the present alone lies happiness ("Die Gegenwart allein—ist unser Glück" [l. 9382]), which is the empiricism of the ancient world, he later unlearns in his inveterate striving as Western man, who is unsatisfied every moment: "Er, unbefriedigt jeden Augenblick:" (l. 11,452).

65. *Die natürliche Tochter,* begun in 1799, is the first part of a trilogy which was not completed. With the exception of the heroine, Eugenie, the characters in the play have no personal names—further evidence of a move toward the objective or abstract.

And thus to theirs dilate my individual mind,
And share at length with them the shipwreck of mankind.[66]

So begins, in a sense, the fragment of *Faust* which Goethe
published in the last volume of a collected works that appeared between 1787 and 1790. These are not in fact the
first lines, the fragment beginning, as did *Urfaust,* with the
introductory monologue and continuing unchanged, except
in the punctuation an *Ur*-manuscript is not likely to have, to
this point. But an ellipsis precedes the lines to indicate a
gap, and it is here that we begin when we know the earlier
version and wish to see what new has developed.

New proved to be this scene, and two complete scenes, the
"Witches' Kitchen" and "Forest and Cavern."[67] "Auerbach's
Cellar" has been rendered into blank verse; and the part
played by Faust in it reduced to a greeting and, at the high
point of the joviality, a suggestion that he and Mephistopheles depart. The scene between Mephistopheles and the
student is made more sharply satirical of academic learning,
and the simpler humor in the spirit of early university days
takes second place. The fragment ends with the scene in
the cathedral, where Gretchen faints.

Where the fragment begins (in our sense) and where it
ends are both important. The present scene introduces the
first exchange on a philosophical level between Mephistopheles and Faust. In the early version, they had related to
each other only "dramatically," that is, as the dramatic, not
the thematic, action required. Not that they now fall out

---

66. "Und was der ganzen Menschheit zugeteilt ist,/Will ich in meinem
innern Selbst genießen,/Mit meinem Geist das Höchst' und Tiefste
greifen,/Ihr Wohl und Weh auf meinen Busen häufen,/Und so mein
eigen Selbst zu Ihrem Selbst erweitern,/Und, wie sie selbst, am End'
auch ich zerscheitern" (Witkowski, ll. 249–54). The English translation
is by Anna Swanwick, from whose *Faust: A Tragedy by Goethe in
Two Parts* (New York, 1882 and later) I now quote throughout, except
where otherwise noted.

67. Though a passage from *Urfaust* is affixed to its end.

of character. We hear Faust clearly in the above lines, and as
the scene progresses there are distinct recollections of his
opening monologue:

> What then am I, if I aspire in vain
> The crown of our humanity to gain,
> Toward which my every sense doth strain?[68]

The first words that Mephistopheles speaks are in his inimitable vein:

> Oh, credit me, who still as ages roll,
> Have chew'd this bitter fare from year to year,
> No mortal from the cradle to the bier,
> Digests the ancient leaven![69]

Goethe himself believed he had recaptured the tone and
thread of the original so well that were he to smoke the
edges of his present manuscript, as he wrote from Rome,
March 1, 1788, no one could tell it from the old.

But because the thread was deliberately sought and the
theme consciously rejoined in its central issue, we expect
the *Fragment* to take the next necessary step and produce
a pact. The traditional treatment of the theme, except in
the case of the pragmatic puppet plays which immediately get
down to business, typically includes a philosophical or theological discussion touching upon the human condition and
its incompleteness as prelude to an agreement. That occurs here,
in more than token fashion. The frustrations that drove Faust
in the opening monologue to seek truth and deeper experience in magic are repeated, and Mephistopheles, as if assuming the role that the Earth Spirit played in *Urfaust,* compounds
the frustration by noting its futility: "Thou'rt after all—

68. "Was bin ich denn, wenn es nicht möglich ist / Der Menschheit Kronen zu erringen, / Nach der sich alle Sinne dringen?" (Witkowski,
ll. 282–84; in the final version, ll. 1803–05).

69. "O glaube mir, der manche tausend Jahre / An dieser harten
Speise kaut, / Daß in der Wieg' und auf der Bahre / Kein Mensch den
alten Sauerteig verdaut!" (Witkowski, ll. 255–58; in the final version,
ll. 1776–79).

just what thou art."[70] But the scene ends without a pact or
any allusion to a pact. The scene is important in its own
right, however, as we shall see directly.

There is another reason for our expecting a pact. The comparison of the *Fragment* with the early version provides the
clearest evidence in perhaps the whole of Goethe of the artist
deliberately at work. Each change or development that we
noted has its strict purpose. The drastic reduction in the role
that Faust plays in "Auerbach's Cellar" not only reflects a
distaste for frivolity more in keeping with his character but
serves to make dramatically real, and not merely preliminary,
the rejuvenation scene which immediately follows. There is
no dealing for Mephistopheles with a staid scholar. The
"Witches' Kitchen," in turn, which effects the rejuvenation
and anticipates the meeting with Gretchen in the next scene,
at the same time further commits the work to an approach
through the fantastical as the perspective and measure of things,
destructive or positive. In this scene, the monkeys roll out
a large ball and, as if in parody of the earlier Earth Spirit's
song, we hear the rhyme: "The world behold / Unceasingly
roll'd / It riseth and falleth ever."[71] The ball is empty. Goethe
reintroduces a passage from *Urfaust* in the new context of
"Forest and Cavern," and we find that the lines repeat in the
particular the generalized urge to self-destruction contained
in our quotation from the "beginning" of the *Fragment*. As he
envisions the destruction of Gretchen through his own fault,
Faust says "Her direful doom fall crushing on my head / And
into ruin let her plunge with me!"[72] In short, if no pact was

70. "Du bist am Ende—was du bist" (Witkowski, l. 285; in the final
version, l. 1806).

71. "Das ist die Welt; / Sie steigt und fällt / Und rollt beständig"
(Witkowski, l. 865–67; final version ll. 2402–04).

72. "Mag ihr Geschick auf mich zusammenstürzen / Und sie mit mir
zu Grunde gehn!" (ll. 2037–38; final version ll. 3364–65). The lines
at the "beginning" of the *Fragment,* referring to the destruction of the
world, read: "Und so mein eigen Selbst zu Ihrem Selbst erweitern, / Und,
wie sie selbst, am End' auch ich zerscheitern," as we just saw. There is
the same transformation of a particularized to a generalized urge here

included in this version, which in other respects seems wholly
intent upon further developing the theme and motivating the
action, it cannot have been by chance. And our expectations
are correct in the sense that the pact, when finally included,
will appear in the main scene in question, just prior to the
lines with which it began.

Goethe seems still to have conceived of Faust as damned,
or better, doomed, at this stage in the development of the
work. I say doomed, because damnation in the context of the
legend would imply transgression against an established order,
and such transgression in the view of the Storm and Stress
author of *Urfaust* would have been not only tolerable, but
almost requisite in a hero. Tragedy for the new Faust would
follow from the very freedom of thought and action which
brings him unhampered, but unguided, into the realm of the
unknown. One of the difficulties in devising a pact now
would be that none was really needed. Nature, both in the
sense of natural laws and human characteristics, would doom
or save. For as much as Goethe acclaimed freedom in the
early years, he was aware of a force that inevitably redressed
imbalance, as witness Werther. We may see the early Faust
as an inverted Werther, doomed from excess without.[73] And
by the time of the *Fragment,* not only had the natural
process of maturing lent Goethe a certain further caution,
but his scientific studies had made concrete what was first
intuited, and he seemed deliberately to distance himself
from his hero. Character development at this point consisted
mainly in emphasizing the unwieldy and unreasoning element
in Faust, in contrast to the cynical rationalism of Mephistopheles, though there is no hint that Goethe could side with
the latter point of view. Mephistopheles best makes the case

---

as in the urge to suicide in Orestes; from the "characteristic," that is,
emanating from character or personality, to the symbolic, belonging to
all.

73. The *Tag- und Jahreshefte* for 1760–75 (Artemis edition, vol.
11) note *Faust* among the literary undertakings that were "deeply
and truly felt but often one-sided and falsely expressed," p. 618.

for us when he notes that Faust would be doomed even if
he had not given himself over to the Devil: "And were
he not the devil's by his bond,/Yet must his soul infallibly
be lost!"[74] These lines are not in *Urfaust*.

But by the time of the *Fragment* Goethe had also
developed an urge toward a broader view that might
ignore caution in its will to comprehend, to take in all.
The urge had been there from the beginning, most notably
in *Urfaust* itself, where, for that matter, it is given as the
reason for turning to magic: "That I the force may recog-
nize/That finds creation's inmost energies."[75] But again the
difference lay in the confirmation in nature of intuition
and words, if considerably less concretely than before. The
trip to Italy had intervened. Goethe, of course, had anticipated this. "What I always told myself has occurred—that
only in this land would I understand . . . a number of phenomena of nature and complexities of ideas,"[76] he wrote
from Naples, March 17, 1787. He eventually had to abandon
his most spectacular thought, which was to discover in Italy
an actual example of a plant that represents all plants, his
Urpflanze, but he did not forsake the spirit that prompted
the search, which was a "recognizing of the essential form
with which nature, as it were, never fails to play and playing
brings forth manifold life," as he wrote to Frau von Stein,
July 10, 1786, before Italy. "And it is not a dream, not a
fantasy," he added. At the same time, his fascination with
the violence and apparent disorder in nature began to reassert
itself, if it ever lay truly dormant. When the occasion presented itself, Goethe made three consecutive visits to Vesuvius,

74. "Und hätt' er sich nicht dem Teufel Uebergeben,/Er
müßte doch zu Grunde gehn!" (Witkowski, ll. 345–46; final
version, ll. 1866–67). The German is more accurate in speaking
of perdition without using the word "soul."

75. "Daß ich erkenne, was die Welt/Im Innersten zusammenhält,"
already quoted from *Urfaust* in a more literal translation (Witkowski,
Urfaust, ll. 29–30; final version, ll. 382–83).

76. "Verworrenheit der Meinungen": "confusion of opinions" might
be better.

and climbed the volcanic mountain to a height where only
the younger guides would go. It was the scientist who, in the
last visit, was pleased to make certain geological observations,
but it was the poet who found lyric strength in settings of
night and storm—"Wanderers Sturmlied" ("Wanderer's Storm
Song")[77] —and who retained an attraction to a "formless
mass that time after time consumes itself and has declared
war on all sense of beauty," as he said of the volcano on
March 6, 1787; this in contrast to his portraitist, and companion at Vesuvius, Tischbein, whose sensibilities he saw as
justifiably offended. The image of Goethe in Italy turning his
his back on all undefined thought and feeling applies more to
the artist than the man. He could still speak of Hamann, to
whose all-but-mystical philosophy he had been early attracted,
as one day gaining recognition, like Vico in Italy, as the
father of a national mode of thought.[78]

Goethe remained open, especially to nature. "Nature is
always right and most fundamentally so at those very points
where we do not understand her."[79] He himself could never
again go the murky path of his Faust, for he had come to see
clearly, and, he believed, for a lifetime. "It seems to me, at
least, as if I have never judged things so well as here," he

77. 1771. "Wanderers Nachtlied" I and II (1776 and 1780) are
at the opposite pole from "Wanderers Sturmlied," the former in its
longing for peace, the latter, with its celebrated beginning lines, "Ueber
allen Gipfeln / Ist Ruh," in the at least momentary attainment of it.
For English versions of the poems, see the most complete collection,
The Poems of Goethe, which is translated by Edgar Alfred Bowring
(2nd ed., London, 1874). The Penguin collection, *Goethe: Selected
Verse*, ed. David Luke (Baltimore, 1964), with prose translations accompanying the originals, is more serviceable—by implication it respects the definition of poetry attributed to Robert Frost: poetry is
that which is lost in translation.
78. Giovanni Battista Vico (1668–1744), philosopher of history.
"Es ist gar schön, wenn ein Volk solch einen Aeltervater besitzt; den
Deutschen wird einst Hamann ein ähnlicher Kodex werden," are
Goethe's words in *The Italian Journey*, March 5, 1787.
79. This from "Ueber die Natur," however.

wrote in the *Italian Journey* under November 10, 1786. "I
look forward to the blessed consequence for my whole
life." But he was eventually forced to define rather than
reject the instincts that dominated his life and art in an
earlier period and to trust nature in its dark workings within
man as well as in the phenomenal world. This would speak
for his saving rather than damning Faust.

It is as if Goethe consciously anticipated damnation, but
instinctively, and by the very instincts he would otherwise
deny, had begun to commit himself to the salvation of his
hero. There is no evidence of a decision on the point, or even
of debate in his own mind, but there is in the *Fragment*
itself a passage that suggests the potential conflict. It occurs
at the beginning of "Forest and Cavern," the scene from
which we quoted subsequent lines to illustrate the self-
destructive tendency in Faust. Here his mood and tone are
different—so unmistakably the mood and tone of Goethe
outside the play that we wonder whether author and character
have not again become one. Also, the content of the passage,
which is in monologue form, reflects the same intimate
relation to nature we find in the early poems, though now,
if anything, more poignant, because more mature. The
same kind of spirit or god who in the early poetry seems
to represent a force in the universe and yet to exist solely
for the poet himself[80] reappears: "Spirit sublime! Thou
gav'st me, gav'st me all / For which I prayed!"[81] The spirit
is praised for the special communication with nature it
provides, the insight into her secrets: "Thou dost permit me
in her depths profound / As in the bosom of a friend to gaze."[82]
Of course, this sense of harmony with nature and the universe contradicts the assumption we have made up to this

80. These are not muses who relate to the poet as poet, but patron
saints of nature, as it were, who guide his being, not merely his talent.
See "Wanderers Sturmlied" or "Harzreise im Winter" (1777).

81. "Erhabner Geist, du gabst mir, gabst mir alles, / Worum ich
bat" (ll. 1890–91; final version, ll. 3217–19).

82. "Vergönnest mir in ihre tiefe Brust, / Wie in den Busen eines
Freund's, zu schauen" (ll. 1896–97; final version, ll. 3223–24).

point, that *want* of access to deeper truth is the definitive problem in the play. Goethe seems aware of the potential discrepancy, for he moves immediately to resolve it. "With this exalted joy," he has Faust continue in an abrupt change of thought, "Thou gav'st me this companion [Mephistopheles] who degrades me to myself and turns/Thy glorious gifts to nothing, with a breath."[83]

But in so motivating or redefining the conflict, he has heightened and greatly broadened the theme. In place of the particular problem of the overweening individual who in his despair with human limitations turns to magic in search of truth and enlightening experience, we have the general question of the duality within man himself. For we can no longer see Mephistopheles as a figure summoned or sent from another realm when he is now presented as a force inimically, but inseparably, related to the force from which is seen to derive all true communion and knowledge. We must see him as representing simply the negative counterpart of the positive qualities we identify in Faust—the striving, the visionary hope. This does not mean that Faust must be saved, nor that his tragedy will be less, since the evil of which he partakes is merely the concomitant of the good he pursues. One of the reasons the play may logically retain the title of tragedy despite its ultimate resolution is that it uncompromisingly insists on an inherent contradiction in the human condition. But to the extent that the fate of Faust as an individual is equated with the fate of mankind, his actions are the less damnable, if his tragedy no less profound. And if I am right in assuming that the passage in question was more immediately the product of independent inspiration or insight on the part of the author than deliberate development of character or thematics in his play, then it will stand as perhaps the best illustration thus far of the creative process

83. "Du gabst zu dieser Wonne,/Die mich den Göttern nah' und näher bringt,/Mir den Gefährten, den ich schon nicht mehr/Entbehren kann . . . [der] mich vor mir selbst erniedrigt, und zu Nichts,/Mit einem Worthauch, deine Gaben wandelt" (ll. 1914–19; final version, ll. 3241–46); similar lines in *Urfaust*, Witkowski, ll. 19ff.

I am attempting to discern in *Faust*. We remember from
Urfaust how the instinct for characterization led Goethe to
anticipate perfectly naturally the abstract purport the figures
and actions would come to have in his completed play. We
even questioned his claim to have foreseen the general
treatment of his theme from the beginning, so unpremeditated, so ripe in coming seems the thought as it enters the
work. But here it is Goethe as Goethe, not as author, who
seems directly to intervene, forcing, wittingly or unwittingly,
a new beginning. For while the concept of polarity could
account for the phenomenon of opposition in nature, it could
not justify the phenomenon in the moral world, the world of
the mind, which is the realm the play at this point reenters
and where the question of purpose will obtain. There are,
outside the play, indications of the resolution to the problem
that will ultimately emerge. There is a letter from Italy, for
example, dated October 20, 1786, in which Goethe likens
himself to the god Antaeus, who "always feels newly strength-
ened the more directly one brings him in touch with his
mother, Earth."[84] The reference is to his own experience
on his geological excursions, yet the image anticipates one
of the "souls" or polar urges in Faust which will be described as "clinging to the world with obstinate desire"
(l. 1115).

A clearer, and earlier, indication is afforded by the three
philosophical poems, "Song of the Spirits above the Waters,"
"The Limits of Man," and "The Divine," all written some
time before the publication of the *Fragment*, between 1779
and 1785. The first envisions man in his constant turmoil,
rushing like the pure stream headlong into the still lake, where
it will then be tossed by the wind. The poem entertains no
thought of consolation or rest, any more than will the spirit
of man as it is reflected in *Faust*.[85] The second conceives

84. Antaeus, the son of Poseidon and Gaea, the Earth, is invincible
in wrestling. Hercules overpowers him by lifting him from the ground.

85. "Gesang der Geister über den Wassern" (1779). The first
stanza reads: "Des Menschen Seele / Gleicht dem Wasser: / Vom Himmel steigt es, / Und wieder nieder / Aur Erde muß es, / Ewig wechselnd";

the problem in slightly different terms, setting the instinct of man to strive upward and the attendant loss of equilibrium—"And with him play/The clouds and the winds"—against the opposite urge to secure himself upon solid ground, where he will not reach heights "comparable/Even to the tree or the vine."[86] The poem ends with the philosophically optimistic projection of individual existence as limited, yet extended eternally: "A little ring encompasses our life/And generations ceaselessly form themselves/On the unending chain of being,"[87] but it does not relate the resolution to the specific nature of the problem it raises. Nor does "The Divine," which, after noting the apparent indifference of the larger scheme of things to human endeavor ("The sun will shine/Alike on good and evil"), almost despite that fact exhorts man to "Be noble and good,/For that alone/Distinguishes him/From all beings/That we know." The poem is morally exhortative but not philosophically convincing.[88]

However, raising and resolving of the problem within the framework of a philosophical poem[89] is not the same as incorporating and resolving it in a dramatic work in progress.

---

the last: "Seele des Menschen,/Wie gleichst du dem Wasser:/Schicksal des Menschen,/Wie gleichst du dem Wind!"

86. "Grenzen der Menschheit" (1778), from the Bowring translation, p. 184.

87. This from the last stanza. The original is clearer as to the "limited" nature of man: "Ein kleiner Ring/Begrenzt unser Leben,/Und viele Geschlechter/Reihen sich dauernd/An ihres Daseins/Unendliche Kette."

88. I quote from the Bowring translation, pp. 184-85. The title of the poem in the original is "Das Göttliche," which does not have so strong a religous connotation as "The Divine," in my opinion.

89. In his edition of Goethe's poems (Cambridge, 1966), Ronald Gray calls these lyrics "hymns" (in the German sense—not *Kirchenlieder*), which they are, and which may account for the not wholly logical development they at times follow. Also, to think of them as hymns makes clearer the acknowledged but not so readily apparent influence of Klopstock on Goethe. See *Poetry and Truth*, Book ten, at the very beginning.

The truly surprising thing about the pact eventually formulated in *Faust* is not that it provides the means to explore
the basic contradictions in the human condition, which is
also the theme of the poems, but that it provides the perfect
means, against all expectation. To have *consciously* conceived
a pact that would not only meet the demands of the legend
but also assure its modern interpretation, not only generate
objective action but itself form the measure of inner truth,
not only allow for the saving of the hero but predicate his
salvation on the very nature of the agreement into which he
enters, seems, in fact, so unlikely that we are led to assume
the opposite. We imagine, not an intelligence devising a single
solution to a complex of problems, but the creative mind
producing answers from a resource where art and thought
have roots in common and no intent is without its form. The
intention to save Faust may have partaken of this process.
When there was the means there was the reason for his salvation, we may say. But that is a subject for the next chapter.

And, finally, when we ask why the *Fragment* was made to
end where it did, with the scene in the cathedral, we find that
questions of form of the kind we have raised throughout this
chapter again pertain. Made to end, we must say, because we
know that the Gretchen episode was complete, yet not included in its entirety. Technical matters were not a factor,
since the final version would present the episode substantially
unchanged and would insert only one new scene between
"Cathedral" and "Dungeon," with which Part I, like *Urfaust,*
will end. It is with this insertion that we are concerned, and,
for the present, with its form rather than its content, which
will be discussed in its proper place. (See chapter 6.)

For "Walpurgis Night," whatever its intent, has the effect
of altering the work categorically. The realism of the Gretchen
tragedy is interrupted by a fantastic sequence which is not
quite comic relief, in that the comedy is satire that has
little relation to the world in which the drama takes place,
nor wholly symbolism, for few of its motifs will be so
recognized. The lyric sequel, "Walpurgis Night's Dream,"
carries the separation of plot and play to the breaking point.

By making reference in the opening lines to the "stout sons
of Mieding" who had been the carpenter and factotum of
theWeimar theater, it destroys not only the dramatic but also
the artistic illusion. We are taken momentarily to a historical
point in time. Not that this touch of so-called romantic
irony is without purpose, and that is our point. It is merely
the extreme expression of a developing artistic freedom that
would eventually dominate the action as a whole. If other
themes we have discussed in this chapter made demands upon
the form in which Goethe treated them, the Faust theme
would grow to make demands upon form itself. Was the work
to absorb all the thought and feeling that seemed naturally
to accrue to its theme, as if it were destined to be not about
one thing, but everything in life, or was it to remain true to
its initial, single impulse and become the crowning achievement of the Storm and Stress? Ending with "Cathedral,"
the *Fragment* appears suspended, as though it had unconsciously asked this question and, unconsciously hesitating
to answer, had been unable to progress.

Part I resolved the matter. "Formless content in preference
to empty form," read a notation in a generalized scheme to
Faust of 1800, which also mentioned for the first time an
anticipated second part.[90] For at that stage the work had already begun to reveal the problematical along with the
positive aspects of its great regenerative powers and had
proved to "contain in the problem just resolved a new problem
to be resolved," as Goethe remarked of its final stages in a
letter to Johann Heinrich Meyer, July 20, 1831.

But Part I, in going forward, did not attempt to transcend
its own or its author's earlier beginnings, as we suspected may
have been the case in *Tasso*. In including in toto the scenes
from *Urfaust* as well as the *Fragment,* it embodied literally its
past in its present form.

90. "Vorzug dem formlosen Gehalt vor der leeren Form" (see
Thomas's translation of the schemata, cited above). Witkowski dates
the document between 1797 and 1800 (1:511, 2:421), by which latter
date Schiller, in a letter to Goethe of September 13, is alluding to a
second part of the work. For a discussion of the transition, see chapter 6.

5

THE TRAGEDY, PART I

From Rome, on August 11, 1787, Goethe wrote to the Duke
in Weimar: "By Easter I will likely close yet another epoch:
my first (or actually) my second epoch as author. Egmont is
finished, and I hope to have done the final work on Tasso
by New Year, on Faust by Easter, which will only be possible
in this distant seclusion." "Faust on his [magic] mantle
will announce my arrival," the letter ends.

One senses in the passage a probably unwitting desire to
reassure the Duke and others in Weimar that tangible results
would follow from the time spent in Italy, where Goethe
remained longer than was anticipated. We know the measurable and immeasurable results, and may even be persuaded
that nothing remotely compared in influence upon Goethe
with these years that seemed to bring everything together in
his life and thought; after Italy he did not change significantly.[1] But those in Weimar could know only that the
celebrated young poet who had come into their midst some
dozen years before, and whose early work they knew on the
stage and in print, had meanwhile completed only one new
play, *Iphigenia* (*Egmont* had been brought from Frankfurt),
and was promising two more. They would have been aware
of his scientific studies, but as yet would not have seen the
publication of his findings, nor seen the more than one
thousand drawings he had made as artist and as researcher.[2]

1. See, again, Fairley, *A Study of Goethe*, pp. 97–120, on the influence of Frau von Stein, which he considers the turning point, rather
than Italy.

2. Hans Mayer, in "Die Italienische Reise," included in his *Klassik
und Romantik* (Pfullingen, 1963), pp. 57ff., says Goethe saw himself
as "gescheitert" ("failed") at the time.

That a manuscript of *Urfaust* circulated among them would only have whetted their appetite.

Urge or no urge to reassure, it is unlikely that the *Faust* here contemplated would have broadly resembled the finished product we know as Part I and Part II of *Faust*. More likely and more practicably projected would have been a Storm and Stress tragedy, an expanded *Urfaust,* with a conventional pact perhaps, and the damnation of the hero depicted or implied. His salvation would have been unconscionable in any close proximity to the Gretchen tragedy, which remained the moral thorn in the side of the play. Only at the great remove in time and feeling effected by the passage of the action through various phases does the eventual redemption seem justified, and of that some have doubts.[3] An unredeemed Faust tragedy, on the other hand, would have been perfectly conceivable as the culmination of a period that had begun with *Götz* and run through *Egmont* to the present. Hence the end of an epoch. Goethe's afterthought that in fact a second period was coming to a close may reflect his sense that the products of the first, begun in Frankfurt, were only now emerging, along with the later and quite differently conceived *Iphigenia* and *Tasso*. Goethe did not plan any further dramas in the classical vein, and appeared at this very point to abandon his *Nausikaa,* ostensibly under the pressure from scientific concerns. In an entry for *The Italian Journey,* April 17, 1787, he bemusedly reported how an innocent morning walk in the botanical gardens in Palermo shattered his literary plans for the day by reawaking in him the thought of discovering after all a specimen of the "plant primeval." He concluded: "Why are we moderns so distracted, why challenged by demands we can neither meet nor fulfill!" The exclamation would have its reasoned display in Part II, where the ancient and the modern spirit are not only contrasted, but joined, in the union of Faust and Helen of

3. Among others, Alexander Gillies, in *Goethe's Faust: An Interpretation,* p. 220, and Erich Heller, in "Faust's Damnation," included in his *Artist's Journey into the Interior,* pp. 33ff.

Troy, and yet the fruit of their union, in the figure of Euphorion, doomed.

It is not my purpose to attempt to prove an original intent
to damn Faust, which the evidence will not allow. But if we
make this assumption, which the evidence does not disallow,
it provides us with a perspective upon the work that perhaps
best reveals its inner dynamics. Whether or not Goethe saw
his project clearly from the beginning, he probably would
have taken essentially the same steps in completing it. His
tendency to retain and incorporate, rather than to separate
and reject, caused him always to broaden his first concep-
tions, so that a Faust conceived as redeemed might as easily
have developed the tragic dimension that led Goethe so to
name his play, as a Faust conceived as doomed have found a
place in a wider scheme that demanded his salvation. The
tragedy and the salvation will ultimately be comprehended
under the same law of nature, that of time, which is a condition of being that is tragic in the individual, in that we cannot make "the moment stay," but all-saving in the species,
in that rest induces stagnation. But we must be wary of
presuming just how far Goethe had come in his thinking,
if not his writing, on *Faust* at any given time. Surely he was
not merely mocking when he suggested to Schiller that the
latter think through the Faust problem "in a sleepless night,"
formulate the requisites of the theme, "and so, like a true
prophet, relate and explain to me my own dreams." (This in
a letter of June 22, 1797, the year in which Goethe seriously
resumed work on his Faust manuscript.)

On the other hand, almost every new dimension or element
of plot now introduced into the work prepared for and
served to justify the salvation of the hero. *Urfaust* contained
no such anticipation, and the *Fragment* little to imply saving
grace. That suggests design. The exception is the death of
Valentin, who in a duel with Faust is dispatched with Mephistopheles' aid, but that death is an extension of the Gretchen
tragedy, not a new motif, and is presupposed in *Urfaust* in

Gretchen's remark, "Give me thy hand! . . . 'Tis wet! . . .
There's blood thereon . . ." (ll. 39–41).[4]

The "Prologue in Heaven" provides the first new dimension
or frame around the action.[5] Other material—namely a
dedication and the "Prelude in the Theater"—in fact preceded
it when Part I was published in 1808, and this material likewise provides perspective, in the first instance upon the
personal relation of the author to his work, in the second of
the work to the world in which it was to be presented. These
extra dimensions are obviously of importance in my own
approach, which has stressed the development rather than
the autonomy of the work of art, but their analysis will
better suit my general argument if postponed until the very
end.[6]

The "Prologue in Heaven" seems part of a pageant. Its
opening choral song proves more than simply majestic, but
it first makes that impression as it celebrates the works
of Creation while the Lord amid the heavenly hosts awaits
his audience with the Devil. The devil who appears, namely
Mephistopheles, is not of the kind we associate with a miracle
play or religious drama, but there is a precedent for the
meeting in the Book of Job. There, too, an agreement is
reached to tempt an earthly servant, though here it is an
ambitious one, as the Lord almost defensively points out:
"Know'st thou Faust?" Mephistopheles: "The Doctor?"

4. "Deine Hand Heinrich!—Sie ist feucht—Wische sie ab ich bitte
dich! Es ist Blut daran. . . ." (Witkowski, *Urfaust*, ll. 39–41).

5. Harold Jantz, in his article "Patterns and Structures in *Faust*,"
speaks of broad correlations between Part I and Part II, and finds "an
initial set of basic themes that are carried through the whole drama,
varied and developed in dynamic interplay" (p. 363).

6. In a planned study of Part II. It has been argued that the "Prelude
in the Theater" was not originally conceived as a prelude to *Faust*.
See Oskar Seidlin, "Is the 'Prelude in the Theatre' a Prelude to *Faust*?"
PMLA 64 (1949):462–70.

The Lord: "My servant!"[7] And when at the end of the scene
Mephistopheles in his mocking tone has the last word—
"'Tis courteous in so great a lord as he/To speak so kindly
even to the Devil"[8] —we take the humor with the earlier
solemnity as part of the intent to elevate and to entertain,
in the tradition of folk rather than literary drama. It is not
true that with *Faust* Goethe separated himself from the
stage and in the "Prelude in the Theater" wrote his "bill of
divorcement," as August Wilhelm Schlegel claimed.[9] What
we, and even Schlegel as a contemporary, might regard as the
restrictions of the theater paradoxically disappear when the
demands are no longer for realism. The smaller the theater,
in this special sense, the fewer the restrictions, down to the
puppet play in which Goethe perhaps first encountered
Faust. The grandeur and attraction of the "Prologue in Heaven"
reflect Goethe not only in his greatness as a poet but in his
role as the director of the Weimar Theater and the author of
masques, prologues, epilogues, and pageants (*Festspiele*) for
its special occasions.[10]

The choral song in form, and the exchange between God
and the Devil in tone, suggest that admixture of the sacred
and the profane typical of the century in which the Faust
legend was born, but both could only have been conceived
later. The choral song, if we allow a proper margin for poetry,
is steadfastly scientific in its vision, and the exchange between God and the Devil, if we take its moral implications
to their logical end, heretical, perhaps even for the modern

7. "Meinen Knecht!" (1.299). For purposes of rhyme, Swanwick
rearranges the lines slightly.

8. "Es ist gar hübsch von einem großen Herrn,/So menschlich mit
dem Teufel selbst zu sprechen" (ll. 352–53).

9. "Scheidebrief" (Witkowski, 2:98).

10. Goethe's own notes list fifteen (see the index to *Tag- und Jahreshefte* [Artemis edition, vol. 11]). One can safely say that he had
written more choruses than he ever did monologues, which is suggestive
of his concept of theater. Note also his remark to Schiller which I
quoted above to the effect that all poetry should be "occasional"
poetry.

mind.[11] Indeed, the latter grows out of the presuppositions
of the former.

The world, namely, or rather the earth and its atmosphere,
that the archangels describe by way of praising the glories of
Creation is a perplexing phenomenon to behold. Raphael
celebrates the harmony in the universe, as he hears the sun
"Still quiring as in ancient time/With brother spheres in
rival song,"[12] but the remainder of the chorus is concentrated
on the awesome activity of other elements. Gabriel emphasizes the speed ("Swifter than thought [the] rapid flight"),
Michael the violence ("And rival tempests rush amain/From
sea to land, from land to sea,/And raging form a wondrous
chain") with which events take place in the natural order.
There are more, and stronger images in the original, and one
must remind oneself, as the angels remind the Lord, that
it is the "*mild* procession of thy day" that they most revere.[13]
The higher beauty or order in the universe affirmed in the
opening and reaffirmed at the close of the choral song, "Thy
works still shine with splendor bright,/As on creation's
primal day,"[14] seems neither to encompass nor reflect the
lower order here observed. Most important, God appears to
reign not over, so much as amongst, these spheres. He must
be assumed to comprehend the higher, if only in logical contrast to the claim of the angels that none may comprehend
him: "Though fathom thee no angel may."[15] Over the
lower order, however, he exerts no apparent control, yet

11. "[That] the Devil himself finds mercy and pity in God's eyes, that
they will not soon forgive me" (Goethe, in a conversation with Falk, no date).

12. "Die Sonne tönt nach alter Weise/In Brüdersphären Wett-
gesang" (Witkowski, ll. 243-44).

13. "Und schnell und unbegreiflich schnelle/Dreht sich umher der
Erde Pracht;/Es wechselt Paradieseshelle/Mit tiefer, schauervoller
Nacht" . . . "Und Stürme brausen um die Wette,/Vom Meer aufs Land,
vom Land aufs Meer,/Und bilden wütend eine Kette/Der tiefsten
Wirkung rings umher" in contrast to "Doch deine Boten, Herr, ver-
ehren/Das sanfte Wandeln deines Tags" (ll. 251-56).

14. "Und alle deine hohen Werke/Sind herrlich wie am ersten Tag"
(ll. 269-70).

15. "Da keiner dich ergründen mag" (l. 268).

by choice, for it is viewed as his creation. This is the first
indication that the events in *Faust* will be made, not in heaven,
but in nature.

The initial frame around the action—to continue with our
phrase—seems of conscious design. The vision from eternity
corresponds to the vision provided in *Urfaust* from below, in
respect both to the ineffable harmony in the macrocosm and
the contrasting flux in the lower sphere—here seen as the
physical entity Earth, there as the imagined Earth Spirit. I
spoke of this correspondence earlier. What Goethe the poet
first conceived, Goethe the scientist confirmed.[16]

But *Urfaust* had raised a problem the solution to which
only now began to emerge. The problem was both formal and
philosophical. The realism of the Gretchen tragedy had
militated against the further development of the philosophical
import of the theme. What was needed to advance the work
was a "metaphysical exposition of the realistic drama."[17] This
the Prologue provided. The view of Earth, enveloped in its
turbulent atmosphere, not only placed that planet in its
position in the universe but also anticipated the spirit in which
events on it would occur. Conditions seem such that one will
barely see the purpose for the sheer activity.[18]

16. By this time he would allow of no truth that was not grounded
in nature. *The Italian Journey*, under October 5, 1787, reads in part:
"Plato would allow no a-geometric in his school; were I in the same
position, I would allow no one who had not actually and seriously
elected a natural science" (". . . ein Naturstudium ernst und eigentlich
gewählt").

17. Witkowski, 2:84. Here he follows Schiller.

18. Atkins notes the discrepancy between the harmony in the universe and the disharmony on Earth, and points to the fact that it persists to the end (*Goethe, Faust: A Literary Analysis* p. 18). Most com-
commentators stress the ultimate broader harmony, in which Goethe
surely believed, yet in *Faust* may have wished to deemphasize in favor
of the disturbing contrast. A direct influence of Herder on this view
from eternity has been asserted: "In his 'Ideas toward a Philosophy of
History,' [Herder] had set forth the view that the earth is a star among
stars, 'in the chorus of the worlds to which it is subject,' A revolving ball,
changing from light to darkness, surrounded by an atmosphere whose
electric and magnetic currents produce the mightiest effects . . . the earth,

Mephistopheles does not overlook this point. After mocking
the angels' song under the guise of modesty ("Forgive me,
I have no talent for lofty words") and commenting on the
use that man makes of the supreme gift that God has given
him ("Reason he names it and doth so/Use it than brutes
more brutish still to grow"),[19] the first of which remarks is
wholly gratuitous, he draws an analogy we cannot ignore. He
sees man as a long-legged grasshopper ever leaping into the
air, only to land back in the grass, singing the same old song.[20]
We cannot ignore the analogy, not because it is striking and
may seem true (the remark about man's use of his reason
may also seem true), but for the reason that it partakes of
an emerging pattern. The exchange of light and dark, of ebb
and flow, life and death, or any similar set of oppositions
one identifies in the work seems to reflect the central principle
or problem which now, in the realm of human endeavor, as-

---

according to Herder, is the stage upon which man is to live and to
act. . . . But this earth is bound by laws of the great, harmonious universe,
the work of 'omnipotent power, goodness and wisdom'—"The storms
of the sea, often destructive and devastating, are also children of a
harmonious world order and must serve it just as the rustling breeze'"
(notes respectively, to lines 242–70 and 259 in the edition of *Faust:
Erster Teil* [New York, 1907] by J. Goebel). The influence of Herder
on Goethe is important. See, again, Alexander Gillies, "Herder and
Faust" (*Publications of the English Goethe Society*, n.s. 16 [1947]:
90–111); also his study *Herder;* further, Robert T. Clark, *Herder: His
Life and Thought.* The year 1784, in which the "Ideas toward a Philosophy of History" appeared (titled *Reflections on the Philosophy of
the History of Mankind* in an English translation by Frank E. Manuel
[Chicago, 1968]), was the same year in which Goethe seriously began
his meteorological studies. But Herder never took the interest in precise
science that Goethe did.

19. "Verzeih, ich kann nicht hohe Worte machen" (l. 275). I do
not follow Swanwick here, who gives Mephistopheles' intention, not
his words, i.e.: ". . . fine harangue I cannot make." "Er nennt's Vernunft
und braucht's allein/Nur tierischer als jedes Tier zu sein" (ll. 285–86).

20. "Er scheint mir, mit Verlaub von Euer Gnaden,/Wie eine der
langbeinigen Zikaden,/Die immer fleigt und fliegend springt/Und
gleich im Gras ihr altes Liedchen singt" (ll. 287–90).

sumes the aspect of endless effort and constant defeat. Whatever the purpose, the facts of creation seem clear.

Of the purpose God speaks only indirectly; the angels do
not comprehend, and we may anticipate that Faust, or man,
will be seen as still more unguided. Yet the Lord answers
Mephistopheles. He may dismiss the remark in question as
merely querulous ("Is blame/in coming here, as ever, thy
sole aim?"),[21] but his own pronouncements refute the impression of futility, if not of frustration, in the human condition. Of Faust he says: "Though now he serves me with
imperfect sight,/I will ere long conduct him to the light."[22]
Of man in general: "Man still must err, while he doth strive."[23]
And since the frustration would seem to derive from the
height rather than the nature of the aspiration, at least in the
case of Faust ("Not earthly is his food or drink. . . . From
heaven claimeth he its brightest star"),[24] we are confronted
with the paradoxical, and yet, since the romantic era, wholly
familiar, insight into the disproportion between the nobility
of purpose and the possibility of success. This does not imply
futility, at least not in Goethe. He himself will say that
"the highest possible attainment is achieved by postulating
the impossible,"[25] which suggests a simple recognition of the
indirect manner in which nature often works. The Lord here
says: "A good man in his dark ways is conscious of the
right."[26] No more than in the physical would there seem to
be straight lines in the moral world.

21. "Kommst du immer anzuklagen?/Ist auf der Erde ewig dir nichts
recht?" (ll. 294–95).
22. "Wenn er mir jetzt auch nur verworren dient/So werd' ich ihn
bald in die Klarheit führen" (ll. 308–09). God will not directly intervene in the action, however. Faust will come to clarity on his own.
23. "Es irrt der Mensch, so lang' er strebt" (l. 317).
24. "Nicht irdisch ist des Toren Trank noch Speise. . . . Vom Himmel
fordert er die schönsten Sterne" (ll. 301–04).
25. ". . . es werde dadurch das Möglichste erstrebt, daß man das
Unmögliche postuliere" (in a conversation with Friedrich von Müller,
October 19, 1823).
26. "Ein guter Mensch in seinem dunklen Drange/Ist sich des rechten

Mephistopheles' role in the general scheme of things is also defined. He functions as a gadfly. "Ever too prone is man activity to shirk/In unconditioned rest he fain would live," the Lord explains. He must be given "this companion . . . who stirs, excites, and must as devil work."[27] The principle would appear to exclude Faust, who already in the legend exemplifies the active rather than the passive side of man, and as a motif it would suggest folk theater and folk wisdom, were it not for its unexpected interrelating of good and evil. We are made to understand that evil, or the Devil, is here to be equated with negation, not corruption. "Of all the spirits who deny,/The scoffer is least wearisome to me," the Lord says of Mephistopheles.[28] Out of such an equation must grow a free play of forces, like the plus and minus of algebra,[29] and a true wager with the Devil, not a pact, which is simply a foregone conclusion extended in time. We better understand why both the Lord and Mephistopheles appear anxious

---

Weges wohl bewußt" (ll. 328-29, my translation). Swanwick, with "in the direful grasp of ill,/His consciousness of right retaineth still," is again interpretative, as is Passage with "harried in his dark distraction," and Taylor with "in his darkest aberrations." MacIntyre's "A good man, struggling in his darkness, will be aware of the true course," is closest to the original. I stress the point, not in order to fault the translators in their difficult task, but because upon it and the terms of the pact rests the moral resolution of the theme.

27. "Des Menschen Tätigkeit kann allzuleicht erschlaffen,/Er liebt sich bald die unbedingte Ruh;/Drum geb' ich gern ihm den Gesellen zu,/Der reizt und wirkt und muß als Teufel schaffen" (ll. 340-43).

28. "Von allen Geistern, die verneinen,/Ist mir der Schalk am wenigsten zur Last" (ll. 338-39). The contrast with Milton's God is striking. This is a more popular God, in the tradition of Hans Sachs's "Legenden."

29. Heinrich von Kleist uses this analogy to describe the contrast between an active and a passive heroine in two of his dramas, *Penthesilea* and *Kätchen von Heilbronn*, but the idea is common in the age and is found in Novalis, Hegel, and Adam Müller. Müller formulated a theory of opposition in *Die Lehre vom Gegensatze* (1804)—that is, opposition as a governing principle, not as conscious effort.

to stage the contest. The system itself is to be tested through
an exemplary individual. As Job was tried and proved un-
assailable in his faith in an older order, Faust, as representative
of modern man, will be tested against a new concept of life
and the nature of the universe, an evolutionary concept. When
Goethe not only allowed but welcomed the comparison of
his Faust with Job ("If the exposition of my motif has some
resemblance to that of Job, that is quite proper, and I am
rather to be praised than criticised for it" [Eckermann, January 18, 1825]), he was perhaps encouraging the perspective
of the old recurring transformed in the new. Changing contrasts are the mode of the work. The Lord may bid the angels,
who stand outside of time, to arrest the "changeful forms,
around ye flowing . . . in ever-during thought,"[30] but within
time, where mind remains rooted in matter, there is no true
stopping of the flow. Even the work itself, which as art might
strive to fix the impermanent, seems forced time and again in
its development to choose change over order. In that light,
its freedom of form seems almost a burden.

At this point "the heavens close,"[31] leaving Mephistopheles
outside, and with no one to address but the audience, he
delivers himself of the lines quoted above, which end the
scene. Up to this point, theme and design have seemed clearly
in the control of the author. The work had now been some
thirty years in the making. The scientific preoccupations had
unobtrusively insinuated themselves into the poetry and
had become the basis for a resolution to the central problem
in the play—as yet, like the pact, unstated. The principle of
heightening, which Goethe perceived in the natural and applied
to the moral world, though also not stated, is implicit in the
fact that Mephistopheles, as devil, as negating force, cannot
see the spiral effect of the vicious cycle in the hectic rhythms

30. "Und was in schwankender Erscheinung schwebt,/Befestiget
mit daurenden Gedanken" (ll. 348–49).

31. Probably employing the kind of machinery mentioned in the
"Prelude in the Theater" ("Nor scenes nor mechanism spare!" [l.
234]). I have this from Reinhard Buchwald's *Führer durch Goethes
Faust* (p. 15).

of life—witness his analogy of the grasshopper.[32] In that
regard, the angels themselves, who praise without understanding, appear less than wholly enlightened. This heightening, further, is applied to art as to life, and to the development of the artist, as we suggested in the introductory chapter.
Although it appears at the beginning, the "Prologue in
Heaven" actually marks a middle stage in the movement
from realism to the symbolism of Part II, representing a more
comprehensive and comprehending view. It "understands"
the action of *Urfaust*. Also, in departing from the original
form, the Prologue makes possible, almost demands, further
heightening, as in any evolution. Before it was completed, we
noted, Goethe was already contemplating a second part.

But the greatest freedom to accrue to the work would
seem to have been gained almost incidentally. Mephistopheles'
parting remark, which might suggest the folk or puppet play
if we did not know his comic irreverence from *Urfaust,*
takes on an all-important dimension when read with a knowledge of the purpose and effect of this devil, on earth and in
the play. We can now envision his pitting his cynical humor
not only against the idealism and animal earnestness ("Tier-
ernst") of Faust, but, as here, against the seriousness of the
work itself. That is romantic irony, which is the turning of
art back upon itself and upon life. Goethe may not have
followed the contemporary romanticists in their projected
ultimate fusion of life and art,[33] for in that regard his
priorities were different. But the sardonic humor that had
attached to the Mephistophelean character from the beginning
as counterbalance to Faust has now assumed the broader
role of levity opposing gravity in general. The crude comic

32. See Trunz, Hamburg edition, vol. 3, note to ll. 281 ff.
33. "Die romantische Poesie ist eine progressive Universalpoesie"—
"Romantic poetry is a progressive universal poetry," is Schlegel's
formulation. See, again, Eichner, *Friedrich Schlegel;* further, *Friedrich
Schlegel: The Dialogue on Poetry and Literary Aphorisms,* trans. with
an introduction and notes by Ernst Behler and Roman Struc; also,
Friedrich Schlegel: Lucinde and the Fragments, trans. with an introduction by Peter Firchow.

function Mephistopheles inherited from the Pickelhäring and
Hanswurst of folk drama has been "heightened" and has
come to serve a higher purpose. For we will soon be told that
Mephistopheles' will to evil always effects good, and we may
logically anticipate that his destruction of illusion in some
like way will effect truth. In that light, the description of
Part II as "these very serious jokes" seems less a conceit than
a frank recognition of the strange pass to which this work
eventually brought its creator.

The opening scene of Part I, from its renowned first lines
("I have [studied], alas! Philosophy, Jurisprudence too,/And
to my cost Theology . . .") to the suicide attempt and the
rededication to living (". . . earth, I am thine again!"), is a
monodrama, interrupted only by the exchange with Wagner,
which is retained intact and in place from the early version.
Spirits materialize, at least as voices, at the close, but they are
essentially of the order of the Earth Spirit and not dramatic
presences. They take the form of choruses of angels who
celebrate the resurrection of Christ at Easter and, implicitly,
the revival of Faust from his dark night of the soul. Not that
the drama is being christianized. The present juxtaposition
reflects rather the new tendency of the work to place in context, to motivate event, as it were. The view from eternity
had established for the physical world laws or designs which
now express themselves in the spiritual realm. We may even
begin to see Christ in the light of Faust, whose present spiritual
redemption may appear a truer image of the universal phenomenon of death and rebirth than its corporeal counterpart
in the Bible.

The suicide attempt is placed in the context inherited from
Urfaust, so that when Wagner leaves after his interruption,
whereupon in the earlier versions the scene ends, Faust picks
up the thread of his despairing thought. He recalls his first
reaction to the Earth Spirit ("I felt myself shrink dwarfed as
I surveyed!") and echoes and elaborates upon his earlier
words: "I, God's own image . . . I, more than cherub . . . how
am I punished now! . . . Spirit! I dare not lift me to thy

sphere . . . I am not like the gods! Feel it I must."[34] The intensified feeling of rejection and frustration is intended as motivation to suicide. But here suicide is conceived as the crucible, not the terminus of despair.[35] On the other side of life would dawn a new understanding, perhaps brightest for those who would dare speed, or "heighten," the slower process of nature.[36] The attempt, therefore, is hardly different from the adventure in magic, which at the time was equally prohibited and, in its own lights, equally promising of reward. (The more Faust alters his approach, the more his goal remains the same.) Even after he has reconciled himself to live within the limits of nature (". . . earth, I am thine again!"),[37] he instinctively grasps for the absolute when the occasion again presents itself. "When to the moment I shall say: / Linger awhile, so fair thou art!" is the essential clause he introduces into the pact, and while the words are not so intended, they in fact presuppose the impossible, namely, the arresting of time.[38] And their literal or scientific rather than metaphorical meaning will bear the greater significance, as the nature of human nature, and this its representative figure, are conceived more and more in relation to the laws of the physical universe.

We speak of Faust as character, but to the extent that a general scheme of things is recognizable in his actions and motives (an extent greatly increased at this point), we see him also as part of a whole, as a microcosm in the macrocosm.

34. "Daß ich mich recht als Zwerg empfinden sollte. . . . Ich, Ebenbild der Gottheit . . . Ich, mehr als Cherub . . . wie muß ich's büßen! . . . Nicht darf ich dir zu gleichen mich vermessen! . . . Zu tief ist es gefühlt" (ll. 613-52).

35. "Ich breche durch," in the paralipomena, Witkowski, 1:518.

36. Gray, *Goethe, the Alchemist*, p. 180.

37. "Die Erde hat mich wieder" (l. 784).

38. "Werd' ich zum Augenblicke sagen: / Verweile doch! du bist so schön!" (ll. 1699-1700) is what would be termed today the "operative clause," and what Goethe himself describes as essential: "In the beginning Faust makes an agreement with the Devil from which everything follows" (in a conversation with Boisserée, August 3, 1815, cited above).

"Herr Mikrokosmus," Mephistopheles will call him presently.
Our earlier identification of the laws of nature with the
rhythms of human consciousness and life—and Faust in the
final version is more than ever caught up in a flux of hope
and despair—is advanced to the recognition of a distinct pattern. The work has provided in the "Prologue in Heaven"
a unique perspective that allows us to see in the suicide attempt the will to live as well as the conscious will, in the
moment, to die, "to ebb . . . the floodtide of my spirit," as
Faust says.[39] For it has been made clear by the play, though
not to Faust, that intensity of reaction is a sign of life and
only apparently of disorder, as witness the formidable way
in which nature strikes its own balances. No miracle, therefore,
need be said to have occurred when the Easter bells suddenly
resound and stay Faust from death. All occasions seem to inform the occurrence. It is dawn, the rebirth of the day, and
spring, the rebirth of the year, which underline the Christian
notion of resurrection at Easter.[40] So appropriate, in fact,
is event to idea, and idea to event, that it prompts our ongoing
question about the degree of deliberation with which the
work as a whole was composed. Easter, after all, is wholly
fitting in the sixteenth-century setting, and a church beyond
the walls of the "high, narrow Gothic room" almost requisite. Goethe is developing his figure in context. And Faust
himself attributes his sudden redemption from death to his
associating the tolling bells with youth and childhood: "And
fond remembrance now, doth me, with childlike feeling,/
Back from the last, the solemn step, withhold."[41]

But it is also true that recollections of boyhood, and so of
joy, precede the reversal apparently caused totally from without. The crystal goblet from which Faust would drink the
poison recalls not only a joyous adult world ("Oft at my
father's revels thou didst shine") but his own participation in

39. "Des Geistes Flutstrom ebbet nach und nach" (l. 698).
40. Werther destroys himself at midnight, in the middle of winter,
on Christmas Eve.
41. "Errinnerung hält mich nun mit kindlichem Gefühle/Vom
letzten, ernsten Schritt zurück" (ll. 781–82).

the festivities (". . . hath nights of boyhood to fond memory brought"). These are not morbid thoughts. Moreover, the toast he proposes with this "last draught"[42] is to the dawn, which, for all its aptness in the recollected and in the present setting (for it is becoming day outside the study), is a contradiction in purpose. The intended toast to death emerges as a toast to life, as if nature were working *in* Faust, against his conscious will. The alchemist's anticipation of a dawn of understanding after death we must also allow. But my point is not to prove the importance of the generic over the individual, the symbolic over the real action, but to suggest their oneness here. We might say that Goethe took care not to blur motivation of character and event as he lent them larger meaning. His remark about the newer material in his manuscript being hardly distinguishable from the older except for the color of the paper indicates care, as does that about the burden of completing with conscious purpose what he had begun in spontaneous creativity. Yet the advent of Easter, so artistically and dramatically introduced, seems in the last analysis a stroke of genius, which solves without measurable forethought. We can as well imagine Goethe hitting upon the idea as the fit conclusion of his monodrama,[43] only to discover its symbolic potential, as, conversely, long anticipating the motif for reasons of symbolism, only to realize its dramatic potential in context. Faust could not have been once again interrupted by Wagner.

We imagine, but we do not know, and that again is to my point. We now ask whether even the most assuredly deliberate developments of the theme, such as the view of nature from eternity, were all that consciously conceived. From the beginning Goethe saw nature dynamically. It would not have

42. "Du glänztest bei der Väter Freudenfest/Erheitertest die ernsten Gäste,/Wenn einer dich dem andern zugebracht./Der vielen Bilder künstlich reiche Pracht,/Des Trinkers Pflicht, sie reimweis zu erklären,/Auf e i n e n Zug die Höhlung auszuleeren,/Erinnert mich an manche Jugendnacht" (ll. 724–29).

43. Heffner, Rehder, Twadell (1:60f.) note that a choral song sometimes ended a monodrama.

required any scientific reaffirmation of earlier insight to prompt the celebration of earthly laws that opens the play, merely activation of his basic poetic impulses toward nature. Not to recall the laws of motion in his own personality which would be receptive to such a vitalistic view of the world.

Our problem is not solved. To uncover a pattern is not to define its function. We may perceive the relation between heavenly and earthly designs, but our perception does not alter our experience of the disruption the systems seem to require. Where there is disruption, we assume disorder. When we regard Faust and his actions as symbols, to be sure, we may easily resolve the disorder in our glimpse of a grander harmony, just as he does in contemplating the Sign of the Macrocosm. But when we identify with him as dramatis persona and share his experience, which the work in, and as a result of, its beginnings equally encourages us to do, we react as if to a reality of total despair. For we do not consider his feelings eccentric or his frustrations merely personal. We recognize ourselves in his words. We sense the absurdity of our undefined fears ("Imagined evils chill thy blood") and self-induced anxiety ("And what thou ne'er shalt lose, o'er that doth shed the tear"). We see the limitations of our actions, which as products of choice are made to the exclusion of other actions and so delimit our lives as much as outward occurrences: "What ought I to forego? Ought I that impulse obey?/Alas! our every deed, as well as every woe,/Impedes . . . the way!"[44] We cannot make the basic distinction between opportunity and temptation.

44. "Die uns das Leben gaben, herrliche Gefühle,/Erstarren in dem irdischen Gewühle. . . . Du bebst vor allem, was nicht trifft . . . Und was du nie verlierst, das mußt du stets beweinen. . . ."; "Was lehret mich? Was soll ich meiden?/Soll ich gehorchen jenem Drang?/Ach! unsre Taten selbst, so gut als unsre Leiden,/Sie hemmen unsres Lebens Gang" (ll. 638–39, 650–51, 630–33, respectively). Heffner, Rehder, Twadell remark on l. 632: "*Taten: Leiden.* The two terms are complementary,

These are sufficient reasons for suicide, by means of which
Faust would escape from life. Not to cite, as he does, the
historical record, where one can "read in a thousand tomes
that, everywhere,/Self-torture is the lot of human-kind,/
With but one mortal happy, here and there."[45] But what for
Faust is a torment from which to seek deliverance was for
the author himself a dilemma. Goethe was committed to
resolving the inner conflict in man through nature—that is,
within time. Yet nature and time appeared to know no
resolve or end. It was as if any deliberate conclusion *about*
life would be as unnatural as a deliberate conclusion *to* life,
as through suicide. At this stage, almost certainly, Goethe
held an answer to the question; he could hardly have specified
the terms of the pact, which is about to be made, without
anticipating the specifics of his conclusion. But that conclusion is kept wholly from Faust now and, in its philosophical
implications, later, and it is only dimly seen by us. An author
who objected to the search for abstract profundities in his
work would not have attempted to supply his hero, and so
his audience, with definitive solutions to human questions.
We know only what we need to know, as will Faust in the
end.[46] Goethe was clear as to the purpose of knowledge, no
less than of art, which was to move to action, or, more
accurately, to be sufficient unto action. But knowledge un-
earned, such as through magic, like art unexperienced, as in
the pursuit of mere symbol, is not true knowing. Our uneven
enlightenment thus parallels Faust's. More important, our
viewpoints differ, we comprehending his actions within a

'what we do, and what is done to us.'" The familiar pair *Lust und Leid*
should also be understood as the active and the passive side of experience, not as *desire* and *suffering* in the usual sense of those
words.
    45. ". . . in tausend Büchern lesen,/Daß überall die Menschen
sich gequält,/Daß hie und da ein Glücklicher gewesen?"(ll. 661-63).
    46. Emil Staiger in *Goethe* (3 vols., Zurich and Freiburg, 1956)
notes that Goethe knows more than Faust (2:349).

frame of reference and ourselves being comprehended in a larger frame.

Finally, it should be noted that what we have here called spiritual resurrection becomes in the larger frame a form of death. "Earth, I am thine again!" is a commitment to a limited existence, at least insofar as Faust has known existence. It is at this point that the Devil will be sent to Faust, for this is the first point at which he might conceivably succumb to the urge for peace and comfort against which the Lord in the "Prologue in Heaven" had warned.

There is an inner and an outer chronology in *Faust,* as in many dramas, perhaps in imitation of life, where often effect becomes evident before cause. We have just seen how the outward circumstance of the chiming bells seemed to have kept Faust from death, when in fact forces of a profounder order were already, or at the same time, at work. It *seemed* so to Faust himself: ". . . this sweet strain familiar when a boy,/Back it recalleth me to life once more."[47] Similarly in *Iphigenia,* the salvation of Orestes was less caused than secured by the reunion with his sister, the more significant change having taken place in the traumatic vision which freed him suddenly to accept the truth or light his sister shed. This is not unusual, but it is important to note. A work such as *Faust,* which itself only gradually yielded up its intent to its author, might well reflect that process in its style. Thus, as we shall see now in "Before the Gate," even the revealing of the cause for action already in progress, which is the nature of dramatic exposition, seems more related to truth than to dramaturgy.

"Before the Gate" furthers theme and character more than its opening lines and the setting would lead us to expect. Workers and students, peasants and burghers, servant girls and soldiers gather on the grounds outside the city to

47. ". . . an diesen Klang von Jugend auf gewöhnt,/Ruft er auch jetzt zurück mich in das Leben" (ll. 769–70). See Robert E. Dye, "The Easter Cantata and the Idea of Mediation in Goethe's *Faust, PMLA* 93 (1978):963–76.

celebrate Easter in the secular manner, with song and dance. Faust remarks: "For they themselves have risen, with joy,/ From lowly tenements, from cheerless room,/From bonds of toil. . . ."[48] Of the fact that he himself has been as much moved by primal nature as they, he is perhaps not aware. But that is the point the scene will make, first poetically, then in important, conscious formulation.

Goethe has in Faust a hero of sensibility who can express profound feelings and observations. It falls to him to describe the reawakening of man in nature and nature in man which the peasants and others display but cannot articulate. The result is as vital a descriptive passage as can be found in the poem. "Here I am human, here I dare to be,"[49] is the conclusion of a passage which has so well succeeded in identifying the natural with the human world that we are moved to appreciate the freedom and sense of wholeness evoked in its final line. The so-called natural fallacy, the attributing of motives from the moral realm to the objective world, here becomes a tenet of faith. Of course, the fall from this psychological state of grace is inevitable in the cyclical order of things. As the scene closes and the day ends the people will return to their lowly quarters and their toil. Faust will be found in the following scene again in his "narrow Gothic room."

But the drama is there for Faust no less than Faust for the drama. As obviously intentional as are the contrasts drawn between the darkness and the light, the narrowness and the expanse, the suffering and the joy in this and the preceding scene, it is the sheer feeling for what is described that is important in a separate regard. The work as drama is in the modern, as opposed to the rhetorical, tradition, and attaches only thoughts and sentiments commensurate with the person who expresses them. The feeling, then, is not only part of

48. "Denn sie sind selber aufgestanden,/Aus niedriger Häuser dumpfen Gemächern,/Aus Handwerks- und Gewerbesbanden. . . ." (ll. 922-24). I have changed "sordid" in Swanwick to "lowly."

49. My translation for "Hier bin ich Mensch, hier darf ich's sein" (l. 940). Rousseau's spirit is in this line.

the poetry but a part of Faust. It is the part that he describes
as clinging "to the world with obstinate desire." In contrast,
Wagner, who strolls with Faust before the gate and is a witness
to the same scene but does not respond, knows no such
feeling. His discomfort with the view of joyous humanity in
a natural setting ("I hate the tumult of the vulgar throng;/
They roar as by the evil one possessed,/And call it pleasure,
call it song") is made as clear as his taste for an opposite
environment (". . . ah! when we unroll/Some old and precious
parchment, at the sight/All heaven itself descends upon the
soul").[50] It is this last remark that prompts from Faust the
significant formulation of the "two souls" residing within him:

> Your heart by one sole impulse is possessed. . . .
> Two souls, alas! are lodged within my breast,
> Which struggle there for undivided reign:
> One to the world, with obstinate desire,
> And closely-cleaving organs, still adheres;
> Above the mist, the other doth aspire,
> With sacred vehemence, to purer spheres.[51]

The formulation is crucial in the truest sense, a convergence
of elements forming the crux of the matter. The coinciding
within Faust of the two great impulses of humanity divides
his being and yet extends it to encompass the whole of
human experience: ". . . to know in my heart's core all
human weal and woe." There is no question of duality, only
of process. That he himself, to be sure, still experiences the
process as tragic is implied in the remark to Wagner in which
he wishes his own fate upon no man. But while the poem
dramatically appreciates this dilemma, its new contrasts

50. "Und ach! entrollst du gar ein würdig Pergamen,/So steigt der
ganze Himmel zu dir nieder" (ll. 1108–09).

51. The celebrated lines 1110–17: "Du bist dir nur des einen Triebs
bewußt;/O lerne nie den andern kennen!/Zwei Seelen wohnen, ach!
in meiner Brust,/Die eine will sich von der andern trennen;/Die eine
hält, in derber Liebeslust,/Sich an die Welt mit klammernden Organen;/
Die andre hebt gewaltsam sich vom Dust/Zu den Gefilden hoher
Ahnen."

create a breadth that suggests wholeness, much as its recurrent patterns allow us visions of order in the swirl of events. Faust may even regard his inner impulses as ordered in importance, the one the nobler, the other the baser drive, thus repeating the error he earlier committed in measuring himself against the Earth Spirit in stature, not in kind. Yet we know from the intensity of his feeling for nature that the soul that clings to the earth, in his case, at least, is a vital and revitalizing force, like the soul Goethe sensed within himself and compared, as we saw in his *Italian Journey,* to the god who gained strength from his contact with the earth, Antaeus. Conversely, if we look forward to Part II, we discover that the soul of which Wagner is singly possessed, though it reaches the apparent acme of attainment in creating a human being in a test tube,[52] is doomed to failure for want of a balancing counterpart. Far from representing the superficial rationalist and optimist we see in him in Part I, he will come to stand in Part II for pioneering science that yet proves futile when divorced from nature. He, too, will undergo a kind of heightening. In any event, we are clearly meant to find in Wagner a symbol for all thinking or undertaking that fails to relate to life and is thus merely progress on a closed road.

Thus far the furthering of the theme. The character of Faust is also developed. The perspectives in which we have attempted to measure his actions have produced, in fact, extreme views, as if from opposite ends of the telescope. Against the broad background of the laws and rhythms of nature the actions seem of a piece with the world, while in their own right, regarded up close, they appear willful and overwhelming. In this latter perspective we see Faust almost

52. I.e., Homunculus. Despite its being carried out in the old laboratory we know from *Urfaust,* and performed with equal parts of fantasy and alchemy—the alchemists were the "fathers" of homunculi—the experiment seems the epitome of mechanistic science, which Goethe had already begun to condemn in his own day. His distrust of Newton stemmed from the same aversion to measurable or positivistic learning or understanding, in art no less than science.

as he sees the Earth Spirit. But now an intermediate perspective is insinuated into the play. Faust is set more particularly
in a time and place. We learn of his past, of his father who
was himself given to brooding over the nature of things and
whose occult investigations culminated in a physic, the
effects of which proved fatal when administered in the plague:
"The patients died,/'Who were restored?' none cared to ask."[53]
This same father Faust must now hear praised by a peasant
in the scene who is old enough to have known him, and he
must hear himself extolled for his present ministrations.
Yet as a young man he "the deadly poison did to thousands
give."[54] It is not that his sensitivity makes him more human,
which it does, but that it makes more understandable the
degree of frustration he experiences in his search for truth.
His dilemma is not academic, but moral. The lack of knowledge sufficient unto our actions is the tragedy in the human
condition. The drama will not quite surmount that obstacle
even in the very end—whence *Faust*: "A Tragedy." "What man
knows not, is just what he requires,/And what he knows,
he cannot use for good,"[55] Faust remarks in the immediate
context, to be sure with a pessimism that will finally be
dispelled.

Wagner, again in contrast, conceives of morality as based in
intent, not result ("How can you trouble yourself about such
things?"),[56] and while the concept is traditional, almost

53. "Und niemand fragte: wer genas?" (l. 1049).
54. "Ich habe selbst den Gift [sic] an Tausende gegeben,/Sie welkten
hin, ich muß erleben,/Daß man die frechen Mörder lobt" (ll. 1053–55).
55. The German is not so specific: "Was man nicht nützt, ist eine
schwere Last,/Nur was der Augenblick erschafft, das kann er nützen"
(ll. 684–85). As part of their note on these difficult lines, Heffner,
Rehder, and Twadell interpret as follows: "One can make use of the
wisdom of the past only when one has won this wisdom for oneself.
Then one's mind will produce it when confronted by the need of the
moment, and thus it will be useful." Other commentators make
references to remarks by Goethe that would support the interpretation,
for example, Witkowski (2:200).
56. "Wie könnt Ihr Euch darum betrüben!" (l. 1056).

requisite in the Christian ethic, in its present juxtaposition
and in the mouth of its present representative, its dangers
become apparent. There is all too great convenience and all
too little sense of urgency in the position. "Can man do
more than . . . with firm and conscientious will,/Practise the
art transmitted from the past?" says Wagner.[57] We notice a
peculiar reflection of an earlier, unenlightened age in this form
of eighteenth-century optimism, the belief of the former
in the inevitability of human misery betraying itself in the
latter by the continual postponement of a remedy to the
future. Faust, on the other hand, would appear to have the
roots of his morality and humanity in the Renaissance—
quite appropriately, given the historical figure. But we must
now not think of Renaissance man as happily combining the
needs of the mind with those of the body, but as struggling
to combine them. Goethe was not as removed as we from the
world of the Renaissance, and he felt its influence as a living
force. His early dabbling in the occult is perhaps the best
evidence of the fact, the number of other significant works
with their settings in the period (*Götz, Egmont,* and *Tasso*)
being further evidence. That world, like the past in the Frankfurt of his birth, persisted into his own day. The intervening
Age of Reason, which we might regard as the culmination of
a great intellectual movement, he experienced rather as a
single-minded deviation from more propitious beginnings
that might yet be recovered. We noted his reaction to Voltaire.
Similarly, he would experience the contemporary movements
of romanticism and revolution as extremes and reject them,
not instinctively, for he well knew extremities in himself,
but for the reason that extreme positions have as their aim
an ultimate resolution that would preclude opposition and
thus deny the process of development. Whence the positive
effect of struggle in life and whence the two souls in Faust.

57. "Tut nicht ein braver Mann genug,/Die Kunst, die man ihm
übertrug,/Gewissenhaft und pünktlich auszuüben?" (ll. 1057–59).
One thinks of the medicinal arts called into service for the plague just
mentioned.

The gods give everything, the infinite ones,
To their beloved, completely,
Every pleasure, the infinite ones,
Every suffering, the infinite ones, completely.

These lines, written in 1777, constitute a poem, although
they seem only part of a poem and, like *Urfaust,* in want of
a larger context.[58] Yet Goethe usually began with the particular and immediate, and moved only later to the general.
Moreover, the lines relate to the concept of the two souls in
man in their suggestion of polarity, and while Goethe in
writing them had in mind as the beloved of the gods the poet
or genius, perhaps specifically himself, there would come
lines in the *Fragment,* we recall, where Faust would demand
just such infinite pleasure and infinite suffering, that is,
"all human weal and woe." There are sufficient reasons for
the conflict within Faust, as "Before the Gate" serves further
to make clear, and we need not look to an early poem to
account for a line in the 1790 *Fragment,* nor to either as an
antecedent to a central concept in the play. But we also need
not deny their relevance. The more we try to delineate the
development of an idea in Goethe, the more we become
aware of an almost impenetrable natural unity formed from
diverse considerations and needs in his art. Caroline Herder
said of him (in a letter of February 13, 1789): "He takes
and processes within himself from the totality of nature. . . .";
we may say, from the totality of his experience. For it was
as if in the act of creating there existed for him only an
eternal present, partaking of all that had come before and yet
developing anew. The formulation of the central concept of
the two souls itself reflects the process, being introduced,
not abstractly, as in a monologue (many look for the famous

58. They were originally composed for the Countess Stolberg on
the occasion of the death of her sister. "Alles geben die Götter,
die unendlichen,/Ihren Lieblingen ganz,/Alle Freuden, die unendlichen/
Alle Schmerzen, die unendlichen, ganz." The English version here
quoted is by Stephen Spender and is included in *The Permanent
Goethe,* ed. Thomas Mann.

line in the opening scene) but in mildly annoyed reaction to
the staid Wagner who knows no inner conflict. Again, occasion and cause seem one. The line might never have been
uttered had Faust undertaken the Easter walk with a different
companion.

The problem in the play is still not fully stated. The
negating force that will counteract the conflicting but positive
urges in Faust is still to be introduced. The poodle who
appears at the end of the scene and accompanies Faust to
his study is its harbinger.

The alternating effects of darkness and light, despair and
hope, which we saw in the preceding scenes, are converted
now into a play of gravity and humor. I am not speaking of
comic relief, a term used earlier to describe the exchange
between Mephistopheles and the student and the scene in
"Auerbach's Cellar" in *Urfaust,* which followed directly upon
the opening monologue and appeared to have no clear
thematic functions. Here the humor is part of the exposition.
Through it the nature of Mephistopheles is further revealed,
both as character and representative force. For, like Faust,
the Devil has two aspects. He seems to us real when he speaks,
a symbol when we think about him; both "real" and "ideal,"
as Schiller said.

We do not normally laugh at Mephistopheles, but through
him. The destructive element in his humor seems to free us
for the moment to live without compunction, like himself.
Also, we delight in his magic power. But when he now enters
the dramatic action as a poodle, it is with the instincts and
prejudices of the comic figure. The poodle is made, in turn, to
pace up and down in the study as Faust, in inspiration from
the Easter day, speaks of the charity that "doth warm the
breast,/And love of God . . . inspire"; to growl, as of "inward
light" and "streams of life" are spoken; and to take to outright "barking and howling" as Faust, in search of the spiritual
clarity that still eludes him, reaches for the Bible, which he
begins to translate into his "beloved German."[59]

59. "Es reget sich die Menschenliebe,/Die Liebe Gottes regt sich

There is humor in this progression, but also thematic progression in the humor. The gravity against which it is played
is no mere prop, the translation Faust attempts no mere
period motif. "In the beginning was the *deed*,"[60] he writes,
after weighing the possibility of "sense" or "power," but
not "word," which is the most direct translation of John 1:1,
because he "cannot the mere word so highly prize."[61] And
if deed is the beginning, it will in consequence inform creation
and human destiny—as witness the ceaseless activity in
nature, the restlessness in Faust. Man must realize himself in
action; he will stagnate, like water, when too long at rest.
That is the "final wisdom" of the poem: "Freedom alone he
earns as well as life,/Who day by day must conquer them
anew";[62] but it was also its guiding principle from its early
Storm and Stress stage, when Faust was made to respond to
the active nature of the Earth Spirit, to its present point,
where action is placed at the center of a cosmology. Mephistopheles, whom we know as the negating spirit and the
opposite of Faust, will also be defined in accordance with the
same principle. Faust will call him the "wondrous son of
Chaos"—"Des Chaos wunderlicher Sohn" (l. 1384). The opposite of chaos is not order, which restrains, as we shall learn,
but action, which gives form to life.

Our fondness for Mephistopheles as a poodle might lead us
to assume a direct relation between his own increasing
disquiet at the moment and the heightening clarity of his
newly procured master, but the humor is more broadly
based. A theatrical element and a folk element are also involved. The Devil has been made not only witness, but captive
audience, to this fervent philosophizing and theologizing,

---

nun . . . Dann wird's in unserm Busen helle . . . Man sehnt sich nach des
Lebens Bächen . . . Mich drängt's . . . Das Heilige Original/In mein
geliebtes Deutsch zu übertragen" (ll. 1184–1223).

60. "Im Anfang war die T a t"(l. 1237).

61. "Ich kann das W o r t so hoch unmöglich schätzen" (l. 1226).

62. "Nur der verdient sich Freiheit wie das Leben,/Der täglich sie
erobern muß (ll. 11,575–76).

having entered through a gap in the ingress that was not repeated in the egress of the protective magical symbol at the threshold of the study; devils, he later explains, must go out the way they came in. When bid leave, like the cornered animal he is, he has no choice but to fight. And the transformations he effects in order to daunt Faust, namely, from poodle to hippopotamus, with appropriately reddened eyes and (vestigially?) bared teeth, and then to elephant, add to the popular atmospherics of the legend, as do the spells that Faust casts in order to exorcise him. I see no symbolic importance in this action.[63] Indeed, if there is a deeper connection with the persistent patterns in the work, it is to the monologue in the opening scene, written so many years earlier. There Faust is almost systematically interrupted by his inner doubts and changes of mood, here by palpable intrusion from without, but the dramatic movement is the same. Moreover, since Mephistopheles, once he materializes, will assume precisely the role of opposer and retarder, his present behavior in materializing is fitting. In general, he will preempt the other side and play, literally but not knowingly, the part of the Devil's advocate that the Lord has created for him.

The action has a function, however. A Mephistopheles bound is not only amusing and the butt of his own wit ("In sprang the dog, indeed, observing nought;/Things now assume another shape,/The devil's in the house and can't

63. In a separate action, in "The Witches' Kitchen," however, it would be hard to deny a conscious intent in the "Einmaleins" after the note to these lines (2540–52) by Kathryn S. Levedahl, "The Witches' One-Times-One: Sense or Nonsense?" in *Modern Language Notes* 85 (1970), 380–83. Levedahl has analyzed the "mathematics of Faust's rejuvenation" (as Harold Jantz in an interesting note in support of the view [pp. 383–85] calls it) and concluded that Faust "at the time he stepped into the magic circle was fifty-five, and at the time he stepped out was twenty-six years old. This would be a loss of twenty-nine years—one more than thirty, 'about thirty'" (that is, the round number used by Faust in the lines, "And can [the witch], by these rites abhorred,/Take thirty winters from my frame?"—"Und schafft die Sudelköcherei/Wohl dreißig Jahre mir vom Leibe?" [ll. 341–42]).

escape"),[64] but, for Faust, a more seductive figure. His
reluctance to discuss terms in the present hampered circumstances, whether real or feigned, can only be conducive to
later commitment. Not that we must assume the flaw in the
magic design to have been invented solely with that purpose
in mind. If Mephistopheles as a character sometimes appears
deliberately to manipulate human action, as a symbol or
force he is compelled to obstinacy through negation.[65] It
is not his own fault, we might say, that humans react positively
to his negative instincts. "Did we force ourselves on thee, or
thou on us?" he asks in a subsequent confrontation, and
Faust fails to answer.[66] Nor can we, readily, for the question
becomes progressively more like that of the hen and the egg,
on the metaphysical as well as psychological or moral levels.

First, the metaphysical problem. When asked, once he has
discarded his animal shapes and emerged in the more sober
form of a traveling scholar,[67] Who are you? Mephistopheles
replies: "Part of that power which still/Produceth good,
whilst ever scheming ill." "Part of the part am I which at
first was all,/A part of darkness, which gave birth to light."
He regards light as the usurper of darkness (not conversely,
which is the human viewpoint): "Proud light, who now his
mother would enthrall,/Contesting space and ancient rank
with night."[68] He speaks of a struggle between these forces,
in which light strives to detach itself from matter, but in vain:

64. "Der Pudel merkte nichts, als er hereingesprungen,/Die Sache
sieht jetzt anders aus:/Der Teufel kann nicht aus dem Haus" (ll. 1406-
08).
65. The Faust legend also has Mephistopheles reluctant at first (cf.
Witkowski, 2:209).
66. "Drangen wir uns dir auf, oder du dich uns?"—already in
Urfaust (Witkowski, 1:434).
67. "Das also war des Pudels Kern!" (l. 1323).
68. "Ein Teil von jener Kraft,/Die stets das Böse will und stets das
Gute schafft. . . . Ich bin ein Teil des Teils, der anfangs alles war,/Ein
Teil der Finsternis, die sich das Licht gebar,/Das stolze Licht, das nun
der Mutter Nacht/Den alten Rang, den Raum ihr streitig macht" (ll.
1336-1352).

"To forms material it adhereth still;/From them it streameth,
them it maketh fair,/And still the progress of its beams they
check."[69] He envisions a time when with the destruction of all
existing things, which is his purpose and goal, light too will
be destroyed. "Whate'er to light is brought/Deserves again
to be reduced to naught," he says in a remark the more
devastating for being not only the ultimate expression of his
own nihilism, but also a valid observation on the principle
active in *Faust,* where nature is presented as destroying and
creating with apparently equal purpose, and man, in the
person of its hero, as failing and succeeding with no clear
loss or gain. That Mephistopheles should see each "ray"
of darkness as hope for his cause is no more presumptuous
than that man should anticipate each emanation of light as
reason for joy. One must choose the forces of light and life
over those of darkness and death, but the latter will not be
denied.[70] The fact that Faust in the final scene of Part II is
made to mistake the breaking of ground for his grave as
excavation for a grand new enterprise, and so "anticipate"

69. "Und doch gelingt's ihm nicht, da es, soveil es strebt,/Verhaftet
an den Körpern klebt./Von Körpern strömt's, die Körper macht es
schön,/Ein Körper hemmt's auf seinem Gange . . ." (ll. 1353–56).
The original makes the parallel between light and darkness and the two
souls within man more clear by its image of light *clinging* to matter,
although Goethe may not have consciously intended the analogy.
"Soviel es strebt" reminds us of the grasshopper image in "The Prologue
in Heaven." Again, I alter Swanwick slightly, who in rendering these
lines uses "he" and "him" for the German *es* and *ihm,* which, though
neuter, do not depersonalize.
70. "Denn alles, was entsteht,/Ist wert, daß es zugrunde geht;/
Drum besser wär's, daß nichts entstünde" (ll. 1339–40). The cosmology at back of Mephistopheles' statements is described at the end of
Book Eight of *Truth and Poetry,* where Goethe expands upon his own
view of Creation. On Mephistopheles, see, for example, Eudo Mason,
"The Paths and Powers of Mephistopheles," in *German Studies:
Presented to Walter Horace Bruford,* pp. 81–101; also his "Goethe's
Sense of Evil," *Publications of the English Goethe Society,* n.s. 34
(1964):1–53.

the perfect moment, is an irony that best illustrates the
point.

The moral aspects of our problem lead us to the pact, and
the next scene.

For whom is *Faust* written? This may seem an idle question
to ask in the midst of a discussion of the pertinent matter of
good and evil, but the question relates to form, which is
always at issue in this work.

The dramatic is the moral, at least in traditional drama,
and up to this point Goethe has presented his theme in
visionary fashion in monologue and magnificent song, deeply
from within and from without, but not through the contention of equal forces consciously opposed which we call drama.
The headlong action that was *Urfaust* now seems hedged by
other concerns. The preceding scene, for example, which
was begun with a humorously horrifying magical event, is
made to end in the purest lyricism. A chorus of spirits
lulls Faust to sleep in order that their master, Mephistopheles,
may escape. The chorus forms a direct counterpart to the
angelic or religious voices in the yet preceding scene, the
former celebrating reawakening life, the latter inducing sleep.
At this point the work seems deliberately to have adopted
a musical or operatic approach to its subject.[71]

The metaphysical question[72] is thus couched among considerations apparently equally important to the work. Not
that philosophy, however profound or significant, is drama,
but one suspects that at this stage in its development the
other-than-dramatic, the theatrical, the lyrical, the mystical,
and the symbolic requisites of the play came more easily
to the author. Goethe had lost his sense for drama through

71. Goethe to Eckermann, February 12, 1829: "Mozart should have
written the music to Faust," It is well known that Goethe intended the
play to be accompanied by music; an orchestra is called for in "Walpurgis Night's Dream."

72. Goethe originally planned a long "disputation scene" between
Faust and Mephistopheles (Witkowski, 1:526–27).

his deepening sense of the underlying forces that constitute it, lost his patience with the details of experience in his knowledge of their broader meaning, and only *Faust* forced him to remain true to his earliest beginnings. He did not undertake a serious dramatic project after the completion of Part I, and the *Helena* drama, which was to become Act III or Part II, had been begun earlier and perhaps independently of *Faust*, in 1800. Part II itself, it is generally agreed, is essentially undramatic, and not really predicated upon the dramatic. It does not present, it reflects.

In other words, our present scene, the all-important pact scene, may be said to have been late in coming for reasons of form as well as matter. The scene tests Goethe both as artist and thinker. The task was to reduce to the real world, to persons in moral opposition, forces that were shown to operate on the larger scale of universe or macrocosm, and pit them against each other in a similar but not artificial way. Each was to have its right, as in nature, despite adherence to a whole. Not any pact would do. A pact that presumed the eternal damnation of Faust could not serve as the vehicle for a work that envisioned an endless process in things, any more than could a wager that allowed of, let alone presupposed, his complete success—for the same reason. Neither force nor party was to be able to win, at least not within the framework of the world we can, or Goethe felt that we could, know.[73] The traditional pact, as is often observed, was conceived in a different world, a Ptolemaic universe[74] in which the limits set in the physical realm were matched in the moral, and perhaps vice versa: the restrictiveness of the one reflected the restrictedness of the other.

The world that Goethe inherited was round, and in motion, and the translation—or better, since the process was hardly

73. "Mephistopheles must only half win the bet, and if half the responsibility comes to rest upon Faust, then the elder's right of pardon ["das Begnadigungs-Recht des alten Herrn"] can be immediately evoked, making for a most happy conclusion of the whole" (Goethe to Schubarth, November 3, 1820).

74. See Stawell and Dickinson, *Goethe's Faust* chap. 1.

conscious, the mutation—of his philosophy of nature into
moral philosophy is likewise revealing. He shared with
Rousseau (though he felt the influence rather from Spinoza)
the belief in the natural goodness of man, but neither of
them shared his acute response to nature itself, which he took
whole, violence and all, and not merely as a philosophical
abstraction. Nor could the philosophy of moderation, which
had served so long in a static world, serve well in a world of
movement. If there was to be balance it would have to be
achieved through action, not restraint, in the same way that
nature achieves its balances. Faust will say: "Renounce! renounce! . . . is the everlasting song . . . that our whole life
long/Hoarsely each passing moment sings,"[75] and although
the drama intends the remark as a dangerous prelude to the
crescendo of curses upon all restraint of which he delivers
himself before the pact is made—"Woe! woe!/Thou hast de-
stroyed/The beautiful world,"[76] a chorus will chant in
response—nowhere does the work uphold the golden mean as
the guiding principle for modern man. At the end, Faust will
speak of having first "stormed" through life and only later
proceeded "cautiously," but that will be appropriate to his
advanced age, and natural.[77] Obvious and natural in that
sense *are* the solutions in *Faust,* as I suggested at the beginning, and it is only the significance of the questions they
serve to answer that reveals the philosophical depth in the

75. "Entbehren sollst du! sollst entbehren!/Das ist der ewige
Gesang,/Der jedem an die Ohren klingt,/Den, unser ganzes Leben
lang,/Uns heiser jede Stunde singt" (ll. 1549-53). The theme of
renunciation ("Entsagung") is prominent in *Wilhelm Meisters Wander-
jahre* (1807-29), yet the problem of extremes would appear to be
more lastingly resolved in a work such as *Elective Affinities* (1808-09),
where extremes are regarded as not only necessary, thus tolerable, in
nature and in man, but also as the prelude to balance.
    76. "Weh! weh!/Du hast sie zerstört,/Die schöne Welt/Mit
mächtiger Faust" (ll. 1607-10).
    77. ". . . und so mit Macht/Mein Leben durchgestürmt; erst groß
und mächtig,/Nun aber geht es weise, geht bedächtig" (ll. 11,338-
40).

work. For one sometimes cannot ask proper questions of a
work of art until the answers are known, artistic creation
being more often organic than logical, and remarkably so
here. The questions now being raised, or, rather, now surfac-
ing, are answered in that manner.

The terms of the pact[78] clarify the question that has gone
begging since the moment the Earth Spirit said to Faust:
"You are like the spirit you comprehend, not me." (Shall we
add, some thirty years before?) Who, then, was man like? The
question was of the age. Having rejected the traditional
authority of religion, it was in search of new moral identity.
Schiller, we noted earlier, looked to art, and the instinct
for "play" in man, in an attempt to erect an ethic upon
aesthetic impulses. Kant, with the "categorical imperative,"
re-erected the old morality upon solidly philosophical rather
than religious grounds. There were other solutions, as the
question of the nature of man and the purpose of action
gained ground again on the more abstract question of the
nature of reality that had occupied the previous age. Goethe
as a thinker appears to have contributed less than any to an
ultimate solution, and yet today, more. He simply posited
human consciousness as moral being.

What distinguishes Faust from the Earth Spirit, what makes
him like the spirit he comprehends, as we come to see when
the pact is drawn, is his human awareness. For what the spirit
celebrates in song as ceaseless activity is suffered by him as
restless change, hence pain, if also joy. If the world is round,
the horizon will recede as it is approached, yet always present
itself as attainable. The tragedy in the human condition is
anticipation, which is a direct consequence of being. Man
creates in his mind an image of the world, and with each step
forward he can see that much farther, with the result that a
former goal, when finally reached, will already have become a
means to a new end. When Faust states as condition for his

78. See, for example, Harry Steinhauer, "Faust's Pact with the
Devil," *PMLA* 69 (1956): 180–200; also A. R. Hohlfeld, "Pact and
Wager in Goethe's *Faust*" (*Modern Philology* 18 [1921]: 113–36),
which deals with three essential passages in the pact scene.

defeat that the Devil produce a moment to which he might
say, "Linger awhile, thou art so fair," he may be asking the
impossible, in that time will not stand still, and he may appear
arrogant in his assurance that such could never come to pass,
but the condition reflects the concept of life underlying the
drama. When he makes, further, the price for his defeat simply
his earthly existence, he may seem to offer little, since he
has no faith in an afterlife (". . . small concern I feel for
yonder world"), but he offers only what he must. The end
of striving, success, is death. This paradox is central in the
work, although it is nowhere stated nor ever explicitly resolved.
But we know from the main cycles of action thus far presented that movement is life, and life movement and we shall
learn the proposition in reverse when Faust is finally brought
to utter *in anticipation*[79] the words he thought would never
cross his lips. For it is not only at his death, but because of
impending death, that he will have a presentiment of complete fulfillment in the final act. Only in death will he lower
his sights. Even the supreme irony in his mistaking the digging of his grave for the beginning of a new life "for millions"
(ll. 11,563 ff.), which a moment ago we were inclined to
regard as tragic, will be heightened, and absorbed into the
greater and more positive symbolism of the work. If the
moral world is round, the continually all but full sense of
attainment, which from within will be experienced as
failure, may appear from without as unending conditional
success. Goethe's contribution was not that he secularized
morality, which the eighteenth century had effectively done,
but that he fully naturalized it. There is a sense in his *Faust*
that mankind is not only redeemable, but already redeemed
in nature.

The pact scene does not present itself philosophically.[80]

79. ". . . im Vorgefühl" (l. 11,585).
80. The planned disputation scene might have provided a relevant
philosophical discussion, yet the notes for the scene speak of choruses
of students and suggest broad humor and theatrics still in the vein
of the puppet plays and the legend. A planned monologue between the
spirits of Gretchen and Helen was also never included, and might have

The exchange with Mephistopheles in the preceding scene is
as intellectually abstract as the play will become. Faust himself will be unaware of the implications of the wager he makes,
for he does not enjoy the perspectives from outside the
drama, either the view from eternity or the persuasive symbolism of his own actions, without which we, too, might see
only a purposeless, jagged course of events in the action
presented. Not that such knowledge of itself is important.
Faust would strive without the prospect of true earthly
attainment, in which he has as little faith as in heavenly reward.
He says to Mephistopheles: "What, poor devil, hast thou to
bestow?/Was ever mortal spirit, in its high endeavor,/Fathomed
by Being such as thou? . . . food thou hast which satisfieth
never . . .";[81] and while the presumption forebodes trial, and
will in fact be sorely tested in "Walpurgis Night," it also
serves to define the condition of the common man who
needs the illusion of attainment, in this or in an other world,
to prompt his striving. Faust's present delusion is that he has
no illusions, and yet he is willing to sacrifice his soul to prove
himself right.

What is being tested in this Faust parable, we said, is a
system represented in its exemplary proponent, and what will
be thereby illustrated, we begin to see, is a universal law in
particular application. At this stage Goethe might still have
been less than certain as to the precise resolution of his
action, but it is clear that he was applying the natural law of
cyclical progression to man and morals, as systematically as
truth and art would allow. "The end I aim at is not joy,"[82]

---

been enlightening. The omission of both is evidence of Goethe's abiding
instinct not to sacrifice the natural to the demands of understanding.
"There is nothing beautiful in nature which is not true according to the
laws of nature."—"Es ist in der Natur nichts schön, was nicht natur-
gesetzlich als wahr motiviert wäre" (Eckermann, part 3, June 5, 1826).

81. "Was willst du armer Teufel geben?/Ward eines Menschen Geist,
in seinem hohen Streben,/Von deinesgleichen je gefaßt?/Doch hast du
Speise, die nicht sättigt . . ." (ll. 1675–76).

82. "Du hörest ja, von Freud' ist nicht die Rede" (l. 1765).

Faust makes clear to Mephistopheles in a line that now
immediately precedes the passage in the *Fragment* where he
was made to speak of desiring to know "all human weal and
woe"; and whereas we could see this remark in the earlier
version as simply reflecting a titanic urge to comprehend
experience, now we sense a necessary relation between weal
and woe, joy and pain, as between life and death. Faust
knows this experience, but not the design. Not that such
knowledge, either, would affect the course of his actions,
since knowledge as such has not been conceived in the work
as the guide to moral or existential truth. Truth results from
action, wisdom from experience. The round century required
for Faust to recognize a true purpose in existence may be
poetic time, but it is not an exaggerated estimate. Part II, in
surveying symbolically the evolution of man and the antecedents of Western culture, will suggest the necessity not only
to perceive but, like nature, to reabsorb the past in order to
take essential steps to the future. "What you have been given
by your fathers, earn, that you may possess it!"[83] Faust says,
though at a point where he still sees the past as a restraining
and not also containing force. In general, this philosophical
drama does not guide, but exhorts, which is a logical consequence of its sense of truth and freedom not as goals finally
to be attained but as necessities of life always to be won or
regained, by the individual ("Freedom alone he earns as well
as life/Who day by day must conquer them anew") and more
broadly, and implicitly, by each new era in its own fashion
and its own terms.

The reason we can think of *Faust* as universally significant
is that its frame of thought encompasses a central moral and
philosophical problem still not resolved in our age and so to
us seemingly applicable to all times. Yet Part II clearly intends
its contrast of the ancient, medieval, and modern worlds to

---

83. My translation for "Was du ererbt von deinen Vätern hast,/
Erwirb es, um es zu besitzen" (ll. 682–83). Alice Raphael has "All that
your ancestors bequeathed to you,/To make it really yours—earn it
anew" (*Faust: A Tragedy, the First Part*, trans. Alice Raphael, with
an introduction and notes by Jacques Barzun [New York, 1955]).

suggest distinct modes of being, the last charged with the
burden of resolving the conflict that had arisen when the
worldly and the otherworldly views of the former clashed in
the Renaissance. The two souls that Faust finds within him
have their cultural and historical bases. Of course, to the extent that the final resolution of the action takes the form of
a resolving in anticipation and recognition of the need ever
to re-solve, to "conquer anew," in the continuous process
of life, it will transcend the historical and again reveal its orig-
ins in the abiding faith in nature. And to the extent that
Faust himself remains ignorant of this truth, this injunction
to live and, in dying, "dare rebirth," as the poem "Selige
Sehnsucht," written in 1812 after the completion of Part I,
states the moral precept, he will find no purpose or pleasure
in life.[84] Almost pointedly Goethe inserts, before the lines
from the *Fragment* where Faust speaks of heaping all men's
fortunes on his breast and sharing "at length with them the
shipwreck of mankind," the remark, "Purged from the love
of knowledge, my vocation . . . be/To bare my breast to every
pang—."[85] The pessimism now appears to be the direct result
of rejecting one form of knowledge without the perception
of a new form in a newly discovered world.

The dramatic realm is the moral realm, we said, and the
conflict between Mephistopheles and Faust, which takes
place dramatically, not merely symbolically, must be understood in that context. This is important, because there would
appear to be no such conflict. Mephistopheles accommodates—for his own clear purposes—and when he frustrates,
it is likewise with an eye to advantage. He does not take his
opponent "personally."[86] Yet the sheer impersonality of
his attitude, which is reflected in the characteristic by which
we know him first and best, his humor, is only a symptom

84. As Michael Hamburger translates "stirb und werde." This is not
a "dying unto the world."

85. "Mein Busen, der vom Wissensdrang geheilt ist,/Soll keinen
Schmerzen künftig sich verschließen" (ll. 1768–69).

86. Except in "Gloomy Day. A Plain," which was kept over from
Urfaust, and remains the one scene not later turned into verse.

of the more essential conflict, the tip of the iceberg of negation which we sense but, except in the rare flashes of malice,
are not made to see. Rather it is the element for which the
humor and impersonality are the displacement—namely,
feeling—that serves truly to join the issue. This Mephistopheles lacks as much as Faust possesses, so that he is to be
seen not only as generally destructive, but specifically destructive of emotion. All that is not patently rational draws
his attention, and his humor, for which we like him, is
often simply the expression of a truth we find intellectually
acceptable but morally hard to countenance. The paradoxical
recognition of evil as a component of the good implied in
the Lord's attitude to Mephistopheles appears in no way contradictory, when evil, brought down to earth, takes no more
insidious a form than scepticism or critical humor, that is, a
balancing force to feeling. Similarly, the principle of good,
when brought down to earth, emerges as no more admirably
moral a force than the conscious will to life. Thus, the Devil
may be seen as evil in intent, not necessarily in effect, and
Faust good in his deepest instinct, though, like man, not
necessarily in his deeds. Goethe once said of himself, "I wish
to be good *and* evil, like nature" (to Lavater, February 22, 1776).

The pact is conceived, occasioned, and acted upon at the
human level, and so reflects the character and bias of its
participants. The pact seems wholly unpremeditated, whence
its form as wager. We may even wonder if its unique terms
are not again an example of an unconscious idea coming into
being under the pressure from art. For while there is no
doubt that by now Goethe was fully master of his subject,
in the sense of having gained objectivity toward his hero
and conscious recognition of the contours of his theme, it
is also true that no other pact or wager could have been
negotiated between these particular protagonists, whom he
already had in hand from *Urfaust*. The pact does not make
Faust and Mephistopheles, but they the pact, literally and
consequentially.[87] Only a Devil, cavalier and worldly enough

87. In contrast to Marlowe's Faust, who is degraded and diminished,

as we know him from *Urfaust,* could have the arrogance (that he will surely win) and want of pedantry (it would not matter how) to enter into a pact subjective and open-ended enough for this "romantic" Faust to have conceived. In fact, the bargain is struck with such aplomb of character that one might well lose sight of the terms in the involvement with the personalities. It is not uncommon for the specifics of the agreement to go unnoticed on first impression. To be sure, a hand clasp, and something in writing, for which minor request Faust indeed calls Mephistopheles a pedant, seal the wager. But this stage moment occurs in the middle of the scene and is bordered on the one side by the kind of dispersive, penetrating remarks on life we have come to expect of Faust and on the other, as if nothing had intervened, by a resurgence of pessimism that is made to join with the nihilistic passage from the *Fragment* and close the discussion. The satirical scene with the Devil and the student, already complete in *Urfaust,* thus becomes the following scene, so that instead of a subsequent action that would demonstrate and clarify the issue at hand, we are simply newly diverted.

If this is unusual form, it is true psychology, and wholly in the spirit of the work. We were not promised, nor will be given until the very end, a Faust who knows and seeks his own advantage. "Not earthly is his food or drink," Mephistopheles accurately said of him in the "Prologue in Heaven." And since he will not suppress his spiritual will, which thought of renouncing, we just saw, drives him to violent outburst, and since he cannot realize the will in action ("The god who throned within my breast resides . . . With sovereign sway my energies he guides,/[Yet] cannot move external things"),[88] his frustration is complete. Faust is not so much

---

not challenged, by his pact with the Devil; Mountfort's *The Life and Death of Doctor Faustus* (1686) becomes an admitted farce, "Made into a Farce."

88. "Der Gott, der mir im Busen wohnt . . . Der über allen meinen Kräften thront,/Er kann nach außen nichts bewegen" (ll. 1566–69).

drawn as driven into the pact, in desperation and with scorn
for its terms: "Slave am I here, at any rate,/If thine, or
whose, it matters not,"[89] though clearly some form of agreement would have to have been reached after he had so long
"sucked on the atmosphere"[90] of the Devil, as he had on that
of the Earth Spirit. There is even a kind of eeriness, surely
not intended, in the thought of what may have passed through
his mind between the time of the first meeting with Mephistopheles and the present visit, which is unannounced but
obviously expected. In any event, Faust's actions at this point
are motivated dramatically, not logically. In despair he
enters a pact which his author has designed for his salvation.

Nor were we promised an all-knowing Devil: "I own,/
Though not omniscient, much to me is known";[91] nor an
omnipotent one: "Opposed to nothingness, the world,/This
clumsy mass, subsisteth still;/Not yet is it to ruin hurled,/
Despite the efforts of my will."[92] Mephistopheles, too, who
believes he is leading, is being led. His guile is not based in
knowledge, but presumption, as is all unsuccessful guile.
The same scepticism and humor that protect him from his
archenemy, life or reality—"Diese plumpe Welt"—blind
him to the quality in Faust and mankind that distinguishes
their being, the creative will, and that must be satisfied
in order to be conquered. He chooses, or rather, he is *compelled* by his realism and rationalism, to discount the very

Witkowski (2:218) suspects that these lines were subsequently inserted
in order better to motivate the pact.

89. "Wie ich beharre, bin ich Knecht,/Ob dein, was frag' ich, oder
wessen" (ll. 1710-11).

90. "Du hast micht mächtig angezogen,/An meiner Sphäre lang'
gesogen" (ll. 483-84).

91. "Allwissend bin ich nicht; doch viel ist mir bewußt" (l. 1582).

92. "Was sich dem Nichts entgegenstellt,/Das Etwas, diese plumpe
Welt . . . Ich wußt nicht ihr beizukommen . . ." (ll. 1363-66). "Diese
plumpe Welt" is perhaps untranslatable, and reflects precisely the
Devil's attitude toward reality and being. Swanwick has, ". . . this
world, this clumsy mass." The most recent translation, by Arndt, is
strained: "What bids defiance to the Naught,/The clumsy lumber
of the Aught. . . ."

clause in the agreement that defiantly expresses that will: "If
e'er upon my couch, stretched at my ease, I'm found/Then
may my life that instant cease."[93] Again in his scepticism,
but also in his long experience ("Oh, credit me, who still as
ages roll/Have chew'd this bitter fare from year to year,/No
mortal from the cradle to the bier,/Digests the ancient
leaven!"),[94] he must regard such human sentiment as empty.
Mephistopheles is of the past. His appearance as courtier and
cavalier ("A cock's feather for a plume")[95] suggests an old
world, with its refinement, order, and intelligence, but want
of vitality. Faust is of the future; it is only on the threshold
of a newly conceived world that he will find satisfaction and
come to rest. But the arc his life describes will be determined
as much by what has been as what will be. For while these
two figures are not meant to understand, they are intended
to complement each other, like the past the future, the real
the ideal, or the two souls within the breast of man. It is
essential in drama that the circle of action be closed, and by
establishing the same relation between protagonist and antagonist as exists between forces in the encompassing world
of nature and the universe, Goethe provided a point of return
for the almost endless implications of his theme.

Yet voices are heard from outside the circle. Art is long
true before it is consistent, we might say in paraphrase of
Goethe's "Art is long developing before it is beautiful." The
comment upon the action by a Chorus of Spirits in the
present scene, for example, for all its apparent appropriate-
ness as evocation of spirit in song, represents a departure.
The absolute voices in the "Prologue in Heaven" were so
defined by their setting beyond time; and while other voices
have periodically interrupted or accompanied the course of
events, they could usually be rationalized in terms of art,

93. "Werd' ich beruhigt je mich auf ein Faulbett legen,/So sei es
gleich um mich getan" (ll. 1692-93).

94. "O glaube mir, der manche tausend Jahre/An dieser harten
Speise kaut,/Daß von der Wiege bis zur Bahre/Kein Mensch den alten
Sauerteig verdaut" (ll. 1776-79).

95. "Die Hahnenfeder auf dem Hut" (l. 1538).

which is not reality. The spirits that lull Faust to sleep at
the end of the preceding scene, as the Devil makes his first
onslaught upon his senses, are an example, as are those that
provide the atmospherics for the magical occurrences at the
beginning: "Captured there within is one!/Stay without and
follow none!"[96] But neither materially affects the action.
The chorus that has the most dramatic impact, that of angels
accompanying the Easter bells that recall Faust to life, seems,
conversely, a relegation of the potentially realistic to the
spiritual or symbolic realm. The voices could have been more
simply designated a choir from without. The present chorus
is still different. It draws upon an awareness as yet not introduced in the poem. In exhorting Faust to renew his commitment to living after he has cursed human limitation
("Thou 'mong the sons of earth,/Lofty and mighty one,/
Build [the beautiful world] once more!"),[97] it sounds the
central theme of birth and rebirth without recourse to poetic
or dramaturgical device. It speaks directly, as if it were the
voice of the poem itself, or of Goethe. Mephistopheles,[98]
of course, claims these spirits for his own, their exhortations
to living falling on his ears as living of the kind that satisfies,
and so deadens, life, the very kind of living that he himself
has just been advocating: ". . . don at once the same costume
[as Mephistopheles'],/And, free from trammels, speed away,/
That what life is you may essay."[99] Faust pays the spirits
no heed. It is true that his outward lack of response need not
preclude the possibility of an important inner reaction, in
much the same way we believed we saw unconscious retarding forces keeping him from suicide in the very process of

96. "Drinnen gefangen ist einer!/Bleibet haußen, folg' ihm keiner!"
(ll. 1259–60).

97. ´Mächtiger/Der Erdensöhne,/Prächtiger/Baue sie wieder,/In
deinem Busen baue sie auf" (ll. 1617–21).

98. The German is winning: "Dies sind die Kleinen/Von den Meinen"
(ll. 1627–28). The nature of these spirits is a matter of controversy,
however.

99. "Dergleichen gleichfalls anzulegen;/Damit du, losgebunden,
frei,/Erfahrest, was das Leben sei" (ll. 1541–43).

his contemplating it, and more exactly in the way, as has been pointed out, that he will be made at the beginning of Part II to sleep off the whole of Part I without knowing it.[100] But the unconscious is more a part of the absolute than of the moral or dramatic.

For whom is *Faust* written? When we earlier asked the question it was with the implication that for all the lyrical, theatrical, folk, and traditional elements that were being gradually introduced in the play (and introduced with the apparent intent to broaden its scope and appeal), the central issue of reducing the theme to dramatic action continued ignored. The pact scene was long in coming. But the reverse may be equally true. Now we may say that the drama produced the pact, literally and chronologically, not the pact the drama. Its terms do not educe events so much as simply reflect a principle already active in what had come before, and fix it at the center of the work. And since the terms are subjective ("When to the moment *I* shall say . . ."), the qualitative rather than the measurable, the spiritual rather than the logical consequences of word and action come to bear the greater weight of meaning and to create the kind of drama that is acted out within, rather than upon a stage.

The recognition of life as process, and its conflicts as the result of inner dynamics more than of opposing forces from the outside world, did not significantly alter the appreciation of traditional drama, which might then simply be seen as a projection of the subjective onto the objective plane or stage, with no changed result. But it did influence, mostly adversely, the dramatic writing newly born of the age. Of the age, not merely in the age, which saw a striking development in the theater, called and experienced as modern, but representing in fact drama unaltered in essential form. *Faust* was the exception. It reflected not only the temper of the times in its language, not only the insights of the times in its visions, but the philosophy of the day in its evolving form. To have invented as the central motif in a drama the search for a

100. See Trunz's remarks in the Hamburg edition, 3:531–33.

perfect moment is to have found the equivalent in human
terms of the process which was believed to inform nature
itself, not merely the social order of which men partook with
their lesser being and upon which traditional drama had
been built. The unnatural form of *Faust* in that respect seems
a natural product of the age. The theme of man in relation
to nature, which is the main theme of the work and major
concern of the period, was not readily adaptable to the con-
ventions of a form that had come almost exclusively to
express the more limited concern of man in relation to other
men and to society. If we regard *Faust* less as an attempt to
dramatize an essentially undramatic, because inward, process
than as an attempt to express through a new form the ultimately dramatic, because endlessly changing, nature of the
human condition, we begin to see sensation, mood, fantasy,
atmosphere, choral song, not as poetic frills on the action,
but as the stuff of which the work was being made. The pact
scene may have been late in coming, that is, not because of
its crucial nature, but simply because, from another point of
view, it may be seen merely as one scene among many. It
does not, after all, serve to pull everything together as might
a central plot element in a conventional play—Goethe himself
to the contrary, in conversation with ʙoisserée, August 3,
1815.

The next scene with which we must deal, "Walpurgis Night,"
breaks with convention totally and so presses even further
our ongoing question of freedom of form in relation to the
development of meaning.

6

WALPURGIS NIGHT

It may seem strange after treating the pact scene to move immediately to "Walpurgis Night," which in the completed text is made to follow the scene in the cathedral, namely the climax, not the onset, of the dramatic action that ensues from the pact. But a special sense of continuity is gained by examining the new material separately from the old, as if it had a life of its own, and regarding what was earlier or later written not as sequence but encompassment. "Walpurgis Night" is different enough as to warrant a chapter to itself.

We must admit that the scene presents difficulties.[1] Its intent and function are not clear. But part of the difficulty results from the position it comes—or, perhaps, is forced—to occupy in the finished play.[2] Its bawdiness and frivolity on the one hand, and what might be called artistic irreverence on the other, result in a blatant contrast with the innocent suffering we have just witnessed in "Cathedral." Furthermore, the murder of Valentin, which, newly introduced, motivates the flight of Mephistopheles and Faust from the town and causes them now to appear almost common criminals as they join the witches' lurid festivities on the Brocken—the mountain where in folklore the Walpurgis Night is celebrated. A reference to these activities is incorporated in the Valentin scene, in anticipation, when Mephistopheles says: "Virtuous withal, I feel, with, I confess,/A touch of thievish joy

1. Witkowski (2: 165–66) notes that the court theater at Braunschweig, in its production of Part I in 1829, omitted the whole of "Walpurgis Night," along with other scenes which were found to be "unstageable, written for the imagination."

2. On the position of the scene in the completed Part I, see Fairley, *Goethe's Faust: Six Essays,* "The Two Walpurgisnachts."

and wantonness./Thus through my limbs already there doth bound/The glorious Walpurgis night!"[3]

The contrast could have been intentional. The Storm and Stress honored extremes, and while "Walpurgis Night" is not a product of that period, it may be seen as emerging from the period, as did the work as a whole. A Dionysian celebration with witches and the Devil in attendance is in any event not unsuited to the Faust theme,[4] and coming after the "Witches' Kitchen," which had been introduced in the *Fragment,* the more to be expected. If we accepted the rejuvenation in the earlier scene as "fact" in the sense of dramatic, artistic reflection of the natural phenomenon of revitalization, we might accept the present fantastic sequence in a similar way and think of its eerie and libidinous movements as the concentration in poetic or dream form of experience too extensive to be treated as an episode, too deep to be represented realistically.

Except for the latter part of the scene. We allow that Faust, after the murder of Valentin and the flight from Gretchen, should enter in despair into the kind of adventure or adventures that would provide him needed forgetfulness, and for which "Walpurgis Night" apparently is the symbol.[5] And he does return inevitably to his responsibility in his projection of a Gretchen with shackled feet, "a single crimson line/ Around [her] lovely neck . . . no broader than a knife's blunt edge,"[6] at the end of the scene. But the social and topical satire which is introduced interrupts the line of dramatic

3. ". . . So spukt mir schon durch alle Glieder/Die herrliche Walpurgisnacht" (ll. 3660–61).

4. Witkowski (2: 272) sees a folk celebration with its masses of people and notes the allusion to the Prater, Vienna's great public park. The Gründgens production of the play represents "Walpurgis Night" as a brothel scene.

5. Upon this one intent and function of the scene, most modern interpreters are agreed.

6. "Wie sonderbar muß diesen schönen Hals/Ein einzig rotes Schnürchen schmücken,/Nicht breiter als ein Messerrücken!" (ll. 4203–05).

action and at the same time seems inappropriate in the atmosphere that has been created. We cannot regard the scene on the one hand as reflecting a morass of cupidity and sexuality into which Faust has been led, and from which he barely escapes, and on the other as a symbolical, therefore free, medium to express other concerns. The social satire, which includes caricatures of a general, a minister, a parvenu, and an author, might conceivably represent a broader adventure that has taken Faust into the great world of human affairs in the manner of Marlowe and the legend (and of Part II).[7] But allegory is rare in Goethe, except where it is patent, as in the numerous minor pieces he wrote for his Weimar friends and their theater.[8] A third Walpurgis Night scene, which was to follow "Walpurgis Night's Dream. Intermezzo," was planned but not written, and may have had the purpose of extending the vision that sees beneath the surface of life beyond Faust, or through him, to the mass of mankind. Some details in the outline for the scene suggest such a development, as we shall see later. But the topical satire on the rationalist Friedrich Nicolai (1733–1811) in the figure of the Proctophantasmist, that is, the Prophet of the Posterior, cannot be so explained. It points forward to the development in the Intermezzo, where the work will begin to reflect outwardly upon its times, and upon itself and its own presence in the theater, but the satire has no organic connection to what has come before.[9]

7. In the note to ll. 4076–91, Heffner, Rehder, and Twadell say: "In sum, we have a group of caricatures of the reactionaries of Goethe's day."

8. For examples, see the Hamburg edition, vol. 5; the Weimar edition, more fully, vols. 10–17; also, M. Carlson, *Goethe and the Weimar Theatre*.

9. Nicolai had written a travesty of *Werther*. Instead of having the hero romantically commit suicide, he has Werther (with the blessings of Albert, who now wishes to disentangle himself from the whole affair) marry Lotte, and end, after facing many unromantic difficulties, as a bourgeois landowner and father of eight children.

The question is one of thematics and "dramatics," the reflection in the theater of the question of art in general in
the age as to the rendering of things immaterial or unseen,
the things with which the age was concerned. We appreciate
the more the contribution of Lessing when we recall that
his directing the Germans toward Shakespeare as a kindred
literary spirit was at the same time a rejection of the tyranny
of realism and rationalism that had emanated from France.[10]
And when we recall that the developments in the science of
the day likewise reflect a concern with the underlying and
progressive rather than apparent and particular aspects of the
real world, in philosophy and history no less than botany
and zoology, we think the broad revolution in the unreal
world of art the less willful or surprising. The concept of romantic as equivalent to modern, which I mentioned above,
might as easily have had its base in a sense of true contemporaneity in the intellectual world as in the common fallacy
of calling new what one simply favors. The opposition of
romantic and real derives from the refusal of the realist to
accept the romantic view of reality, to which he has every
right. But the romantic view as such is not unreal.[11]

A new conception of reality does not explain the presence
of satire in the midst of an emotionally charged drama, but
it makes more understandable the emergence of a new form
that would allow, or believe it could allow, such contrast
and change. We must look deeper here than to comic relief,
which this satire is not, and more cautiously than to say
that the contrast simply parallels the breaks with the tradition prevalent at the time in the other arts and genres. We
are dealing with drama, which, as we noted, was adversely

10. In his view; whereas at the same time he himself would remain
fully linked to the past, at least in terms of artistic form. See his seventeenth "Literary Letter" (included in Arndt/Hamlin, pp. 389–93); also
Henry Garland, *Lessing, the Founder of Modern German Literature.*

11. See Silz, *Early German Romanticism,* where the supposedly
separate concepts of romantic and classic reveal striking similarities
under scrutiny of facts; also Willoughby, *The Classical Age of German
Literature 1748–1805.*

affected by the new perception of experience while other
forms flourished within it. The difficult question posed by
Faust is not whether its form fits its content, but whether
we can see the form for the content, and vice versa. Convention is a large part of understanding. If we see the work as
drama, as we must with part of the mind, we will not only
experience as interruptive those motifs and developments
in "Walpurgis Night" that do not further the action but also
might lend them false meaning. The scene, read as drama,
seems in general unfeeling, and, in its sequel, to repeat a word
we used earlier, cavalier. Read thematically, as a development in a *Faust* perceived as a philosophical poem, it gains in
relevance without losing wholly its connection with the
dramatically real; the image of Gretchen at its close is a powerful binding agent. Yet the scene seems also bound by its
own logic to a further development that would vitiate its philosophical, no less than its dramatic, import, when it begins
to become almost a satire of satire in its sequel, a playful
mockery of itself. The *Xenien,* that collection of satirical
epigrams written by Goethe himself and Schiller, are introduced as allegorical characters. The stage hands of the
Weimar theater, where Goethe would envision his play performed, are saluted in a comradely fashion with the remark
that they may rest for a change, the present scene requiring
few theatrical props for its parade of figures from past and
contemporary literature—the author himself not excluded.[12]
Here, art comes before life on the stage.

Conversely, however, real life, the *present* in the theater
or in the awareness of the reader, comes before art, the illusion on the stage, in that the references to a reality outside
the play return us to our own reality, make us suddenly
think differently than we have just thought, yet in manner,
not in kind. In other words, read in its own right, there
emerges a *Faust* better able to absorb a Walpurgis Night and
its sequel, not because we thus grant it its freedom but

12. *Xenien,* satirical epigrams that Schiller and Goethe wrote for
their *Musenalmanach* (1795–96); ". . . brave sons of Mieding [today
may rest] " (l. 4223–24).

because, the freedom allowed, we can begin to see broader
connections between the parts and the whole. If Goethe
the scientist could attempt to reflect the inner laws of nature
in this "poetic production," and Goethe the moralist could
suggest their relation to the unseen workings of the human
soul and mind, we might expect Goethe the artist, with the
same sense of dynamics, at one point to turn his own creation inside-out to show whence and from whom it came. The
romantic irony of the "Walpurgis Night's Dream," in which
in its title from Shakespeare it already partly indulges, need
not compromise the seriousness of the work, any more than
the humor need compromise the passion of the drama, or
the visions of chaos those of order in the universe. There
would appear to be an obverse and reverse to everything. Not
that this principle will inform every movement of *Faust,*
which in its artistic nature is naive and in its development
organic rather than logical. Yet if *Faust* is naive in nature, it
is not simple, but complex, in its "innocent" or unconven-
tional juxtaposing of diverse elements, and if organic in development, not unguided, in that, its source of inspiration
being largely unconscious and therefore constant, it could
end by forming a meaningful, if less than philosophical, whole.
Goethe warned against the search for a single unifying idea
or principle in *Faust* but not against the search for continuity
amongst things apparently different because separated in
time, which rather he encouraged.

I am repeating what I said at the end of the first chapter.
But it is only with the Walpurgis Night sequence that we
reach the point where the question of form, however we
attempt to answer it, does not satisfy our needs, and we must
turn to the question of development in time.[13] The new

13. German drama of the period produced nothing so original in
form. Tieck's *Genoveva* (1799), despite its mingling of the epic, lyrical, and fantastic, today seems less the product of a pioneering spirit
than an adaptive talent. The religious-medieval theme was highly popular at the time. On the other hand, his "Puss in Boots" (1797), still
included among German theater classics, breaks truly new ground in

frames, as we called them, that Goethe appeared to place
around his older material as he progressed with *Faust,* if they
altered the form of the work, did not present difficulties of
understanding. The "Prologue in Heaven," for example, as
prologue, hardly broke with the traditions of form, and in
content, while showing a remarkable development and ad-
vancement of the theme, was not puzzling. We did not, and
perhaps cannot, say whether its vision from eternity was
intended as cosmic paradigm for the laws of nature and in
man, or whether the correspondence simply resulted from
the spontaneous creation of images similar because stemming
from a common source of creativity. But if the relationship
of thinker and poet was difficult to define, the recognition of
a relationship alone served as an assurance to understanding.
The new monologue in "Forest and Cavern," as a further example, introduced a perspective previously unknown in the
work, a subjective, almost mystical access to a "knowledge"
nature has in common with man, and while the medium
of the knowledge, the mysterious Sublime Spirit, may have
been hard to place dramaturgically in the poem, the knowledge itself could readily be attributed to an author who
elsewhere time and again so expressed himself on the subject.
At such moments we read Goethe instead of *Faust,* or
better, *along* with Faust the character, who is not Goethe,
but not too small to become him, if necessary, for a
moment. And if other perspectives or voices were newly introduced, they were usually insinuated into the work as
echo or anticipation, variant or parallel, and so began further
to serve one another, though none had ever truly gained the
right, dramaturgically speaking, to enter the action. The
voice "from above" that pronounces Gretchen saved at the
end of Part I may be seen as the culmination of the development of a Strom and Stress drama into a symbolical poem.

But nothing in the play, or elsewhere in Goethe, prepares
us for "Walpurgis Night." This fact, and the fact that Goethe

---

introducing audience and author as parts of the play. See Edwin H.
Zeydel, *Ludwig Tieck, the German Romanticist.*

was not an apprentice at the time he wrote the scene, make
it the best, if most difficult, measure of the unique nature
of *Faust*. We witness in this work a form coming into being.
To the extent that we identify the form, as we must, even
unconsciously, as an aid to comprehension, we diminish the
spontaneity of response, which "Walpurgis Night" in its
strange vividness will not allow. Not that the scene stands un-
attached. An attempt has obviously been made to join it,
if not to the action, at least to the thematics of the poem—
not, we sense, in order to be contained or absorbed in the
greater movements of the work, but somehow to justify its
own equally important purpose. The nature of that purpose
we shall leave aside for the moment, and later may have to
be no more precise than to describe the scene as a view from
the bowels (or darker side) of life intended to complement
the nobler vision from Paradise. But the manner in which the
material is presented reflects the struggle of the work at
this stage, not only to serve the forces that be, or were, in its
dramatic and thematic movements but also to anticipate
those to come in its almost endlessly fertile projections.

First as to the time of the scene and in the scene—that is,
when it was written and when it occurs in the play. It pre-
sumably was written in 1797, when Goethe took up *Faust*
again and attempted, as he said, to make progress "by un-
doing what is in print and broadly arranging it together with
what has already been written or invented and so bring the
plan, which actually is only an idea, closer to completion."
Since in this letter, of June 22 of that year, and in a following letter, Goethe speaks of the "mist and fog"[14] of the
world into which *Faust* leads him, and his correspondent
Schiller in an interim letter speaks of a "duality in human
nature"[15] that might well allude to the two souls of which
Faust himself speaks, we may suppose that the former

14. June 22, "Dunst- und Nebelweg," June 24, "Symbol- Ideen-
und Nebelwelt."
15. June 23, "Die Duplizität des menschlichen Natur." The context justifies the translation of "Duplizität" as "duality," a meaning
the word still has in Adelung and Grimm.

reference is to "Walpurgis Night," the latter to "Before the Gate," and that the two scenes were composed in some proximity.[16] For Schiller is still in the dark as to the intent in *Faust,* and calls upon "imagination to submit itself to the service of a rational idea" (June 23, 1797), which suggests that he does not know the material that in fact rationally develops the theme, namely, the "Prologue in Heaven" and the scenes in the study, if any have as yet been written, but does know "Before the Gate."

If it is true that "Walpurgis Night" followed "Before the Gate" in composition and was the first thing that Goethe took up in returning to his *Faust,* the fact would neatly illustrate the conflict and attempt at resolution of what I have been calling the dramatics and thematics in the work. Both scenes are set in spring. This device not only served to introduce the factor of time into a dramatic action that by its dispersive nature, as Schiller immediately saw, sorely needed a guiding principle, but served to introduce it in Goethe's own way. Recurrence is a theme that has taken hold by this point, and the recurrence of Easter and Walpurgis Night, which marks the time that has elapsed between the meeting with Gretchen and the impending catastrophe, also resumes the grand cycle of life and death in nature and in man to which the poem has persistently returned. The thematic becomes the dramatic. We begin to see "Walpurgis Night" as the anticipation, no less than the negation, of the higher purpose that Faust pursues, as if this were a dark night of the other soul in his breast from which he would also rise. We might even take this strange adventure as a peculiarly fine solution to the almost always difficult progression in classical drama, the fourth act, which depicts the futile, hence not readily dramatic, attempt to escape a foregone catastrophe—here Gretchen, pregnant, in the cathedral. In effect, "Walpurgis Night" is the penultimate "act"

16. This is not the conventional assumption, which does not bring the scenes together in time, though it does not insist in placing them apart. I follow here, as in all matters of chronology, Mason, *Faust: Its Genesis and Purport.*

of Part I. And if we assume the abstract—or, as Schiller described it, "ideal"—as opposed to the realistic aspect of
Mephistopheles' character as already conceived, if not yet
defined, as "Part of the power that still/Produceth good,
whilst ever scheming ill," we may also imagine "Before the
Gate" and "Walpurgis Night" as representing the upper-
and the under-worlds of nature and society, each with its
rightful sabbath.

We are not speaking of symbolism, but we are seeking
order in apparent disorder. Goethe may have composed these
and the other scenes from this period with varying awareness of their relation as parts to a whole, but the extent to
which we can join or separate them in conjecture may add
to our sense of coherence in the actual text. For example,
the deployment of persons in the scenes in question is
similar, and new to the play. It is occasional, not dramatic.
When we find soldier and servant, beggar and burgher produced for display in "Before the Gate," which is so known a
convention that we might almost take it as realism, we
may find the darker antics of "Walpurgis Night" less demanding of explanation, more to the point in their simple abandon. Some of the material Goethe omitted in his final version
of this scene suggests pure ribaldry as its first intent. For
example, a Satan was to address a throng of women with the
words: "For you are two things/Of delightful splendor,/
Shining gold/And a glowing member," after he has addressed
a throng of men: "To you are two things/Of utmost service,/
Gleaming gold/And a woman's crevice," in conclusion to
which a chorus in mock ritual would entone: "Fall on your
knees/On this hallowed ground!/O blessed who is near/
And heareth the word!"[17] The material was not used,

17. My translation, since the defunct material has not been translated into English. I have not resisted the temptation to rhyme in the
Mephistopheles passages. Humor suffers in prose, and my point has
to do with spirit and tone. The original reads: "Für euch sind zwey
Dinge/Von köstlichem Glanz/Das leuchtende Gold/Und ein glänzender
Schwanz." "Euch giebt es zwey Dinge/So herrlich und groß/Das
glänzende Gold/Und der weibliche Schoos." The Chorus: "Aufs

perhaps in deference to a future Weimar audience. But its existence furthers the impression of equally strong impulses to creativity from the idealistic as from the destructive side of the work. When it is said that there was as much of Mephistopheles as Faust in Goethe himself, the remark usually rests upon such impressions, more than upon real evidence from his life, which is scant.[18]

There is an example of this impartial creativity, as it were, in material that *was* used. It appears at the beginning of the scene, as Faust and Mephistopheles mount the Brocken in near darkness—just as Faust and Wagner had walked the field in the glory of day. Both settings evoke poetry. Here, "How sadly, yonder, with belated glow/Rises the ruddy moon's imperfect round . . . ," are lines which Goethe himself singled out as truly poetic yet requiring "some observation of nature,"[19] which was the source of his lyrical inspiration. The lines are given to Mephistopheles, but that is not unjustifiable in the rhetorical tradition. My point, rather, is that the demands made upon poetry by "Walpurgis Night" as it moves from night in the real world to the glow of the satanic realm are met to a degree where the scene seems to acquire a life of its own, like a dream, which it is sometimes said to represent.[20] We substitute the illusion of fantasy for the illusion of reality. The setting of night

---

Angesicht nieder/Am heiligen Ort/O glücklich wer nah steht/Und höret das Wort." (Witkowski, 1: 530). Not since "Hans Wurst's Wedding," more than twenty years earlier (1775), have we heard Goethe so profane.

18. As opposed to evidence of a certain aloofness and coldness, which is in plenty. However, in his official capacity Goethe met many personages who later proved unimportant, and it is often upon evidence derived from reports of such probably less than captivating people that the claim of aloofness is made.

19. To Eckermann, February 26, 1824. "Wie traurig steigt die unvollkommne Scheibe/Des roten Monds mit später Glut heran" (ll. 3851–52).

20. Atkins so speaks of it directly (*Goethe's Faust: A Literary Analysis*, p. 91).

gives way to a stranger evocation, as Faust, Mephistopheles,
and a will-o'-the-wisp whom they have asked to light their
way move through a "dream and magic sphere" inhabited by
"mice, in myriads, thousand-hued" and "paunchy salaman-
ders, too," and come to stand before "rocky walls/Ablaze in
all their towering height." "Sir Mammon for this festival/
Grandly illumines his palace hall!"²¹ says Mephistopheles.

So vivid is this last passage that, when read in its own
light, it may make, in complete reversal, certain motifs obviously intended as thematic links with the whole, seem
out of place. It is as if in attaching this fantastic limb to the
natural body of the poem, Goethe himself momentarily
lost faith in his own best instincts and became somewhat obvious. The Devil's response to the enthusiasm that Faust
expresses at the beginning of the scene we may accept as suf-
ficiently in character to bear its symbolic weight, in that
the change in nature would seem as inevitably to prompt a
positive reaction in Faust ("Spring weaves already in the
birchen trees") as a retarding reaction in himself ("Naught of
this genial influence do I sense/Within me all is wintry").²²
But his response to the comment by the will-o'-wisp on its
characteristic zigzag course ("So man, forsooth, he thinks to
imitate!") is schoolmasterly, a stance we will allow Mephistopheles only in mockery.²³

On the other hand, the remark we have had occasion to
quote earlier as a telling, if negative, perspective upon the
process of introversion and extroversion, the breathing in and
out of nature and of man, "You think you are pushing, and
are being pushed,"²⁴ grows so directly out of the tumultuous

21. "In die Traum- und Zaubersphäre/Sind wir, scheint es, ein-
gegangen. . . . Erleuchtet nicht zu diesem Feste/Herr Mammon prächtig
den Palast?" (ll. 3871–3933).

22. "Der Frühling webt schon in den Birken. . . ." "Fürwahr, ich
spüre nichts davon!/Mir ist es winterlich im Leibe" (ll. 3845–49).

23. "Ei! Ei! Er denkt's den Menschen nachzuahmen" (l. 3863).
However, the next line may be said to redeem him: "Now in the Devil's
name, for once go straight"—"Geh' Er nur grad' in's Teufels Namen!"

24. "[Goethe] spoke of the inhaling and exhaling of the earth

movement in the scene that we relate it to our own common experience in crowds rather than to basic laws in the universe. The kind of unity we seek in *Faust,* the "idea that has inspired the poet and which unites the parts of the poem with the whole and is law for the parts and lends them meaning," to speak again with Goethe,[25] is implicit. We seek such unity, partly because the work often lacks more explicit unity, but also because its essential nature is best revealed in this way.

Of course, the social satire that we earlier found at odds with the dramatic import of the poem may appear equally incongruous in its own setting. We are in a witches' element, where all is "crowd and jostle, whirl and flutter . . . whisper, babble, twirl and splutter . . . glimmer, sparkle, stink and flare," as Mephistopheles describes the present activities, again, perhaps, in a negative mirror image of the activities of humanity at large.[26] We are not in a forum for reason, let alone the subtle form of reason that is satire. Not that we must disallow in art what may not obtain in life. But we may also feel that the freedom newly won in the departure from realism, the abandonment of a soul reflected in an abandonment in art, is now casually squandered on concerns

according to eternal laws . . ." (Eckermann, March 22, 1824); ". . . the inhalation and exhalation of the world in which we live, function, and have our being" (*Entwurf einer Farbenlehre*, part 5); and, in connection with our line from *Faust,* "Thank God when he forces you,/ And thank him when he lets you go again."—"Du danke Gott, wenn er dich presst,/Und dank ihm, wenn er dich wieder lässt" (from *West-East Divan*, "Book of Singers," my translation).

25. ". . . die Idee, welche das Einzelne des Gedichts zum Ganzen verknüpft, für das Einzelne Gesetz ist und dem Einzelnen seine Bedeutung gibt" (in a conversation with H. Luden, August 19, 1806; the complete conversation is given in the Artemis edition of the *Gespräche*, 2:98–99).

26. The original is more suggestive of the sexual: "Das drängt und stößt . . ." (ll. 4016–20), etc. The word "stößt" implies fornication, as witness the earlier line in the same scene, "Es f--t die Hexe, es st--t der Bock" (l. 3961, Goethe's deletions).

unrelated to the main action and, as topical, soon to lose significance.

But that would be the result of looking backward. If we look forward, not simply to the sequel, which continues without justifying the light satirical tone, but to the whole of the poem yet to come, we find a mode of creating predicated upon the very kind of freedom that here seems mere willfulness. We are already in spirit in Part II, if we have not quite finished Part I.[27] And since we know that the period that produced this scene produced also the plan for a second part, we may look to a deeper relation. The departure from realism, we saw, was not occasioned by any urge to levity but by the need not only to concentrate in one episode what must stand for many, but also, and more importantly for our present point, to represent what is known in the mind yet cannot be seen, therefore not depicted, only evoked. That need also underlay Part II and largely determined its content and form. It determined its content insofar as the salvation of the hero, which is the reason for there being a second part, could not be effected in itself but, as we noted, only in mankind, whence the greatly broadened perspective that ensued. And it determined its form, in that the representation of the evolution of modern man in an even remotely realistic manner was itself unthinkable, let alone the envisioning of the evolution of the species, which was the depth to which the work would eventually force its author. With Part II, the tension between what we have called the dramatics and thematics will not simply increase, but erupt, with the dramatic giving so far way to the thematic and symbolic that we will sometimes find the central figure long absented from the action, or present but reduced to an observer.[28]

The play generally will become less and less the imitation of an action presumed to be real, and more the projection of

27. Jantz, "Patterns and Structures in *Faust*," notes the impossibility of studying the form of Part II separately from Part I.

28. Fairley, *Goethe's Faust: Six Essays*, remarks on the extent to which Faust is forced to stand around in Part II, pp. 11, 18.

images intended to make visible to the hero, no less than to the audience, the great forces by which they have been invisibly and collectively formed. ("What you have been given by your fathers, earn, that you may possess it.") With these considerations in mind, we may find the insinuating of anomalous satire between the climax and denouement of a moral tragedy less a frivolous conceit than a vain attempt to join two broadly incompatible parts of a major undertaking, and to cover up the abyss between them. We may think of the poet as so far removed from the beginnings of his drama[29] in sentiment and charged feeling that he could be blinded by what he planned to write to the spirit and implications of what he had already written.

But the contradictions inherent in the Walpurgis Night sequence reflect the workings of the poem at an even deeper level. It is for that reason we have sought them out.[30] *Faust* is of its age, not only of its author, in the sense that we used the phrase earlier: that is, to suggest that the work helped to create, not merely to exemplify, the currents in thought and spirit of the times, and so it offers them as they came into being—fresh, as yet not named. If into its earliest stages went the revolt against a spiritually and socially oppressive order, and into its middle phase the new and abiding faith in experience as the medium of truth[31] ("In the beginning was the deed"), into its final development

29. Goethe remarked in later years: "I no longer like to read Faust [in German], but in this French translation [by Gérard de Nerval] everything again seems thoroughly fresh, new, and imaginative" (to Eckermann, January 3, 1830).

30. Although we need not agree with Goethe when he says, "In poetry there are no contradictions. These exist only in the real world, not in the world of poetry. What the poet creates has to be taken as he made it" (in a conversation with H. Luden, August 19, 1806).

31. This may further help to explain his intemperate reaction to Newton's optics, which was founded on mathematics, in contrast to his own theories. See, for example, Erich Heller, "Goethe and the Idea of Scientific Truth," in *The Disinherited Mind* (New York, 1957 and later).

went the concept, likewise as yet unnamed, that would restore order, but in living form, the concept of evolution.
When Darwin in his introduction to the *Origin of Species*
cites Goethe[32] among those who anticipated his own findings, he has in mind, of course, the scientist, but it is the poet
Goethe, if the poet whose vision is now imbued with scientific knowledge, who conceives Part II. For while others
who shared this view of existence as becoming rather than
being—*Werden* as opposed to *Sein*[33] —pursued their insight at the level of culture and history, such as Herder, or
welcomed the thought philosophically without weighing
its implications for art, such as Friedrich Schlegel, who envisioned but never attempted a "world poem," "ein Weltgedicht," Goethe chose to represent the view, not merely discuss it, in his art. The total *Faust* is not a philosophical
poem in any strict sense but it may come close to being a
Weltgedicht, with its inward scope, the thoughts and visions to which it gives rise, touching on limitlessness. What
marks this work of art as a product of its age is the manner in which character and setting are continuously transformed in the flow of identities and images, of masks and
masques, that constitute its action, which action in Part

32. In the first footnote, which reads in part: ". . . Goethe was an
extreme partisan of similar views, as shown in the introduction of
a work written in 1794 and 1795 [probably the comparative anatomy
studies] but not published till long afterward; he has pointedly remarked that the future question for the naturalists will be how, for
instance, cattle got their horns, and not for what they are used. It
is rather a singular instance of the manner in which similar views arise
at about the same time, that Goethe in Germany, Dr. Darwin [Eras-
mus Darwin, the grandfather of the author] in England, and Geoffroy
Saint-Hilaire . . . in France, came to the same conclusion on the origin of species, in the years 1794–95." Darwin had his knowledge of
Goethe's views from Karl Meding, *Goethe als Naturforscher in Beziehung
zur Gegenwart* (Dresden, 1861); see, for example, George Wells, "Goethe
and Evolution," *Journal of the History of Ideas* 28 (1967): 537–50.

33. The concepts upon which the distinction between the romantic
and the classical view of life and of art is often built.

II is then ennobled, and its philosophical importance restored, in the remark of the final Chorus: "Everything transitory/Is but a symbol"—"Alles Vergängliche/Ist nur ein Gleichnis." Here is a drama, not of objective conflict, but of unimpeded movement, as if in the mind.

What further marks the work as a product of an age is the reluctance, uneasiness, or peculiar mixture of distrust and confidence ("the whole composition is subjective") with which over the years its author approached his subject. Goethe would rather have remained, we feel, with the beauty of balanced form and thought he had attained in *Iphigenia*. But neither his time, with its displacing of the concept of progress with the idea of eternal progression, which made the eighteenth into the nineteenth century, nor he himself, who had found the same principle only confirmed in his own experience and his studies of nature, would properly allow it. The times move, they do not guide, and here they no more supplied the form to express this new vision of the causes and interrelationship of things than had an earlier time supplied the form to express the different sense of life that went uncontained into the first version of the play. Goethe had once again to take his own counsel, and at the point where he allowed his *Faust,* whether by intent or from deeper potentials within the poem, to enter the realm of the fantastic in its own right, which occurs for the first time in "Walpurgis Night," he may have done harm to the original conception of his theme as drama, and added insult with the frivolous "Walpurgis Night's Dream,"[34] but his act freed the play to

34. The remarks, ". . . viewed in its connection as a link in the drama ["Walpurgis Night's Dream"] can only be explained as a wanton freak of poetic cynicism" (Thomas, 1:lxv), and "[That] Faust should . . . listen to that sort of thing just after his conscience has been awakened by the vision of Gretchen is intolerable" (Mason, *Goethe's Faust: Its Genesis and Purport*, p. 210), may be said to represent the opinion on one side; on the other is Jantz, "The Function of the 'Walpurgis Night's Dream' in the Faust Drama" (*Monatshefte* 44 [1952]: 397–408), where it is argued that the intermezzo should be seen not as an interruption within Part I but as a link between the two parts of the

become what it had to in order to reflect the new consciousness of the age, that is, symbolical. Not dramatic action
but the play of fantasy and image will become the play in
Part II, and spread itself broadly and sporadically, until
it once again finds anchor in the towering tragic figure of the
blinded Faust at the end. "The first part ended with Gretchen's
death; now it must, *par richochet,* begin again," we quoted
Goethe as saying, and to the extent that he had in mind the
moral horror of the tragedy on the one hand and his intent
nevertheless to save Faust, the metaphor would seem appropriate, though there will still be horrors to witness in Act V,
Part II. But to the extent that his understanding of the dynamics of his own creativity prompted the remark, he might
as well have cited "Walpurgis Night" as the propellent to new
movement: whence its disruptiveness in the economy of
the drama, whence its important impetus in the development
of the whole, which is not cumulative, but revolutionary,
at each telling stage.

But it is to the attempt already in Part I to prepare for the
salvation of the hero that we must now in conclusion briefly
turn.

---

drama, "as a transition from the limitations of space and time in Part I
to the freedom of space and time in Part II" (p. 401).

THE DUNGEON REVISITED. CONCLUSION

*I have never admitted the right of an elderly author to
alter the work of a younger author, even when the
author happens to be his former self.*

—George Bernard Shaw in the 1913 preface to
The Quintessence of Ibsenism

It is not my purpose to examine in detail the changes that
Goethe made when he decided to turn the original prose of
the dungeon scene into verse. Not that the details are unimportant. Reflected in them are essential developments of
the kind that have concerned us throughout, and so must
at the end. But I do not mean to evaluate the changes, some
of which, it can be argued, proved betterments for the
worse—*Verschlimmbesserungen*. We look to what was gained
in the losses, if such they were.[1]

At the end of Part I, one senses at first an approach on the
part of the author that may be described as awkward, as
with someone who has returned to a familiar setting and fails
to respond to the intimacy it once bore. It is true that we
cannot help reading into formerly unrhymed lines a certain
formality that lies in the nature of poetry, but to which
the attention is not normally drawn, except in bad verse. But
here the intent was precisely to formalize, ". . . to mute the

---

1. It has been suggested that earlier scholars in their delight in the
discovery of the original manuscript (in 1887) became overzealous
and read into it more positive features than it in fact possessed; see
Bernd von Heiseler, "Ueber die Möglichkeiten der Sprache," in *Ahnung
und Aussage*. Witkowski speaks of the "powerful" prose of the original scene, 2:285.

effect . . . by turning into verse some tragic scenes which
through their naturalness and strength have become quite
unbearable in relation to the [new] whole," as Goethe
wrote to Schiller, May 5, 1798. Among these scenes was
"Dungeon."

The first change in the scene provides a good illustration.
To be muted were the sentiments of fear and horror—the
Storm and Stress "unwonted fear" and "inner human horror"—which accompany Faust to the door of the prison,
where he has come to rescue Gretchen. These sentiments are
retained in effect: "A fear unwonted o'er my spirit falls;/
Man's concentrated woe o'erwhelms me here!"[2] But in the
need to rhyme, and, one feels, initially mainly in that need,
other contrasting sentiments are produced. Faust seems
suddenly aware of a reality outside his own torment, and
senses a Gretchen in her own world and own right: "She
dwells within these dripping walls;/Her only trespass a delusion dear!"[3] This is not the Faust who had come hot from
the "Witches' Kitchen" onto the "Street," nor who later
blindly thinks: "And into ruin let her plunge with me!" Rather it is the more mature tragic figure who, in both his
sensual and spiritual experience, within his "two souls," must
test each extreme before he can arrive at truth. In the spiritual realm it is the attempted suicide that serves to renew his
will to live, and in the sensual, it is the libidinous adventure
of the "Walpurgis Night" that returns him to his moral self,
and to Gretchen and the present point in the play.

Not that the simple need to rhyme of itself resulted in the
introduction of an important transformation of character.
What this glimpse of an isolated particular of development in
the work affords is not so much a measure of the degree as
of the kind of consciousness that entered in the creative process, here, as broadly, in *Faust*. We begin to recognize less

2. "Mich faßt ein längst entwohnter Schauer,/Der Menschheit
ganzer Jammer faßt mich an" (ll. 4405–06).
3. "Hier wohnt sie, hinter dieser feuchten Mauer,/Und ihr Ver-
brechen war ein guter Wahn!" (ll. 4407–08).

a "naive" than an acquired instinct informing its conception after the early beginnings, and at each stage differently because progressively. The Faust of *Urfaust* would not have expressed or felt the present sentiments, not having undergone either the agony of "Forest and Cavern," which first appeared in the *Fragment,* or the strange catharsis of "Walpurgis Night," although in terms of time or "reality" within the play itself he is not to be construed as a less mature figure. Nor would the Goethe of *Urfaust* have expressed those sentiments. The work grew with the author, we have had occasion to say and no reason to doubt, yet this simple, concrete example of change suggests how the wealth and accumulation, no longer the mere specifics, of experience began to influence its growth, how the confessional mode gave way to objectivity.

The same hand[4] made other minor changes in the text, in our next example, by elimination. The Gretchen who had addressed Faust so often (eight times) as Heinrich is now made to use the given name only four times, in a cluster at the end of the scene, as in the original version. There is a restraint here that has nothing to do with verse or rhyme but which serves to place Gretchen (as Faust momentarily in our previous example) at an ever-so-slight remove from the passion and drama in which she is held. For in place of the personal name, Goethe has her address Faust with a term that adds an unexpected dimension to their relationship—namely, "friend."[5] It is as if she also has matured in the tragedy through the author's rather than her own experience, and yet justifiably, with the condemnation by her brother in death

4. Goethe likened himself in his difficulties with *Faust* to the painter working on the same subject with a quite different brush or hand— "[Der Maler] habe jetzt eine andre Hand, einen andern Pinsel" (in a conversation with Boisserée, August 3, 1815).

5. German "Freund" has a connotation it perhaps does not possess in English. Some translators will use "my love," "my beloved," along with "friend." On the use of vocabulary in "Dungeon," see W. F. Twadell, "The Kerker Lexicon and the Gretchen Episode" (*Monatshefte* 45 [1953] : 354-370.

("Let me tell you in confidence,/You are simply a whore"),[6]
which is absent from the early version, perhaps serving as
further purgation.

In general, Gretchen is made more rational in her thought,
if not in her actions. What in *Urfaust* had been the instinctive responses of a mind at moments unbalanced become now
more integrated, "rationalized," in the dramatic scheme.
The Gretchen who had been restrained from escaping with
Faust by a fear of "[those who] lie in wait for me at the
road by the woods" retains the fear, but of the actual author-
ities. Beyond the first image she projects the rational alternative of a life of begging, "and with a bad conscience," of
straying in foreign lands, only ultimately to be caught:
"And me they will catch, do what I may!"[7] What had been
a purely spontaneous reaction, and for that reason so striking
in Gretchen, becomes broadened and measured, as when
the anticipation of her own execution comes to include, beyond the sound of death knell, the broken judicial staff,
and the quiver of fear, an ordered vision of her end:

> The crowd doth gather, in silence it rolls;
> The squares, the streets,
> Scarce hold the throng.
> The staff is broken—the death-bell tolls—
> They bind and seize me! I'm hurried along,
> To the seat of blood already I'm bound!
> Quivers each neck as the naked steel
> Quivers on mine the blow to deal—[8]

6. My translation. Swanwick omits the word "whore": "Let this in
confidence be said;/Since thou the path of shame doth tread,/Tread
it with right good will!" (for "Ich sag dir's im Vertrauen nur:/Du bist
doch nun einmal eine Hur' . . ." [ll. 3729–30]).

7. "Was hilft es fliehn? Sie lauern doch mir auf,/Es ist so elend,
betteln zu müssen,/Und noch dazu mit bösem Gewissen!/Es ist so
elend, in der Fremde schweifen,/Und sie werden mich doch ergreifen!"
(ll. 4545–49)

8. "Die Menge drängt sich, man hört sie nicht./Der Platz, die Gassen/
Können sie nicht fassen./Die Glocke ruft, das Stäbchen bricht./Wie

We see that verse is made not only of meter or rhyme but
also of content, as though the order in its form promotes
ordered thought. But ordered thought is the matter of the
dungeon scene. A heroine who can see beyond her torment
to the necessity of her fate, and can herself seal it, as it
were, by living her death in advance, is not the heroine who
in the intensity of her feelings bares truths, yet truths unknown to herself—for example in the song: "My mother, the
harlot,/She took me and slew!" This is not to distinguish
between the tragic and the pathetic (with which evaluative
distinction, even if it can be made, we are not concerned),
but between a younger and an older author seeing through
the eyes of the same character, with the older author seeing
in a somewhat different, clearer, and more forebearing way.

And if in turning this scene into verse, Goethe himself was
aware only of muting its effect rather than altering it in
content, our examples become the more telling. They suggest
that the important changes he underwent in his relationship
to Frau von Stein, in the journey to Italy and the exposure to
classical art, and above all in the writing of the works that
grew out of these experiences, had become so much a part of
his nature as to cause him, acting as poet, to express himself unavoidably as thinker. If muting the effect could include such developments as he allows to occur in the changed
"Dungeon," we can understand how he might have claimed
that the conception of *Faust* was clear to him from the
beginning, with only the sequence of events undecided, for
from such changes a new world could emerge. What we
sense—indeed, know to be from our knowledge of his life and
his other works—as surely unforeseen evolutions in *Faust,*
he himself may have experienced as simple extensions, elab-
orations, and modifications of a primary concept so long
lived with that it appeared never to have changed. It was he,
after all, who had replied to Eckermann's natural assumption

sie mich binden und packen!/Zum Blutstuhl bin ich schon entrückt./
Schon zuckt nach jedem Nacken/Die Schärfe, die nach meinem zückt"
(ll. 4587-94).

that a thorough knowledge of the world and life must have
gone into the creation of *Faust,* "Could be. . . . But had I
not already borne a world within me through anticipation, I
would have remained blind with seeing eyes, and all searching and experience would have been nothing but quite dead,
vain effort" (February 26, 1824, cited above).

There are some less than spontaneous, theatrical, or
"period" motifs introduced in the revised scene, but I have
cited changes that better reflect the true inner growth of
the whole in their suggestion of meaning emerging in the
creative act, reason emerging through rhyme. One further example. It has to do with physical action. On two occasions
in *Urfaust,* Faust tries to force a distraught, resistant Gretchen
to flee with him, "drawing her away," "grasping her and
attempting to carry her away," and these actions are elimat-
ed, obviously in the interest of muting the effect. The significance of the change only becomes clear in context,
however. For the original purpose of the action has been
obviated by a Gretchen now not only emotionally but rationally opposed to flight, and not to be moved simply
by force; and by a Faust who, having demonstrated his feelings in his vision at the end of "Walpurgis Night," needs
no Storm and Stress impetuousness to convince us of his sin-
cerity. Force is now the very last resort: "Since here avails
nor argument nor prayer,/Thee hence by force I needs must
bear,"[9] and while we must assume that Faust begins to
carry out the threat, in effect stage direction has been translated into dialogue, action into words.[10] This suggests a
development beyond the movement toward objectivity to

9. "Hilft hier kein Flehen, hilft kein Sagen,/So wag' ich's, dich
hinweg zu tragen" (ll. 4574-75).

10. *Urfaust* was written with the stage hardly in mind, as Meyer-
Benfey, for one, has pointed out. The stage direction, "He *hears* the
chains clatter and the straw rustle" in the original (my italics), had
to be changed, and becomes: *Faust.* "She forebodes not that her
lover's near,/The clanking chains, the rustling straw, to hear." See
Heinrich Meyer-Benfey, "Die Kerkerszene in Goethe's *Faust,*"
Zeitschrift für Deutschkunde 38 (1924): 364-70.

the conception of a world, to be sure with objective existence, but better comprehended in its endless nature through
the medium of words and their associated images, through
the play of poetry and idea, not persons and action. That is
the world of Part II.

I have not restated the most important, yet most obvious,
fact, which is that little *was* altered. Given the opportunity
over so many years to rethink the work, Goethe chose to
retain and add rather than to change, to accomplish through
growth rather than rearrangement. To choose not to change
is still a decision, yet one senses in *Faust* a consistent artistic
instinct rather than conscious deliberation guiding its course.
To be sure, the mature author must have been fully aware
of the nature of his talent, able to watch himself create, before Schiller explained that talent to himself and literary
history. And Schiller, in turn, though he may not have directly influenced the course of *Faust,* surely through his criticism made Goethe more aware of the paths he had chosen
not to take. We may even like to think that this slowly
evolved and unwieldy Part I might never have come into
being without the constant prodding from the friend;
and so think, not in order to relate its existence to chance, or
to lend Schiller reflected glory, of which he has no need,
but in order not to detach the work from life itself, which
was its subject matter first and last. Yet in the final analysis it must have been his own inner sense of rightness in his
manner of creating that pressed Goethe forward in the
main stages of *Faust,* if not at every turn. We must see him
in his instinctive—or, as he continued to describe it, subjective—approach to his subject as ever uncovering broader
meanings for the whole that would confirm his faith in
a communion of the laws of art with the hidden truths of
life which he shared with his age, and, as the scientist
gained sway in his mind, of these with the controlling forces
of nature.

Throughout I have cited examples of the concentricity
of elements that suggest a deeper core or wholeness in his
view of life, an organic quality, as it is often called, a quality

implying growth through addition and retention. But thus far we have not had the opportunity to illustrate the point in the concrete terms which a simple addition to "Dungeon" now affords. At the beginning of the scene, Faust throws himself to the ground in the same Storm and Stress gesture from the early version, but he is made to relieve its starkness by accompanying the gesture with words, "A lover at thy feet bends low," and Gretchen, in her crazed conscience, to mistake the posture and throw herself on her knees beside him: "Oh, let us kneel and move the saints by prayer!"[11] Earlier, we had sometimes to speak of a stroke of genius to account for the coinciding of varied meanings in a single moment or action, as with the tolling of the Easter bells in "Before the Gate," but here we can see more clearly the making of such moments and actions. We cannot say that this particular development emerged in the process of creation, for the exposing of the unconscious through error was already given in the character and the scene when Gretchen was made to mistake the wetness on Faust's hands for blood, symbolically, the murder of her brother. The genius lay in the first instance, which is retained. Yet we cannot quite claim that that identification of the posture of piety with the posture of love, which is the new striking feature, was conceived in the deliberate manner of the later Goethe, who had "long since chosen to place images opposite and, as it were, mirroring each other, in order to reveal deeper meaning."[12] For the action remains functional, not poetically suggestive, and could owe part of its existence simply to contemporary theatrical tastes.[13] We *may* say, which is more to the point, that this example of the past reflected in a present that anticipates further development illustrates the sense with which we have approached *Faust* throughout and so may stand as one example for the whole.

11. "O laß uns knien, die Heil'gen anzurufen!" (l. 4453).
12. "den geheimeren Sinn," in a letter of September 27, 1827, to a scholar who had commented on the "Helena" act in Part II.
13. "Jammerknechtschaft" of l. 4452, for example, is theatrical.

We have come back to our point of departure, and must
conclude. But concluding will be a matter of difficulty
in an author the effect of whose art, as we claimed, is to bend
our thought and mode of experiencing imperceptibly to
his own. When we asked at the beginning, for example,
whether *Faust* was essentially dramatic, epic, or lyrical in nature, we did not soon conclude that one of these formal
elements predominated, or that the evidence of all of them
in the composition suggested a fusion or extension of traditional forms. Rather the reverse was true. We began to
sense that this drama, epic, or poem before us, whatever we
might call it, most resembled itself; it was not simply new,
but represented a unique literary and artistic development.
For while its variety of form did not create a sense of a
broader whole, as would new dimensions added to an original
design, the parts themselves displayed action, vision, and
poetry of such high resolve and grandeur that we could assume an order or purpose in the splendid diversity. We did
not immediately describe that order. Indeed, as Goethe
warned, we can never uncover a single "[principle or idea]
that [lies] at the base of the whole and each scene in particular." That role, if anything, has fallen to freedom of form
as such. But we have taken the first important step toward
analyzing *Faust* in its own right by no longer asking *why* it
has unusual characteristics, which presupposes an established and accepted norm, but, more in the evolutionist spirit
of the work itself, *how* it has come to possess them.

We are able to answer this question to an exceptional degree. We know the stages of composition in *Faust*. Moreover, the dramas and philosophical poems that Goethe wrote,
and the scientific studies he undertook, in the great intervals in the composition of *Faust* also served as a measure and
reflection of the creative process in *Faust* itself, and in
their own wide variety cause the latter to appear more natural, and thus comprehensible, by association. But it is the
deeper unities and correspondences within *Faust* itself that
provide the clearest insights into its essential meaning and,
ultimately, the essential genius of its author. Indeed, at times

these correspondences seem almost accidental. Poet and work
grew together, and mainly instinctively, and their inward
growth joined what was separated in time. Being thus compelled always to look forward and backward in the poem
(and sometimes outside to other elements and influences) in
our attempt to determine what went deliberately, what
more spontaneously, into its making at the major turns, we
are afforded an insight not usually provided by the analysis of a great literary classic. We can glimpse, or believe we
glimpse, not only genius at work in the realm of poetry,
but also the genius or dynamics of the age which this poem,
in exemplifying and dramatizing its spirit and tendencies,
seems to place before us as a living event.

Part I of *Faust* completed, Goethe began Part II, and the
new project causes us to see the earlier undertaking in a
different light. The tragedy recedes. The concerns of the real
and immediate world give way to the concerns of the mind
and imagination. But the problems of form and art persist. If
Part I was a drama in search of a theme, in that its initial
dramatic action had to be absorbed into a broader philosophical scheme, Part II is a theme in search of a drama. The
great knowledge and the sense of culture, art, and thought
that Goethe accumulated in a long life and saw fit to relate to his central masterpiece have to be concentrated into
character and setting, poetry and motif, playful action and
high seriousness. The new work was not so long in the
making as the older; it was accomplished mainly in the last
years of Goethe's life. But the problems it presents are
equally formidable and the solutions it offers equally unique.

It lies in the nature of true development and evolution
that it must not only contain in the past the potential for
what is to come, but must actually exert it in the future. Part
II completed, other great works and developments in literature will emerge that will cause us to see it in turn in new
ways. There is and will be no ending. All classic works of art
have their existence in such a context. Yet *Faust,* with its
very nature and form in process and change, helps to remind
us of this fact which is sometimes forgotten.

SELECT BIBLIOGRAPHY

The list includes only those titles to which I have referred in the text. The preponderance of English titles is explained in the preface and in n. 5 to chapter 1.

Bibliographies

Henning, Hans, ed. *Faust-Bibliographie*. 5 vols. Weimar, 1966-76.
Morgan, B. Q. *A Critical Bibliography of German Literature in English Translation*. 3 vols. New York, 1932 and 1965. Second supplement, edited by Murray F. Smith. Metuchen, N.J., 1972.
Pyritz, Hans, et al., ed. *Goethe-Bibliographie*. 2 vols. Heidelberg, 1965 and 1968.

Goethe's Works

Arndt, Walter, trans., and Hamlin, Cyril, ed. *Faust: A Tragedy*. New York, 1976.
Beutler, Ernst, et al., ed. *Gedenkausgabe der Werke, Briefe, und Gespräche*. Artemis Edition. 24 vols. Zurich, 1949-62.
Goethes Werke. Weimar Edition. Published under the auspices of the Grand Duchess of Saxony. 1887-1919. Vols. 10-17, which include the minor pieces Goethe prepared for the Weimar Theater.
Heffner, R.-M. S.; Rehder, H.; and Twadell, W. F. *Goethe's Faust*. Vol. 1, *Part I: Introduction, Text, and Notes*. Lexington, Mass., 1954. Vol. 2, *Part II*. Boston, 1955.
Morris, Max, ed. *Der junge Goethe*. 6 vols. Leipzig, 1909-12.
Swanwick, Anna. *Faust: A Tragedy by Goethe in Two Parts*. New York, 1882.
Thomas, Calvin. *Goethe's Faust*. Vol. 1, *The First Part*. Boston, 1892. Vol. 2, *The Second Part*. Boston, 1897.
Trunz, Erich, et al., ed. *Goethes Werke*. Hamburg Edition. 14 vols. Hamburg, 1949-60.
Witkowski, Georg. *Goethes Faust*. 2 vols. Leipzig, 1907. Reprint. Leiden, 1949-50.

Faust Reference, Commentary, and Critical Analysis

Atkins, Stuart. *Goethe's Faust: A Literary Analysis.* Cambridge, Mass., 1964.

——. "Schlecht und Modern? Englische *Faust*-Uebersetzungen seit 1949." *Aussichten zu Faust.* Edited by Günther Mahal, Stuttgart, 1973.

——. "Studies of Goethe's *Faust* since 1959." *German Quarterly* 39 (1966): 303–10.

Barber, C. L. "The Form of Faustus' Fortunes Good or Bad." In *Faust: Sources, Works, Criticism.* Edited by Paul E. Bates. New York, 1969.

Bates, Paul E., ed. *Faust: Sources, Works, Criticism.* New York, 1969.

Buchwald, Reinhard. *Führer durch Goethes Faust.* Stuttgart, 1964.

Butler, E. M. *The Fortunes of Faust.* Cambridge, 1952.

Dieckmann, Liselotte. *Goethe's Faust: A Critical Reading.* Englewood, N.J., 1972.

Dye, Robert E. "The Easter Cantata and the Idea of Mediation in Goethe's *Faust.*" *PMLA* 93 (1978): 963–76.

Fairley, Barker. *Goethe's Faust: Six Essays.* Oxford, 1953.

Fischer, Kuno. *Goethes Faust: Ueber die Entstehung und Komposition des Gedichts.* 4 vols. Heidelberg, 1902–03.

Frantz, A. I. *Half a Hundred Thralls to Faust: A Study Based on the British and American Translations of Goethe's "Faust."* Chapel Hill, 1949.

Gillies, Alexander. *Goethe's Faust: An Interpretation.* Oxford, 1957.

Haile, H. G. *The History of Doctor Johann Faustus.* Recovered from the German by H. G. Haile. Urbana, 1965.

Heiseler, Bernd von. "Ueber die Möglichkeiten der Sprache," in *Ahnung und Aussage.* Gütersloh, 1952.

Heller, Erich. "Faust's Damnation." In *The Artist's Journey into the Interior and Other Essays.* New York, 1965.

Heller, Otto. *Faust and Faustus.* St. Louis, 1931.

Hohlfeld, A. R. "Pact and Wager in Goethe's *Faust.*" *Modern Philology* 18 (1921): 113–36.

Jantz, Harold. "The Function of the Walpurgis Night's Dream." *Monatshefte* 44 (1952): 359–408.

——. *Goethe's Faust as a Renaissance Man: Parallels and Prototypes.* Princeton, 1951.

——. "The Mathematics of Faust's Rejuvenation." *Modern Language Notes* 85 (1970): 383–85.

——. "Patterns and Structure in *Faust.* A Preliminary Inquiry." *Modern Language Notes* 83 (1968): 359–87.

———. *The Form of Goethe's Faust*. Baltimore and London, 1978.

Levedahl, Kathryn S. "The Witches' One-Times-One: Sense or Non-sense?" *Modern Language Notes* 85 (1970): 380–83.

Mason, Eudo. *Goethe's Faust: Its Genesis and Purport*. Berkeley, 1967.

———. "Goethe's Sense of Evil." *Publications of the English Goethe Society*, n.s. 34 (1964): 1–53.

———. "The Paths and Powers of Mephistopheles." *German Studies: Presented to Walter Horace Bruford*. London, 1962.

Meyer, Herman. *Diese sehr ernsten Scherze: Eine Studie zu "Faust II."* Heidelberg, 1970.

Meyer-Benfey, Heinrich. "Die Kerkerszene in Goethe's *Faust*." *Zeitschrift für Deutschkunde* 38 (1924): 364–70.

Palmer, P. M., and More, R. P. *The Sources of the Faust Tradition: From Simon Magus to Lessing*. New York, 1965.

Pniower, Otto. "Fausts zweiter Teil." In *Dichtungen und Dichter: Essays und Studien*. Berlin, 1912.

Rickert, Heinrich. *Goethes Faust: Die dramatische Einheit der Dichtung*. Tübingen, 1932.

Salm, Peter. *The Poem as Plant: A Biological View of Goethe's Faust*. Cleveland, 1971.

Seidlin, Oskar. "Is the 'Prelude in the Theater' a Prelude to *Faust*?" *PMLA* 64 (1949): 462–70.

Stawell, F. M., and Dickinson, G. Lowes. *Goethe's Faust*. London, 1928.

Steinhauer, Harry. "Faust's Pact with the Devil." *PMLA* 69 (1956): 180–200.

Twadell, W. F. "The Kerker Lexicon and the Gretchen Episode." *Monatshefte* 45 (1953): 354–70.

Weinberg, Kurt. *The Figure of Faust in Valéry and Goethe*. Princeton, 1976.

Wendriner, Georg, ed. *Die Faustdichtung, vor, neben, und nach Goethe*. 4 vols. Berlin, 1913.

Willoughby, L. A. "Faust: A Morphological Approach." In *Goethe, Poet and Thinker*. Edited by E. M. Wilkinson and L. A. Willoughby. London, 1962.

General Reference

Alexander, William M. *J. G. Hamann*. The Hague, 1960.

Atkins, Stuart. *The Testament of Werther in Poetry and Drama*. Cambridge, Mass., 1949.

Behler, Ernst, and Struc, R., ed. and trans. *Friedrich Schlegel: The*

Dialogue on Poetry and Literary Aphorisms. University Park, Pa., 1968.

Bergstraesser, Arnold. *Goethe's Image of Man and Society*. Chicago, 1949.

Bielschowsky, Albert. *Goethe: Sein Leben und seine Werke*. 1896. Translated by William A. Cooper. 3 vols. 1905ff.

Blunden, A. G. "Schiller's *Egmont.*" *Seminar* 14 (1978): 31-44.

Brednow, Walter. "Goethe und die Langeweile." *Neue Sammlung* 4 (1964): 1-9.

Bruford, Walter H. *Theatre, Drama, and Audience in Goethe's Germany*. London, 1950.

Butler, E. M. *Byron and Goethe*. London, 1956.

Carlson, Marvin. *Goethe and the Weimar Theater*. Ithaca and London, 1978.

Cassirer, Ernst. *The Philosophy of the Enlightenment*. Translated by Fritz C. A. Koelln and James P. Pettegrove. Princeton, 1951.

———. *Rousseau, Kant, Goethe*. Translated by James Gutman, Paul O. Kristeller, and John Herman Randall. Princeton, 1945.

Clark, Robert T. *Herder: His Life and Thought*. Berkeley, 1955.

Cottrell, Allan P. "On Speaking the Good. Goethe's *Iphigenie* as 'Moralisches Urphänomen.'" *Modern Language Quarterly* 41 (1980): 162-80.

Eichner, Hans. *Friedrich Schlegel*. New York, 1970.

———, ed. *"Romantic" and its Cognates*. Toronto, 1972.

Eisler, K. R. *Goethe: A Psychoanalytic Study, 1775-1786*. 2 vols. Detroit, 1963.

Elias, Julias, trans. and ed. *Schiller's "On Naive and Sentimental Poetry" and "On the Sublime."* New York, 1966.

Fairley, Barker. "Goethe's Last Letter." *University of Toronto Quarterly* 28 (1957-58): 1-9.

———. *A Study of Goethe*. Oxford, 1947.

Firchow, Peter, trans. *Friedrich Schlegel: Lucinde and the Fragments*. Minneapolis, 1971.

Friedenthal, Richard. *Goethe: His Life and Times*. New York, 1965.

Garland, H. *Lessing, the Founder of Modern German Literature*. Cambridge, 1937.

Gearey, John. "Heinrich Heine." In *Einführung in die deutsche Literatur*, edited by John Gearey and Willy Schumann, pp. 147-66. New York, 1964.

Gillies, Alexander. *Herder*. Oxford, 1945.

——. "Herder and Faust." *Publications of the English Goethe Society.* n.s. 16 (1947): 90–111.

——. "Herder and Goethe." *German Studies: Presented to Leonard Ashley Willoughby,* pp. 82–95. Oxford, 1952.

Graham, Ilse. *Goethe: Portrait of the Artist.* Berlin and New York, 1977.

Gray, Ronald. *Goethe, the Alchemist.* Cambridge, 1952.

——. *Goethe: A Critical Introduction.* London, 1967.

——, ed. *Poems of Goethe: A Selection with Introduction and Notes by R. G.* Cambridge, 1966.

Hammer, Carl. *Goethe and Rousseau: Resonances of the Mind.* Lexington, 1973.

——, ed. *Goethe after Two Centuries.* Port Washington, N.Y., 1969.

Hatfield, Henry. *Goethe: A Critical Introduction.* Cambridge, Mass., 1964.

Heller, Erich. "Goethe and the Idea of Scientific Truth." In *The Disinherited Mind,* pp. 3–34. New York, 1965.

Henel, Heinrich. "Type and Proto-phenomenon in Goethe's Science." *PMLA* 72 (1956): 651–68.

Jackson, Naomi. "Goethe's Drawings." *Harvard Germanic Museum Bulletin* 1, nos. 7 and 8, 1938.

Kantor, J. R. "Goethe's Place in Modern Science." In *Goethe Bicentennial Studies,* edited by Hubert J. Meessen, pp. 61–82. Urbana, 1949.

Kaufmann, Walter. *Hegel: A Reinterpretation.* New York, 1965.

Lange, Victor, ed. *Goethe: A Collection of Critical Essays.* Englewood Cliffs, N.J., 1968.

Löwith, Karl. *From Hegel to Nietzsche: The Revolution in Nineteenth-Century Thought.* Translated by David E. Green. New York, 1964.

Mandelkow, K. R., ed. *Goethe im Urteil seiner Kritiker.* Munich, 1975.

Mann, Thomas, ed. *The Permanent Goethe.* New York, 1948.

Mayer, Hans. *Klassik und Romantik.* Pfullingen, 1963.

Meding, Karl. *Goethe als Naturforscher in Beziehung zur Gegenwart.* Dresden, 1861.

Meessen, Hubert J., ed. *Goethe Bicentennial Studies,* Urbana, 1949.

O'Flaherty, James C. *Unity and Language: A Study in the Philosophy of Johann Georg Hamann.* New York, 1952.

Oppenheimer, Ernst M. *Goethe's Poetry for Occasions.* Toronto, 1974.

Pascal, Roy. *The German Sturm und Drang.* Manchester, 1959.

Peacock, Ronald. *Goethe's Major Plays.* Manchester, 1959.

Pringer, William R. *Laurence Sterne and Goethe.* Berkeley, 1930.

Raphael, Alice. *Goethe and the Philosopher's Stone.* London, 1965.

Santayana, George. *Three Philosophical Poets: Lucretius, Dante, and Goethe.* Cambridge, Mass., 1910.

Schmidt, Gerhard. *Die Krankheit zum Tode: Goethe's Todeneurose.* Stuttgart, 1968.

Seidlin, Oskar. "Goethe's *Iphigenia* and the Humane Ideal." In *Goethe: A Collection of Critical Essays.* Edited by Victor Lange. Englewood Cliffs, N.J., 1968.

Sherrington, Sir Charles. *Goethe on Nature and Science.* 2nd rev. ed. Cambridge, 1949.

Silz, Walter. *Early German Romanticism: Its Founders and Heinrich von Kleist.* Cambridge, Mass., 1929.

Simmel, Georg. *Goethe.* Leipzig, 1918.

Stahl, E. L., ed. *Goethe's Torquato Tasso.* Oxford, 1962.

Staiger, Emil. *Goethe.* Zurich and Freiburg, 1956.

Steiner, Rudolph. *Goethe's Weltanschauung.* Weimar, 1897.

——. *The Theory of Knowledge Implicit in Goethe's World View.* Translated by O. D. Wannamaker. New York, 1940.

Steinfeld, Frederick. *Goethe and Music.* New York, 1954.

Urzidil, Johannes. "Goethe and Art." *Germanic Review* 24 (1949): 184–99.

Vaget, Hans Rudolf. *Dillettantismus und Meisterschaft: Zum Problem des Dilettantismus bei Goethe.* Munich, 1971.

Viëtor, Karl. *Goethe, the Poet.* Translated by Moses Hadas. Cambridge, Mass., 1949.

——. *Goethe, the Thinker.* Translated by B. Q. Morgan. Cambridge, Mass., 1950.

Weigand, Hermann, ed. and trans. *Goethe's Wisdom and Experience.* New York, 1949.

Wellek, René. "The Conception of Romanticism in Literary History." *Comparative Literature* 1 (1949): 1–23; 147–72.

Wells, George. "Goethe and Evolution." *Journal of the History of Ideas* 28 (1967): 537–50.

Werner, Oscar H. *The Unmarried Mother in German Literature, with Special Reference to the Period 1770–1800.* New York, 1917.

Wilkinson, E. M. "*Tasso*—ein gesteigerter *Werther.*" *Modern Language Review* 44 (1949): 305–28.

——, and Willoughby, L. A. *Goethe: Poet and Thinker.* London, 1962.

Willoughby, L. A. *The Classical Age of German Literature, 1747–1805.* New York, 1966.

Zedyel, Edwin E. *Ludwig Tieck, the German Romanticist.* Princeton, 1935.

INDEX